LINUX

Programming

Patrick Volkerding

Eric Foster-Johnson

Kevin Reichard

The MIS:Press Slackware series:

LINUX: Configuration and Installation, 2/e
1-55828-492-3 Available now

The LINUX Database
1-55828-491-5 February 1997

The LINUX Internet Server
1-55828-545-8 March 1997

LINUX in Plain English
1-55828-542-3 April 1997

MIS:
P R E S S

A Subsidiary of
Henry Holt and Co., Inc.

MIS:Press

A Subsidiary of Henry Holt and Company, Inc.

115 West 18th Street

New York, New York 10011

http://www.mispress.com

A Subsidiary of
Henry Holt and Co., Inc.

Limits of Liability and Disclaimer of Warranty

First Edition—1997

Library of Congress Cataloging-in-Publication Data

```
Volkerding, Patrick.
   Linux Programming / by Patrick Volkerding, Eric F. Johnson, Kevin
   Reichard.
      p.      cm.
   ISBN 1-55828-507-5
      1. Linux. 2. Operating systems (Computers)   I. Johnson, Eric F.
   II. Reichard, Kevin.   III. Title.
   QA76.76.063V65      1996
   005.26'8--dc21                                      96-46890
                                                           CIP
```

MIS:Press and M&T Books are available at special discounts for bulk purchases for sales promotions, premiums, and fundraising. Special editions or book excerpts can also be created to specification.

For details contact: Special Sales Director
                          MIS:Press and M&T Books
                          Subsidiaries of Henry Holt and Company, Inc.
                          115 West 18th Street
                          New York, New York 10011

10 9 8 7 6 5 4 3 2 1

Associate Publisher: *Paul Farrell*   **Executive Editor:** *Cary Sullivan*
Production Editor: *Joe McPartland*   **Editor:** *Laura Lewin*
Copy Editor: *Shari Chappell*   **Copy Edit Manager:** *Shari Chappell*

Table of Contents

Introduction..xvii

What Is Linux? xviii

What Makes Slackware96 Linux Special? xix

Linux, Slackware96, and This Book xix

The FSF GNU Public License xx

Conventions Used in the Book xxi

Contacting the Authors xxi

Chapter 1

Installing Linux and XFree86 1

Installing and Configuring Linux and XFree86 2

Creating Boot and Root Floppies 3

Choosing Bootdisk and Rootdisk Images 3

Creating the Diskettes 10

Preparing Your Hard Drive for Linux 11

Using FIPS to Divide Your Hard Drive 13

Using DOS Utilities to Divide Your Hard Drive 15

Using the DOS FDISK Utility 16

FDISK and OS/2 21

Booting Linux with the Bootdisk 21

Linux and Hard-Disk Names 23

Linux and a Swap Disk 25

Creating the Main Linux Partition 28

Installing Linux from the Setup Program 30

Setting Up the Swap Space 31

Selecting the Target for Linux 31

Selecting the Source for Linux 32

Choosing the Disk Sets to Install 33

Installing Linux 35

Configuring the Installed Software 37

Other Installation Methods 41

Installing from Hard Drive 41

Installing from 3.25-Inch Floppy Disk 41

Installing from 5.25-Inch Floppy Drive 42

Installing from Tape 42

Recompiling a Kernel 50

Upgrading from a Previous Version of Linux 51

Booting the System 54

Adding Users 55

Using Kernel Modules 58

Looking for Help 59

Shutting Linux Down 60

What to Do If Things Go Wrong 60

Other Configuration Procedures 61

    Setting Up a Printer 61

    Working with PCMCIA Devices 62

    Working with a UPS 63

The X Window System 63

    X on the Network 64

    The Window Manager 65

X on Linux 66

    How XFree86 Works 66

Setting Up the XF86Config File 72

    Hardware, Hardware, Hardware 72

    Laptops and X 73

Automating the Configuration Process 75

    Setting Up Paths in the Configuration File 75

    Configuring the Server Flags Section 77

    Configuring the Keyboard Section 78

    Configuring the Pointer Section 80

    Configuring the Monitor Section 83

    Configuring the Graphics-Card Section 86

Combining the Graphics Card with the Monitor to
Make a Working X Setup 87

    Virtual Screens 88

Running the Xf86config Program 89

    Testing Your Configuration 92

Starting X 92

    VGA to the Rescue 95

    Using the Default Super VGA 95

Making the Most of X 96

    Setting Up Your X Account 96

    Configuring the Xterm Program 97

    Controlling the Size of the Xterm Window 98

Copying and Pasting between Xterm Windows 102

Starting X Automatically at Boot-Up and
Creating an X Login Screen 102

UNIX Run Levels 103

User Accounts Under Xdm 105

Starting X Automatically on Login 107

The X Font Server 108

The Fvwm Window Manager 110

Configuring Fvwm 110

Configuring Fonts and Colors 111

Testing Your Fvwm Configuration 113

Placing Icons 113

Exiting X from Fvwm 114

Summary 114

Chapter 2

C Programming Tools and Linux **115**

C Programming Tools in Linux 116

The Linux C Compiler: GNU cc 117

C Programming 118

The Cc Command 119

Using the Cc Command 122

Linking with Libraries 123

ELF Files 124

Linux Libraries 125

Creating Your Own Libraries with ar 126

Building Programs with Make 127

Debuggers 131

Parsers and Lexers 132

Other Tools 132

Other Programming Languages 133
Summary 133

Chapter 3

X Window Programming 135
What is X? 136
   Why X? 136
Imake 139
   X Window Tools 142
Programming for X on Linux 142
Programming with Toolkits 144
   Xt-Based Toolkits 144
   Installing LessTif 145
   Differences from Motif 147
   Compiling and Linking with LessTif 148
   The Xt Intrinsics and Motif 149
What Is a Widget? 149
   The Basic Format of Motif Programs 150
   XtAppInitialize 151
   Creating Widgets 152
   XmCreatePushButton 152
Xt Event Handling 153
   Setting Up Callback Functions 153
   Callback-Function Parameters 154
Container Widgets and Complex Programs 155
   Label Widgets 156
   Managing Widgets 156
   XtRealizeWidget 157
   XtAppMainLoop 158

Using Make with the Exmotif.c File 163
Athena 165
XForms 168
XView 174
Fresco, a C++ Toolkit 176
Glyphs 176
Toolkits for Other Languages 178
Summary 178

Chapter 4

Using Tcl..**181**
Linux Scripting Languages 182
Tcl 182
Scripting with Tcl 185
Tcl Variables 187
Variables and Substitutions 188
Command Substitution 189
Array Variables 190
Controlling the Flow of the Script 191
Writing Your Own Procedures 192
Summary 201

Chapter 5

Using Perl...**203**
Perl 204
A First Perl Script 205
Variables 206
Scalar Variables 206

Arrays 206

Associative Arrays 208

Working with Linux 209

The Environment Associative Array 209

Assessing the Password File 210

Executing Programs 211

Controlling the Flow of Your Scripts 211

Subroutines 214

Summary 215

Chapter 6

Java **217**

Insert Bad Coffee Pun Here: A Look at Java 218

What Is Java? 218

Creating Java Applications 220

The Inevitable "Hello World!" Application 220

Creating an Applet 222

Distributing Your Applications 224

Kaffe 224

Guavac 225

For More Information 225

Summary 226

Chapter 7

Miscellaneous Tools and Languages............................**227**

Programming Linux 228

BASIC 228

Fortran 231

Objective C 232

Pascal, Modula, and Oberon 233

    Pascal 233

    Modula 235

    Oberon 236

LISP 236

    Emacs and LISP 237

    Common LISP 237

Eiffel 238

    Small Eiffel 239

    Programming in Eiffel 240

    Compiling Eiffel Programs with Small Eiffel 241

    For More Information on Eiffel 242

Summary 242

Chapter 8

Programmer Information Sources..............................243

Looking for the Elusive Needle 244

Manual Pages 244

Documentation 244

    Frequently Asked Questions 246

    How-Tos 246

    Info Tools and Documents 247

Summary 251

Chapter 9

Debugging on Linux...253

Debugging 254

Debuggers 254

    Compiling with Debugging Options 254

Using Gdb 255

    Trying Out Gdb 256

    Gdb Commands 264

    Graphical Front Ends To Debuggers 265

    Emacs and Gdb 266

    Other Debugging Techniques 267

Debugging Java Applications 268

Summary 273

Chapter 10

More Linux Commands for Programmers............................275

Handy Linux Commands 276

Comparing Files 276

    Other File-Comparison Programs 278

Searching For Files in All the Wrong Places 282

    Searching For Data In Files 282

    Finding Files 283

Tools To Work With Object Modules and Binary Files 287

    Checking for Shared Libraries 290

    Examining Binary Files 290

Managing Versions with RCS 292

    How Version Control Systems Work 293

RCS: The Revision Control System 294

    The Only RCS Commands You Really Need 294

    More RCS Commands 296

    Working in Groups With RCS 297

    Checking the RCS Log 300

Abandoning Changes 301

Locking Without Overwriting 301

Breaking Locks 302

Version Numbers 302

Branching 303

Placing RCS IDs in Your Code 304

Checking the Differences Between Versions 306

Merging Versions 307

Using RCS From Emacs 308

Working with Image Files 308

Making Screen Shots on Linux 308

Converting Images 312

Creating Program Icons 312

Remote Connections 314

Remote Connections 315

Copying Files From Remote Machines 316

Summary 317

Appendix A

Linux Hardware Compatibility.................................319

Bus 320

Processor 320

Graphics Card 320

Hard-Drive Controllers 322

SCSI Controllers 323

Floppy Drive 324

Tape Drives 325

CD-ROM 325

Removable Drives 326

I/O Controllers 326
Network Cards 326
Multiport Controllers 328
Modems 329
ISDN Cards 329
ATM Network Adapters 330
Frame Relay Cards 330
Sound Boards 330
Mouse and Joystick 331
Printers 332
Scanners 333
Video-Capture Boards 333
Uninterruptible Power Systems 334
Data-Acquisition Equipment 334
Linux on Laptops 335
  PCMCIA and Laptops 336

Appendix B

For More Information...337
Internet Resources 338
  The Linux Documentation Project 338
  Linux.org 338
  Walnut Creek CD-ROM 339
  The Linux Applications and Utilities Page 339
  The Linux Software Map 339
  The Linux FAQ 339
  LessTif 340
  The XFree86 Project 340
  The Java-Linux Page 340

The Linux Configuration Page 340

The Linux Laptop Page 341

Linux PCMCIA Information 341

Slackware Mirrors 341

Usenet Newsgroups 343

Books 345

Other Linux Books 346

UNIX Books 346

Programming Books 347

X Window Books 347

Motif Books 347

Java Books 348

Magazines 348

OSF/Motif and Linux 348

Linux How-Tos 349

Appendix C

Linux Text Editors 351

Using the Elvis Text Editor 352

Elvis and Memory 354

Creating a Text File 354

Moving Through Your Document 355

Undoing the Last Command 356

elvis Information 356

Using Emacs 356

Emacs and Commands 358

The Many Modes of Emacs 360

Creating and Editing Files 361

Emacs and Help 363

A Basic Emacs Tutorial 363
Xedit 367
    Textedit 369
    Other Text-Editing Tools 369

Index..**371**

Introduction

Welcome to the world of programming with the Linux operating system! This book will guide you through the many programming tools available with the Slackware Linux distribution, which is contained on the accompanying CD-ROM.

What you have is a full, working implementation of Slackware Linux that's been optimized for programmers. We've included a full set of programming tools on the accompanying CD-ROM, including C, C++, Tcl, Perl, LessTif (a Motif workalike), XForms, the X Window System, Java, and more. With this book and CD-ROM, you're ready to install Linux on your PC and create applications in a variety of languages.

What Is Linux?

Linux (pronounced *lih-nux*) is a 32-bit operating system designed for use on Intel 80386 (or better) PCs. Technically, Linux is a UNIX workalike, which means that it responds to standard UNIX commands and will run UNIX programs. It's not a UNIX clone that makes use of UNIX code (and the accompanying payments for their use), which means that Linux can be made freely available to users everywhere.

Linux began life as the project of a single man, Linus Torvalds (then a student at the University of Finland at Helsinki), who wanted his own alternative to another UNIX alternative—the Minix operating system. He designed Linux to be similar to Minix (to the point where the original Minix filesystem was used in Linux), yet more stable and freely available.

For a long time, Linux was an operating system under development; many beta versions of Linux circulated throughout the computer world—mostly distributed on bulletin-board systems (BBSes) and the Internet. Version 0.2 was released to the world in the middle of 1991; in 1994, version 1.0 of Linux was finally made available. A ready and willing group of volunteers (including one of the authors of this book, Patrick Volkerding) helped create the add-on software that helps make Linux so popular. The CD-ROM accompanying this book is based on Linux 2.0 and Slackware96.

Linux, as an operating system, is actually rather trim and fit. For example, the installation system for Slackware utilizes a small Linux installation contained on just two floppy disks. So why do we use a CD-ROM with this book? Because the core operating system, as such, doesn't offer much more than a command line and a few commands. You'll need additional software, ranging from utilities and commands from the Free Software Foundation to editors and graphics programs. Because this additional software is different from distribution to distribution, there are many differences between the available Linux distributions. For example, the menu-driven installation program—so critical for many users—is unique to Slackware96. And Linux features its own graphical interface, based on the X Window System

This leads us to one essential truth about Linux: Linux is a series of tools. You use one tool to do one thing and another tool to perform another function. That's why it's important to remember that Slackware96 is more than just Linux.

What Makes Slackware96 Linux Special?

Why use Linux for your programming tasks? The following features make Linux special in the operating-system world:

- **Linux is an alternative to the commercial operating-system world**. There's something to be said for striking a blow against the Empire, especially the Empire from Redmond. Linux is the result of many hours of volunteer workers who believe that a grass-roots approach to software development is a more harmonic approach than commercial offerings. Whether you buy into this ethos is up to you, but you cannot help but be impressed that such an outstanding computer operating system, rich in complexity and features, is the work of so many.

- **Linux is completely open**. You get the source code for the Linux operating system on the accompanying CD-ROM. If you want to make changes to the operating system, you can do so.

- **Linux contains a full set of programming tools**. Slackware96 contains all the major programming tools you'll need in the computer world, ranging from powerful C and C++ compilers from the Free Software Foundation to Perl, Tcl, XForms, and LessTif. These tools can be used to create applications for any version of UNIX and portable applications that can be used on the Internet.

Linux, Slackware96, and This Book

This book and the accompanying version of Slackware96 are specifically geared toward programmers. We're not going to explain the in-depth usage of these programming tools, because almost all of the programming tools discussed in this book (C, Perl, Tcl, Java, X Window System) are the subject of many programming books on the market (some of which we'll cover in Appendix B).

You can think of this book as a roadmap to the programming resources in Slackware96 on the accompanying CD-ROM, rather than as an in-depth primer on programming. We're not going to tell you with a straight face that you can learn all about C, C++, Perl, Tcl, Java, X Window System, and Motif/LessTif programming through this book.

A full, working implementation of Slackware96 is included on the accompanying CD-ROM. Installation directions are included in Chapter 1.

The FSF GNU Public License

Anyone developing applications on Linux will need to deal with the GNU Public Licenses if they use Free Software Foundation. This isn't something to dismiss, but it's not necessarily something to worry about, either.

Basically, there are two FSF licenses:

- The GNU General Public License (GPL) covers the Linux kernel, the GNU C compiler (GCC), and many Linux applications.
- The GNU Library General Public License (LGPL) covers most Linux libraries.

There are some strings attached to these licenses. Basically, these licenses specify that any software created with GNU tools be distributed in source-code form (and not in binary form, as is the case with most commercial applications). They also allow for anyone else to copy and distribute the software in source-code form.

If you're using Linux for corporate internal application development, you won't need to worry too much about these restrictions, because you're not preparing applications for public consumption. If you're a shareware/freeware programmer, you've probably already bought into the Linux ethos and will be distributing your applications along with source code.

If you're using Linux for commercial development and don't really relish releasing the source code along with your application, you'll need to make sure your applications don't run afoul of these licenses.

Conventions Used in the Book

To make this book more usable, we've incorporated a few formatting conventions that should make it easier for you to find what you need. These include the following icons:

 The *Note* icon indicates something that you should pay attention to.

 The *Warning* icon warns you about actions that could be hazardous to the health of your Linux installation.

 The *CD-ROM* icon refers to items found on the accompanying CD-ROM.

Contacting the Authors

Feel free to drop us a line via electronic mail at *reichard@mr.net*. However, we must warn you that we promise no further guidance to Linux than what's printed in this book. Among the three of us, we receive a lot of electronic mail, and at times it's impossible to keep up with it. Please don't assume that this electronic-mail address will bring you instant help—or any help at all.

You can also find more information about Linux, this book, and other Linux texts at *http://www.kreichard.com*.

Installing Linux and XFree86

This chapter covers:

- Preparing your PC for Linux
- Creating new partitions under DOS
- Creating your bootdisk and rootdisk
- Installing from the **setup** command
- Selecting the software to install
- Logging onto the virgin Linux system
- Adding hardware drivers with kernel modules
- Configuring X and XFree86
- Working with the **fvwm** window manager
- Shutting down Linux and X

Installing and Configuring Linux and XFree86

Installing Linux isn't a terribly complicated process, provided you have a rather generic computer system. If not, installation complexity can range from mildly annoying to moderately troublesome.

In this chapter, we'll cover the steps needed to install and configure Linux on your computer. This is the streamlined version of the installation instructions; for a more complete guide, we recommend you check out a book on the subject, *Linux Installation and Configuration*, second edition (MIS:Press, 1996).

N O T E No, we're not merely trying to force you to buy another book that we happened to write. Linux is a complex operating system (as all operating systems tend to be), and it takes a whole book to explain its many facets and capabilities. Still, the truncated installation instructions here should suffice for most experienced users, especially if all you want to get out of Linux is its programming capabilities. If you're not really conversant with operating systems and/or UNIX, you'll want to check out *Linux Installation and Configuration*.

Linux installation is somewhat involved. You can't install Linux directly from the accompanying CD-ROM; you must first configure your hard drive, create boot floppies, run a trimmed-down Linux kernel, and then install Linux from the CD-ROM drive. None of these steps is particularly difficult. The actual installation process is:

- Create boot and root floppies.
- Prepare your hard drive for installation.
- Boot Linux from the boot and root floppies.
- Install Linux from the CD-ROM.

In the following steps, we're assuming you already have a PC up and running with the MS-DOS operating system and a CD-ROM drive installed correctly, because you'll need to copy some files from the CD-ROM onto your hard drive. This doesn't need to be the PC you plan on installing Linux on; it just needs to be a PC with a DOS command line and access to the CD-ROM drive.

The procedures in this chapter are specific to the installation and configuration routines found on the accompanying CD-ROM. Other distributions of Linux are not the same.

Creating Boot and Root Floppies

Your first steps will be to create two floppy disks used to boot Linux: the boot and root diskettes. The *boot diskette* is the diskette used (as the name implies) to boot the PC, while the *root diskette* contains a set of Linux commands (actually, a complete mini-Linux system). Creating these disks is probably the best way to install Linux, although it is possible to install Linux without using any floppy disks using **LOADLIN.EXE**, a DOS program that loads Linux from an MS-DOS prompt. We'll cover this option a little later, but unless your floppy disk doesn't work under Linux, it is recommended that you install using a bootdisk and rootdisk.

Your next step is to determine which bootdisk and rootdisk images you'll be using to write writing the images onto formatted floppy disks. Because deciding which disk images to use (especially on the bootdisk) can be a relatively large task, it warrants its own section.

Choosing Bootdisk and Rootdisk Images

Linux needs to know a lot about your PC's hardware, and that knowledge begins the second you boot the system. That's why you need to put some thought into selecting your bootdisk and rootdisk images.

Before we go any further, we should explain what bootdisk and rootdisk images are. Linux needs to boot from floppies initially, and it needs to know what sort of hardware it's working with. When you boot Linux for the first time, the information is contained on the bootdisk and the rootdisk. To create a bootdisk and a rootdisk, you need to select the proper images. You'll then use the **RAWRITE.EXE** utility to copy the images byte for byte to the diskettes.

How do you select the proper image? The first step is to determine the disk size of your drive **A:**, which you boot the system from. If you're using a 3.5-inch disk drive as **A:**, you'll need to grab an image from the **bootdsks.144** directory. (This is so labeled because the capacity of a 3.5-inch high-density floppy is 1.44 megabytes.) If you're using a 5.25-inch disk drive to boot from, you'll need to grab an image from the **bootdsks.12** directory. (This is so labeled because the capacity of a 5.25-inch high-density floppy is 1.2 megabytes.)

If you look inside either directory, you'll see a list of filenames ending in **.I** (for *IDE*) or **.S** (for *SCSI*). (The filenames are the same in both directories; it doesn't matter from this point which directory you grab the image from.) Each image supports a different set of hardware; a list of the files and supported hardware is in Tables 1.1 (for IDE bootdisks) and 1.2 (for SCSI bootdisks).

Table 1.1 Linux IDE bootdisks and supported hardware. All IDE bootdisks support IDE hard drives and CD-ROM drives, plus additional support listed here.

Filename	Supported Hardware
aztech.i	CD-ROM drives: Aztech CDA268-01A, Orchid CD-3110, Okano/Wearnes CDD110, Conrad TXC, CyCDROM CR520, CR540
bare.i	IDE hard-drive only
cdu31a.i	Sony CDU31/33a CD-ROM
cdu535.i	Sony CDU531/535 CD-ROM
cm206.i	Philips/LMS cm206 CD-ROM with cm260 adapter card
goldstar.i	Goldstar R420 CD-ROM (sometimes sold in a Reveal Multimedia Kit)
mcd.i	Non-IDE Mitsumi CD-ROM
mcdx.i	Improved non-IDE Mitsumi CD-ROM support
net.i	Ethernet support
optics.i	Optics Storage 8000 AT CD-ROM (know as the "Dolphin" drive)
sanyo.i	Sanyo CDR-H94A CD-ROM
sbpcd.i	Matsushita, Kotobuki, Panasonic, Creative Labs (SoundBlaster), Longshine, TEAC non-IDE CD-ROM
xt.i	MFM hard drive

Table 1.2 Linux SCSI bootdisks and hardware support. All SCSI bootdisks feature full IDE hard-drive and CD-ROM support, plus additional drivers listed here.

Filename	Supported Hardware
7000fast.s	Western Digital 7000FASST SCSI
advansys.s	AdvanSys SCSI support
aha152x.s	Adaptec 152x SCSI
aha1542.s	Adaptec 1542 SCSI
aha1740.s	Adaptec 1740 SCSI
aha2x4x.s	Adaptec AIC7xxx SCSI (including AHA-274x, AHA-2842, AHA-2940, AHA-2940W, AHA-2940U, AHA-2940UW, AHA-2944D, AHA-2944WD, AHA-3940, AHA-3940W, AHA-3985, AHA-3985W
am53c974.s	AMD AM53/79C974 SCSI
aztech.s	All supported SCSI controllers, plus CD-ROM support for Aztech CDA268-01A, Orchid CD-3110, Okano/Wearnes CDD110, Conrad TXC, CyCDROM CR520, CR540
buslogic.s	Buslogic MultiMaster SCSI
cdu31a.s	All supported SCSI controllers, plus CD-ROM support for Sony CDU31/33a
cdu535.s	All supported SCSI controllers, plus CD-ROM support for Sony CDU531/535
cm206.s	All supported SCSI controllers, plus Philips/LMS cm206 CD-ROM with cm260 adapter card
dtc3280.s	DTC (Data Technology Corp.) 3180/3280 SCSI
eata_dma.s	DPT EATA-DMA SCSI (boards such as PM2011, PM2021, PM2041, PM3021, PM2012B, PM2022, PM2122, PM2322, PM2042, PM3122, PM3222, PM3332, PM2024, PM2124, PM2044, PM2144, PM3224, PM3334)
eata_isa.s	DPT EATA-ISA/EISA SCSI support (boards such as PM2011B/9X, PM2021A/9X, PM2012A, PM2012B, PM2022A/9X, PM2122A/9X, PM2322A/9X)
eata_pio.s	DPT EATA-PIO SCSI (PM2001, PM2012A)
fdomain.s	Future Domain TMC-16x0 SCSI
goldstar.s	All supported SCSI controllers, plus Goldstar R420 CD-ROM (sometimes sold in a Reveal Multimedia Kit)
in2000.s	Always IN2000 SCSI
iomega.s	IOMEGA PPA3 parallel-port SCSI (also supports parallel-port version of the ZIP drive)
mcd.s	All supported SCSI controllers, plus standard non-IDE Mitsumi CD-ROM

continued...

Filename	Supported Hardware
mcdx.s	All supported SCSI controllers, plus enhanced non-IDE Mitsumi CD-ROM
n53c406a.s	NCR 53c406a SCSI
n_5380.s	NCR 5380 and 53c400 SCSI
n_53c7xx.s	NCR 53c7xx, 53c8xx SCSI (most NCR PCI SCSI controllers use this driver)
optics.s	All supported SCSI controllers, plus support for the Optics Storage 8000 AT CD-ROM (the "Dolphin" drive)
pas16.s	Pro Audio Spectrum/Studio 16 SCSI
qlog_fas.s	ISA/VLB/PCMCIA Qlogic FastSCSI! (also supports the Control Concepts SCSI cards based on the Qlogic FASXXX chip)
qlog_isp.s	Supports all Qlogic PCI SCSI controllers, except the PCI-basic, which is supported by the AMD SCSI driver
sanyo.s	All supported SCSI controllers, plus Sanyo CDR-H94A CD-ROM
sbpcd.s	All supported SCSI controllers, plus Matsushita, Kotobuki, Panasonic, Creative Labs (SoundBlaster), Longshine, and TEAC NON-IDE CD-ROMs
scsinet.s	All supported SCSI controllers, plus full Ethernet
seagate.s	Seagate ST01/ST02 and Future Domain TMC-885/950 SCSI
trantor.s	Trantor T128/T128F/T228 SCSI
ultrastr.s	UltraStor 14F, 24F, 34F SCSI
ustor14f.s	UltraStor 14F, 34F SCSI

N O T E   All of these images support UMSDOS, if you prefer this method of installation. UMSDOS will be covered later in this chapter in the section, "Should You Use UMSDOS?"

You'll need one of these to get Linux started on your system so that you can install the full operating system. Because of the possibility of collisions between the various Linux drivers, several bootkernel disk images are provided. You should use the one with the least drivers possible to maximize your chances of success. All of these disks support UMSDOS.

At first glance, Tables 1.1 and 1.2 can be a little confusing. To clear things up, Table 1.3 contains a handy little guide that matches installation medium and hard-disk format to the preferred image (in **bold**).

Table 1.3 A chart for choosing bootdisk images.

Installation Medium	IDE Destination	SCSI Destination	MFM Destination
Hard drive	**bare.i**	Use a SCSI controller bootdisk from the list following the table	**xt.i**
SCSI CD-ROM	Use a SCSI controller bootdisk from the list following the table		Use a SCSI controller bootdisk from the list following the table
IDE/ATAPI CD-ROM	**bare.i**	Use a SCSI controller bootdisk from the list following the table	
Aztech, Orchid, Okano, Wearnes, Conrad, CyCDROM non-IDE CD-ROM	**aztech.i**	**aztech.s**	
Sony CDU31a, Sony CDU33a CD-ROM	**cdu31a.i**	**cdu31a.s**	
Sony CDU531, Sony CDU535 CD-ROM	**cdu535.i**	**cdu535.s**	
Philips/LMS cm 206 CD-ROM	**cm206.i**	**cm206.s**	
Goldstar R420 CD-ROM	**goldstar.i**	**goldstar.s**	
Mitsumi non-IDE CD-ROM	**mcdx.i, mcd.i**	**mcdx.s, mcd.i**	
Optics Storage 8000 AT CD-ROM ("Dolphin")	**optics.i**	**optics.s**	

continued...

Installation Medium	IDE Destination	SCSI Destination	MFM Destination
Sanyo CDR-H94A CD-ROM	**sanyo.i**	**sanyo.s**	
Matsushita, Kotobuki, Panasonic, Creative Labs (SoundBlaster), Longshine, TEAC non-IDE CD-ROM	**sbpcd.i**	**sbpcd.s**	
NFS	**net.i**	**scsinet.i**	
Tape	**bare.i** (for floppy tape); for SCSI tape, use a SCSI controller bootdisk from the list following the table	Use a SCSI controller bootdisk from the list following the table	**xt.i** (for floppy tape)

SCSI controller bootdisks: **7000fast.s, advansys.s, aha152x.s, aha1542.s, aha1740.s, aha2x4x.s, am53c974.s, buslogic.s, dtc3280.s, eata_dma.s, eata_isa.s, eata_pio.s, fdomain.s, in2000.s, iomega.s, n53c406a.s, n_5380.s, n_53c7xx.s, pas16.s, qlog_fas.s, qlog_isp.s, seagate.s, trantor.s, ultrastr.s, ustor14f.s.**

Choosing the Proper Rootdisk Image

After selecting the proper bootdisk image, you'll need to select the proper rootdisk image. The selections are more limited, so you won't have to put too much work into this selection. The rootdisks are stored in the **ROOTDSKS** directory and will work with either 3.5-inch or 5.25-inch high-density diskettes.

Your rootdisk image selections are listed in Table 1.4.

Table 1.4 Rootdisk selections.

Filename	Purpose
COLOR.GZ	This image contains a full-screen color install program and should be considered the default rootdisk image. This version of the install system has some known bugs, however; in particular, it is not forgiving of extra keystrokes entered between screens. This is probably the file you'll want to use.
UMSDOS.GZ	This is similar to the COLOR disk, but installs using UMSDOS, a filesystem that allows you to install Linux into a directory on an existing MS-DOS partition. This filesystem is not as fast as a native Linux filesystem but it works, and you don't have to repartition your hard drive.
TEXT.GZ	This is a text-based version of the install program derived from scripts used in previous Slackware releases.
TAPE.GZ	This image is designed to support installation from tape. See the section "Installing from Tape" later in this chapter.

N O T E You'll notice that these filenames end in the **.GZ** extension; this indicates that the files have been compressed with GNU **zip**. Some older distributions of Linux required that the files be decompressed prior to use, but this is not necessary anymore. The kernel on the bootdisk will detect that the rootdisk is compressed and will automatically decompress the disk as it is loaded into RAM. This allows the use of a 1.44MB uncompressed image size for both 1.44MB and 1.2MB floppy drives.

Most users will use the **COLOR.GZ** rootdisk image.

Should You Use UMSDOS?

The UMSDOS filesystem allows you to install Linux in an MS-DOS directory on an existing DOS partition. The advantage of this is that you won't need to reformat or repartition your existing system. There are two disadvantages to using this system, however.

First, the UMSDOS system is somewhat slower than using a native Linux filesystem. This is especially true of machines with 8 megabytes of memory or less; UMSDOS is virtually unusable on a 4MB machine. The second disadvantage of UMSDOS has to do with a shortcoming of the MS-DOS FAT filesystem. MS-DOS allocates space for files in units called *clusters*. A cluster is usually 4 or 8 kilobytes. This means that the smallest file that can be created on a UMSDOS filesystem takes up a full cluster (4096+ bytes), even if the file is much smaller. Linux contains many such small files, including symbolic links and device entries. As a result, installing with UMSDOS can require a good bit more drive space than installing with a native Linux filesystem.

Now that you've chosen your bootdisk and rootdisk images, it's time to create the bootdisk and rootdisk.

Creating the Diskettes

For this step, you'll need two high-density diskettes. It doesn't matter what's on the diskettes, but they must be formatted. Just be warned that this process will completely wipe out anything currently stored on the diskettes. You might also wish to format a third high-density floppy disk at this time for the installation program to use later when preparing your system bootdisk.

NOTE   As you'll recall from an earlier note, the images for the rootdisks do not need to be decompressed; the kernel will automatically decompress them as it loads them into memory.

In these examples, we'll be using the **BARE.I** and **COLOR.GZ** images. If you're using a different set of images, just substitute those filenames.

NOTE   The procedures in this section do not need to be done on the computer you're planning to use as your Linux workstation. You can create the files on a different PC or even use a UNIX workstation to create the floppies. On a UNIX workstation the **dd** command is used to write an image to the floppy drive. When using **dd** on Suns, and possibly on other UNIX workstations, you must provide an approximate block size. Here's an example:

```
dd if=bare.i of=/dev/(rdfd0, rdf0c, fd0, or whatever) obs=18k
```

Now it's time to make your bootdisk. First, move into the **bootdisks.144** directory (or **bootdisks.12** if you use a 1.2-MB floppy drive) on your Slackware CD-ROM.

Assuming your CD-ROM drive has the drive letter **E:** assigned to it, you'd move into the directory like this:

```
C:\> E:
E:\> CD BOOTDSKS.144
E:\BOOTDSKS.144>
```

Now you'll actually create the bootdisk. Put the eventual bootdisk diskette in drive **A:** and type the following command:

```
E:\> RAWRITE BARE.I A:
```

This will use the **RAWRITE** command (there's a copy of this in each of the **BOOTDSKS** and **ROOTDSKS** directories) to copy the **BARE.I** disk image to the **A:** floppy drive. As it writes, **RAWRITE** will give you a status report. After it's finished writing the bootdisk, remove it from the drive and put it aside.

Then insert another blank formatted high-density floppy and use the same procedure to write out the rootdisk. In this case, you'll need to move into the **ROOTDSKS** directory and write out the **COLOR.GZ** image using **RAWRITE**:

```
E:\BOOTDSKS.144> cd \ROOTDSKS
E:\ROOTDSKS> RAWRITE COLOR.GZ A:
```

There's really not much to the **RAWRITE** command; the only things that can go wrong would be if you're not using a high-density diskette or if the diskette is flawed.

Preparing Your Hard Drive for Linux

Now that you've created your bootdisks, it's time to prepare your hard drive for Linux. In order to install Linux, you must create a Linux partition on your hard drive. You should also consider creating a DOS partition on your hard drive in addition to the Linux partition—a step that's not necessary, but that we follow for many reasons (which we'll explain later).

If you're a UNIX workstation user, you're not going to be familiar with some of the concepts and operations we describe here. If, after reading this section, you're still a little fuzzy about the IBM PC and its many quirks, you may want to head for your **N O T E**   local bookstore and purchase a good guide to the PC.

Intel-based PCs can divide a hard drive into *partitions*. This is why you may have several different drive letters (**C:, D:, E:**) even though you have only one physical hard drive. (This dates from the early versions of MS-DOS, which lacked the ability to recognize hard-disk partitions larger than 33 megabytes; MS-DOS 4.0 was the first version to do away with this restriction.) The ability to create partitions also yields a bonus (as far as a Linux user is concerned): You can install different operating systems on a hard drive, and these different operating systems won't conflict. As a matter of fact, they can coexist quite nicely; you can configure Linux to give you your choice of operating systems when you boot your PC, and you can access DOS-formatted partitions from within Linux. Linux is relatively good about coexisting with other operating systems—primarily, DOS, Windows, Windows 95, and OS/2. Linux requires at least one partition for itself.

You must physically create partitions, as Intel-based PCs need to know what type of operating system is residing on a portion of the hard drive. If you purchased your PC from a clone vendor or superstore and started using it immediately, chances are that you've treated the hard disk as one contiguous drive without partitioning it into smaller drives. In a perfect world, of course, you're installing Linux on a brand-new system, and there's little of importance currently installed on your hard disk. This is the route we try to follow, because there's little chance of damaging anything important.

However, if you've been using your PC for a while, you've probably accumulated software, data files, and configurations that you're loathe to give up. In this case, you'll want to retain as much of the DOS configuration as possible, while making room for Linux. There are two routes you can take:

- Use the **FIPS** utility to partition the hard drive without (theoretically) destroying the existing data.
- Backing up the DOS data, creating the new Linux and DOS partitions, and then reinstalling the backup. (This is our preferred method.) You'll need to make sure that the new partition is large enough to contain all the data from the old DOS partition, of course.

In either case, you'll want to first make a backup of your hard disk, either on floppy disks or some tape-based medium (Bernoulli drive, Syquest tape, DAT tape). Depending on your system configuration, you'll either want to back up everything or just those directories that can't easily be reinstalled from floppy or CD-ROM. (We find that a good system cleansing is a good thing every once in a while, so we tend to back up data and irreplaceable configuration files and reinstall applications from scratch.) Yes, we know backing up your hard drive is a pain (and we probably don't do it as often as we should), but you should make a backup every time you do something to your hard drive that could destroy data.

Using FIPS to Divide Your Hard Drive

After you make your backup, you'll need to decide which route to take. The **FIPS** utility described earlier is stored in the root directory of the accompanying CD-ROM as **FIPS.EXE**; the guide to using **FIPS** is stored in the same location as **FIPS.DOC**. (If you plan on using the **FIPS** utility, we *strongly* advise you to read through this file a couple of times; it contains far more information and detail than here.)

Basically, **FIPS** works by creating a new partition on the physical end of the hard drive. Before the **FIPS** utility does so, you must first defragment your hard drive. A word about how a PC's hard drive stores data is in order here.

When a PC writes to a hard disk, it writes to clusters on disk. Generally speaking, this writing is done sequentially; the first clusters appear at the physical beginning of the disk. As you use the system, you inevitably write more and more to the hard drive, and you probably delete data as well. As you delete the data, the clusters it occupied are freed; at the same time, new data is written to the end of the disk. Any hard disk that's been in use for a while will have data scattered throughout the physical drive. (This is why hard drives slow down when they fill with data; the drive head must physically hop around the drive to retrieve scattered data.)

When you *defragment* your hard drive, you're replacing the freed clusters at the beginning of the drive with data from the end of the drive. While not purely sequential, your data is all crammed at the beginning of the hard drive. This improves disk performance; because your data is physically closer together, the drive head spends less time retrieving data that had been scattered.

 Newer versions of MS-DOS and PC-DOS (that is, versions 6.0 and later) contain a defragmenting utility. (Check your operating system documentation for specifics; the utilities differ.) If you're using an older version of MS-DOS, you'll need to use a general-purpose utility package (such as the Norton Utilities or PC Tools Deluxe) to defragment your hard drive.

The **FIPS** utility takes advantage of the fact that the data is crammed at the beginning of the hard drive. It allows you to create a point past the end of the DOS data to begin the new Linux partition (if you use this method, remember to leave room for more data in the DOS partition!).

We're not going to spend a lot of time on **FIPS** here because the documentation on the accompanying CD-ROM more than adequately explains how **FIPS** works, its limitations, and the exact procedures for dividing a hard drive. The only caveat we offer is that you should know a little about how PCs deal with hard drive partitions before using **FIPS**; if you're a PC neophyte, we suggest you follow the steps detailed in the next section.

 FIPS will not work with OS/2. The details are contained in the **FIPS.DOC** file. In addition, you should run **FIPS** from DOS, rather than from a multitasking environment like Windows or DESQview.

Using DOS Utilities to Divide Your Hard Drive

The second method to prepare your hard drive for Linux involves various DOS utilities, which you'll use to create new partitions and configure a floppy diskette you can use to boot your PC with DOS.

The first step involves creating a DOS boot diskette. (You've already created a Linux boot diskette; the two are different.) This is a rather simple procedure, involving the following command line:

```
C:> format /s A:
```

where **A:** is your boot drive. This command formats a floppy disk and adds the system files (**COMMAND.COM** and the hidden files **IO.SYS** and **MSDOS.SYS**) needed to boot DOS from the floppy. If you install a DOS partition, booting from this diskette will give you access to that partition (which will appear as drive **C:**). It will *not*, however, give you access to the CD-ROM until you install the CD-ROM drivers on the DOS boot diskette.

When you installed DOS, it should have directed you to create an emergency boot floppy. You may need this diskette if something goes wrong in the installation.

N O T E

After doing this, you'll need to copy some additional utilities to the floppy. You'll need to be fairly selective about which files you copy to the floppy, because the sum of all DOS **.EXE** and **.COM** files (essentially, the utility files) in a typical DOS installation won't fit on a floppy disk. You'll need to copy the **FDISK.EXE** and **FORMAT.COM** files to the floppy drive with the following command lines:

```
C:> copy \DOS\FDISK.EXE A:
    1 file(s) copied

C:> copy \DOS\FORMAT.COM A:
    1 file(s) copied
```

You may also want to copy onto floppies the files that restore your system backup, if you used operating system utilities to create the backup. Check your documentation for the specific files; they differ between operating systems.

What are FDISK and FORMAT?

We've told you to copy **FDISK.EXE** and **FORMAT.COM** onto the floppy for future use, so we should take some time to explain what they do.

FDISK.EXE is the program that creates MS-DOS partitions. Every operating system has a program that does something similar (you'll use the Linux **fdisk** command later in this process). You'll need to use the partitioning software specific to the operating system; for example, you can't use the DOS **FDISK** to create Linux or OS/2 partitions. **FDISK.EXE** works very simply: You delete an existing partition or partitions and create new partitions in their place.

Creating a partition merely leaves a portion of your hard disk devoted to that particular operating system. After you've used **FDISK.EXE** to create a new DOS partition, you'll use the **FORMAT.COM** program to format that partition for use under MS-DOS. If you don't format the MS-DOS partition, the operating system won't be able to recognize it.

Using the DOS FDISK Utility

Now that you've created the system backup and a boot diskette, it's time to destroy the data on your hard drive with the **FDISK** utility. Destroy? Yup. The act of creating new partitions is by definition a destructive act. You must destroy the existing partitions and the records of the data contained therein in order to create the new partitions.

You can use **FDISK** if your system has more than one hard drive. In this case, you'll want to make sure you're working on the correct hard drive. **FDISK** does not use the normal DOS drive representations (**C:**, **D:**, **E:**, etc.); rather, **FDISK** uses numerals, such as **1** or **2**.

Begin by booting your PC from the floppy drive you created in the previous section. This vanilla boot will ask for today's date and time (ignore both; they don't matter) and then give you the following command line:

```
A>
```

You're now ready to run the DOS **FDISK** utility:

```
A> fdisk
```

There are no command-line parameters to **FDISK**.

The program loads and displays something like the screen shown in Figure 1.1.

```
MS-DOS Version 5.00
Fixed Disk Setup Program
(C) Copyright Microsoft 1983 - 1991
FDISK OPTIONS


Current fixed disk drive: 1

Choose one of the following:

1. Create DOS partition or Logical DOS Drive
2. Set active partition
3. Delete partition or Logical DOS Drive
4. Display partition information

Enter choice: [1]

Press Esc to exit FDISK
```

Figure 1.1 The opening screen to the **FDISK** utility.

N O T E   The figures is this section are for a specific version of MS-DOS. However, most versions of MS-DOS follow the conventions shown and explained here. If the choices on your system aren't exactly like the ones here, read through them carefully and use the most similar choice. Remember: You are essentially deleting a partition and creating a new one in this procedure.

At this point you need to delete the existing partition, so choose **3**. (If you're not sure about the existing partitions on your disk or whether you're even working on the correct disk if you have more than one, select **4**.)

N O T E   When using the **FDISK** utility, you'll see references to primary and extended partitions, as well as logical drives. Here an explanation:

- The *primary* partition is the partition containing the files (**IO.SYS**, **MSDOS.SYS**, and **COMMAND.COM**) needed to boot MS-DOS. In essence, this is your **C:** drive. The partition cannot be divided into other logical drives.

- The *extended* partition or partitions do not contain these boot files. An extended partition can exist as its own logical drive (such as **D:** or **E:**) or be divided into additional logical drives.

- The *logical drive* is the portion of a partition assigned a drive letter. For example, an extended partition can be divided into up to 23 logical drives (**A:** and **B:** are reserved for floppies, and **C:** is reserved for the primary partition, leaving 23 letters).

Additionally, the *non-DOS partition* is for another operating system, such as Linux.

Chances are that you won't need to deal with more than a primary drive and an extended drive.

After selecting **3**, you'll see the screen shown in Figure 1.2.

What you do at this point depends on how your hard drive has been configured. If you have primary and extended partitions, delete them. If you have only a primary drive, delete it. **FDISK** will confirm that you do indeed want to delete a partition. This is your last chance to chicken out and check the DOS partition one more time before wiping it out.

After deleting a partition, you'll need to create a new DOS partition— a choice that's listed in Figure 1.1 as option **1**. After choosing **1**, you'll be shown a screen like Figure 1.3.

```
Delete DOS Partition or Logical DOS Drive

Current fixed disk drive: 1

Choose one of the following:

1. Delete Primary DOS Partition
2. Delete Extended DOS Partition
3. Delete Logical DOS Drive(s) in the Extended DOS Partition
4. Delete Non-DOS Partition

Enter choice: [ ]

Press Esc to return to FDISK Options
```

Figure 1.2 The delete screen for **FDISK**.

```
Create DOS Partition or Logical DOS Drive

Current fixed disk drive: 1

Choose one of the following:

1. Create Primary DOS Partition
2. Create Extended DOS Partition
3. Create Logical DOS Drive(s) in the Extended DOS Partition

Enter choice: [1]

Press Esc to return to FDISK Options
```

Figure 1.3 Creating a new partition with **FDISK**.

Of course, you'll want to create a new primary partition; this is the partition that will be used for DOS.

The next thing you need to decide is how much of the hard drive to devote to DOS. There are no hard-and-fast rules concerning partition sizes. Obviously, you'll first need to think about how much of a priority Linux is—if you plan on running Linux a lot, you should give it a lot of hard disk space. If you plan on using it as much as DOS, you should equalize the two installations somewhat, keeping in mind that Linux will require far more hard disk space than DOS. And if you plan on using Microsoft Windows along with DOS and Linux, you should assume that Windows will suck up as much hard-disk space as it can get.

Our only advice: Don't be stingy when it comes to Linux hard disk allocation. Remember that Linux applications tend to eat up a *lot* of disk real estate. It's not unusual to run across freely available binaries on the Internet that are more than a megabyte (such as the popular Web browser NCSA Mosaic for X Window), and in time these applications add up. If you're really careful during installation and install only the applications you need, you can keep a Linux installation down to 100 megabytes or so. Realistically, however, by the time you include everything worth having, you'll be up to about 275 megabytes. If you only have a 325MB hard disk, you'll want to keep the DOS partition to about 10 megabytes.

Don't bother with any other partitions—at least none for Linux usage. You probably won't want to create a logical DOS drive; if you do, you can't use it for a Linux installation, because all Linux partitions must be created through Linux later in the installation process.

After deciding how much hard-disk space to give to DOS, you'll want to exit **FDISK**. Go ahead and make the DOS partition active (this means that you can boot from it later, which you'll want to do; you can have multiple partitions than can boot).

After quitting **FDISK**, reboot the system, leaving the DOS diskette in drive **A:**. Now you want to format drive **C:**—or at least the DOS portion of it—with the DOS **FORMAT** command:

```
A> FORMAT /S C:
```

This command formats the DOS partition with the core of the operating system (the **COMMAND.COM**, **IO.SYS**, and **MSDOS.SYS** files). The **FORMAT** command makes sure that you want to go ahead with the format (this is to make sure that DOS neophytes don't accidentally format a partition that contains valuable information); you'll answer in the affirmative when asked whether you want to proceed with the format.

You can use any version of DOS for these steps, as long as it's DOS 4.0 or later. DOS doesn't care if you format the hard drive with one version of DOS and install another version later.

NOTE

Now that you've prepared the DOS side of your hard disk (and after looking back, realizing it's a lot easier than the extended verbiage in the previous sections would make it seem), it's time to boot Linux.

FDISK and OS/2

When preparing a PC for use with OS/2 and Linux, you need to use a slightly different route for preparing your hard drive.

OS/2 has trouble with partitions not originally created with *its* **FDISK** utility. Therefore, you must start by partitioning your hard disk with the OS/2 **FDISK** utility (keeping in mind that OS/2 needs more than 35 megabytes of hard-disk space to run at all). Then you must create the Linux partition with the OS/2 **FDISK** utility—marked as another OS/2 partition—and make that a potential boot partition using OS/2's Boot Manager. (OS/2 lets you select a boot partition every time you boot the PC.)

You'll then boot your PC with the instructions given next. However, later in the process you'll do something a little different when it comes to the Linux **fdisk** command (which we'll cover at that point in the installation process).

Booting Linux with the Bootdisk

Obviously, you boot Linux with the bootdisk you prepared earlier. Put it in your boot drive and restart your PC with a cold or warm boot (it doesn't matter which).

Initially, your PC will do what it normally does when it boots, such as check the memory and run through the BIOS. However, the word *LILO* will soon appear on your screen, followed by a full screen that begins with the line:

```
Welcome to the Slackware96 Linux 3.1.0 bootkernel disk!
```

You'll also see some verbiage about passing parameters along to the kernel. Most users won't need to pass along any additional parameters.

The exceptions are some IBM PS/1, ValuePoint, and ThinkPad users, as Linux will not recognize the hard disks used by these machines. These IBM computers don't store the hard-disk information in the CMOS, which is checked by Linux upon booting up. Because Linux lacks this information, it assumes there's no hard drive present. You must pass along the hard-disk geometry at this point.

If you are using one of these machines, you cannot use the **bare** bootdisk. Instead, you should use **scsi**. When you boot using this bootdisk, you should press down the left **Shift** key, which gives you a menu where you can specify the geometry of the hard disk. Where do you get this information? From the drive's installation guide or by checking the machine's internal setup.

Most users will be able to press the **Enter** key and proceed to load the Linux RAM disk.

There are some cases where *LILO* appears on the screen and the system hangs or rows of *0*s and *1*s cascade down the screen. In these cases, you are probably using the wrong bootdisk for your PC. The first thing to do is to create a few alternate bootdisks and try them; if the problem persists, scan the Usenet newsgroups and FTP archives (see Appendix B for details) to make sure that your PC and its peripherals are indeed supported by Linux.

The bootdisk runs through your system hardware, noting which hard drives and peripherals are present, and scouting out other salient details about your PC. It's at this point Linux discovers any problems with your PC, and if you have problems installing or using Linux, it's a place you'll want to check. (The same information is displayed and gathered every time you boot.)

If there are no problems, you can put in your rootdisk and press **Enter**. A core of the Linux operating system is then copied to the RAM disk, which gives you access to some Linux commands, including the important **fdisk** command. The installation process instructs you to login the Linux system as *root*:

```
slackware login : root
```

There will be no password required.

If you're asked for a password, it means you don't have enough memory to install.

Before you proceed, carefully look through the instructions on the screen. There are a few notes that may apply to your specific computing situation.

Linux and Hard-Disk Names

After logging in, you'll want to directly run the **fdisk** command (ignoring what the screen instructions say about the **setup** command). The **fdisk** command assumes that the first IDE drive is the default drive. If you plan on installing Linux on another drive, you'll need to specify that on the command line. Table 1.5 lists the hard disk device names.

Table 1.5 Linux hard-disk device names.

Name	Meaning
/dev/hda	First IDE hard drive
/dev/hdb	Second IDE hard drive
/dev/sda	First SCSI hard drive
/dev/sdb	Second SCSI hard drive
/dev/fd0	First floppy drive (A:)
/dev/fd1	Second floppy drive (B:)

Note the pattern in Table 1.5? Additionally, Linux allows you to specify the partitions in the device names. For example, the first primary partition on the first IDE drive would be known as **/dev/hda1**, the second primary partition on the first IDE drive would be known as **/dev/hda2**, and so on. If you're installing logical partitions, the first logical partition would appear as **/dev/hda5**, the second logical partition would appear as **/dev/hda6**, and so on.

The files representing these devices will end up in the directory **/dev**.

NOTE

To run **fdisk** on the second SCSI hard drive, you'd use the following command line:

```
# fdisk /dev/sdb
```

For most of you (because most PCs are sold with IDE drives), you'll be told that Linux is using the first hard drive as the default. When you press **m** for a list of options, you'll see the following list:

```
Command   action
   a      toggle a bootable flag
   c      toggle the dos compatibility flag
   d      delete a partition
   l      list known partition types
   m      print this menu
   n      add a new partition
   p      print the partition table
   q      quit without saving changes
   t      change a partition's system id
   u      change display/entry units
   v      verify the partition table
   w      write table to disk and exit
   x      extra functionality (experts only)
```

There are really only three options you'll ever use, unless you run into some esoteric configurations:

- **d**, which deletes a current partition. This will work on non-Linux partitions.

- **n**, which creates a new partition.

- **p**, which prints a rundown of the current partition table. This will list non-Linux partitions as well.

WARNING

Linux allows you to make your hard-disk configuration (as well as *any* configuration) as complex as you want it to be. Our philosophy is to keep it as simple as possible; unless you have a real need for multiple partitions and the like, just keep to the basics; a DOS partition, a Linux partition, and perhaps a partition for an additional operating system (like OS/2).

Some argue that by creating multiple Linux partitions, you'll be able to recover more easily if something happens to the boot partition. (Damage to one partition doesn't automatically mean that all the partitions are damaged.) However, if you're making frequent backups of important files (mostly data and configuration files), you'll have a more reliable setup. Additionally, if there's damage to the PC's File Allocation Table (FAT), you'll have problems with *all* your partitions.

If you select **p**, you'll see the following:

```
  Device Boot  Begin    Start    End  Blocks   Id  System
/dev/hda1    *      1        1     63   20762+   4  DOS 16-bit (32M)
```

This is the DOS partition you created earlier.

Before you actually create the Linux partition, you should decide if you want to install a swap partition.

Linux and a Swap Disk

If you are using a PC with 4 megabytes of RAM, you may want to set up a *swap partition*. This partition is treated by the system as extended RAM; if you run low on memory (and with 4 megabytes of RAM, you're guaranteed to), Linux can treat this hard disk section as RAM, or *virtual memory*. You'll take a performance hit, as a hard-disk will always be slower than real RAM, and you'll have the joy of watching your hard disk churn furiously when you try and use a few applications. However, a swap partition can be used *only* for swap space by Linux; it can't be used for any other storage. Therefore, you need to weigh your RAM needs versus your hard-disk storage needs, keeping in mind that Linux should have as much hard-disk territory for storage as possible.

Additionally, you may want to consider a swap partition if you have more than 4 megabytes of RAM. We've found that XFree86 is a little hampered when running under only 8 megabytes of RAM, and some swap space can't hurt—especially if you have a very large hard disk. (XFree86 won't tell you that it's low on RAM; it simply refuses to do anything, such as failing to load an application.) Some recommend that you have 16 megabytes of virtual memory. If you have only 8 megabytes of RAM, this would mean that you'd want to set up at least an 8MB swap partition.

If you do want to create a swap partition, read on. If you don't, you can skip to the end of this section and on to the next section, "Creating the Main Linux Partition."

Your first move is to create a swap partition with the **fdisk** command. You'll need to decide how large to make this partition. That will depend on how much free space you think you can give up on your hard drive. For the purposes of this chapter, we'll devote 10 megabytes to swap space.

Run the **fdisk** command and choose the **n** option to create a new partition. You'll see the following:

```
Command    action
   e       extended
   p       primary partition (1-4)
```

Type **p** and enter the partition number. If you've already installed a DOS or OS/2 partition, you'll need to enter the number **2**, as partition number 1 is already is use:

```
Partition number (1-4): 2
```

You'll then be asked where to place the partition. Generally speaking, you'll want to place the partition immediately after the previous partition:

```
First cylinder (64-1010): 64
```

Your numbers will undoubtedly be different. The point here is that **fdisk** automatically lists the first unassigned cylinder here (in this case, it was cylinder *64*), and you should go with that number.

You'll then be asked how large you want to make the partition:

```
Last cylinder or +size or +sizeM or +sizeK (64-1010): +10M
```

Because we're not into figuring out how many cylinders or kilobytes it would take to make up 10 megabytes, we take the easy way out and specify 10 megabytes directly as **+10M**.

Fdisk then creates the partition. To make sure everything went correctly, type **p** to see a list of the current partitions:

```
  Device Boot  Begin    Start    End  Blocks   Id  System
/dev/hda1    *     1       1     63  20762+    4   DOS 16-bit (32M)
/dev/hda2         63      64     95  10560    83   Linux native
```

The number of blocks listed here will be handy when you actually make this partition a swap partition. Jot it down.

NOTE

Fdisk then gives you its command prompt; type **w** to exit.

You may notice that the hard disk is pretty quiet when you're making all these changes to the partition. The **fdisk** command doesn't make its changes until you type the **w** command to exit. You can make all the changes you want and change your mind many times, but until you type **w**, it won't matter.

NOTE

You'll then want to use the **mkswap** command to make the partition a swap partition. The command line is quite simple: You list the partition you want to make a swap partition (remembering that Linux lists partitions as **/dev/hda1, /dev/hda2**, and so on and the size of the partition *in blocks*. The command line would look like the following:

```
# mkswap -c /dev/hda2 10560
```

Remember when we told you the number of blocks would come in handy?

The **-c** option checks for bad blocks on the partition. If **mkswap** returns any errors, you can ignore them, as Linux already knows of their existence and will ignore them.

After creating the swap partition, you need to activate it with a command line like:

```
#  swapon /dev/hda2
```

Finally, you need to tell the filesystem that **/dev/hda2** is indeed a swap partition, again using the **fdisk** command. In this instance, you'll need to change the *type* of the partition. When you created this partition, it was set up as a Linux native partition. However, Linux needs to explicitly know that this is a swap partition, so you need to change the type with the **t** command:

```
Partition number (1-4): 2
Hex code (type L to list codes): 82
```

Linux supports a wide range of partition types, as you'd see if you typed **L**. However, you can take our word for it that *82* is the proper hex code. (You don't need to know every single hex code; there's little reason for you to know that *8* is the hex code for AIX or that *75* is the hex code for PC/IX.)

Quit **fdisk** using **w**, making sure that your changes are written to disk. It will take a few seconds for this to happen.

Now you're ready to create your main Linux partition.

Creating the Main Linux Partition

Most of you will want to designate the remainder of the hard drive as the Linux partition, so that's the assumption made in the remainder of this chapter. With *Command (m for help):* on your screen, select **n** for new partition. You'll see the following:

```
Command    action
   e       extended
   p       primary partition (1-4)
```

Type **p** and the partition number. If you've already installed a DOS or OS/2 partition, you'll need to type the number **2**, as partition number 1 is already is use:

```
Partition number (1-4): 2
```

If you've also installed a swap partition, you'll need to designate this partition as **3**.

You'll then be asked where to place the partition. Generally speaking, you'll want to place the partition immediately after the previous partition:

```
First cylinder (64-1010): 64
```

Your numbers will undoubtedly be different. The point here is that **fdisk** automatically lists the first unassigned cylinder (in this case, it was cylinder *64*), and you should go with that number.

You'll then be asked how large you want to make the partition:

```
Last cylinder or +size or +sizeM or +sizeK (64-1010): 1010
```

Because Linux gives us the number of the last cylinder (*1010*), we'll go with that. There are no advantages to creating more than one Linux partition, unless you're using a *very* large hard drive (larger than 4 gigabytes).

Finally, you'll want to make sure that this is a Linux boot partition, so you can boot from the hard disk in the future via LILO. The **a** command toggles whether or not you want to use a partition as a boot partition. Type **a**, and then specify this partition (**2**) as the partition you want to boot from.

Fdisk will then ask for a command. You'll need to make sure your changes are recorded, so select **w**, which writes the partition table to disk and exits **fdisk**. After this is done, Linux gives you a command prompt (#) again. It's time to run the **setup** program.

Installing Linux from the Setup Program

Now comes the fun part: actually installing Linux. For this, you'll run the **setup** command from a command line:

```
# setup
```

You'll then be presented a menu with the following choices:

```
HELP            Read the Slackware Setup Help file
KEYMAP          Remap your keyboard if you're not using a US one
MAKE TAGS       Experts may customize tagfiles to preselect files
ADDSWAP         Set up your swap partition(s)
TARGET          Set up your target partition
SOURCE          Select source media
DISK SETS       Decide which disk sets you wish to install
INSTALL         Install selected disk sets
CONFIGURE       Reconfigure your Linux system
EXIT            Exit Slackware Linux Setup
```

By all means, you should first look through the help file. Some of the steps presented therein may assist you in the Linux installation process.

To move through the selections in this menu, use the cursor (arrow) keys, or type the first letter in each line (such as **H** for help).

Basically, the installation from CD-ROM is pretty simple; it follows these steps:

- Set up swap space for Linux.
- Tell Linux where you want it to be installed.
- Select the source for the files needed to install Linux (in most cases, this will be the CD-ROM).
- Select the software you want to install.
- Install the software.
- Configure the installed software.

Each of these steps will be covered in its own section.

Before you get started on these steps, you should know that the Slackware96 distribution of Linux supports many different keymaps for different languages and setups. If you want access to another language—say, German—or another keyboard layout—such as the Dvorak keyboard—you should select **Keymap** from the Setup menu.

Setting Up the Swap Space

As you've probably guessed by now, much of Linux installation involves the actual installation and then telling Linux about the installation. This is certainly true if you've installed a swap partition. (If you haven't, you can skip this step.) You've already installed the partition, made it active, and changed the partition type to a Linux swap partition. Now you again need to tell Linux about this partition. However, you don't need to format this partition, as you've already done so with the **mkswap** command.

Selecting the Target for Linux

This selection should be rather simple: You'll want to install to the Linux partition you set up earlier in this chapter. When you select **Target** from the Setup menu, you'll be presented with this partition. This section covers the choices you'll make; for the most part, you'll want to use the default choices.

Formatting the Linux partition is the next step. You'll want to format the Linux partition for a new installation; however, if you're using the **setup** program to upgrade from a previous installation, you won't want to format the Linux partition.

Choosing inode density is next. Again, you'll want to use the default, unless you have Linux experience and know that the default won't help you.

After the hard disk chugs and formats the Linux partition, you'll be asked if you want to make a DOS or OS/2 partition visible (or, more technically speaking, mounted) from Linux, assuming you've created such a partition. Making this partition visible won't affect Linux performance, nor will it eat away at the size of the Linux partition. Because you may find it handy to move files via the DOS or OS/2 partition, you'll probably want to make it visible. You'll also be asked to provide a name for the drive; the name doesn't really matter, so we use **dos** or **dosc**. When you run the **ls** command later in your Linux usage, you'll see **dos** or **dosc** listed as just another directory, and the files within will appear as Linux files.

Selecting the Source for Linux

You have five choices for where you want to install Linux from:

- hard-drive partition
- floppy disks
- NFS
- premounted directory
- CD-ROM

Since you've bought this book, we'll assume you want to use the accompanying CD-ROM for installation. However, other installation methods will be discussed later in this chapter.

 There may be cases where DOS sees a CD-ROM drive with no problems, but Linux cannot. In these cases you won't necessarily know about this problem until you install Linux from the CD-ROM and are told that the CD-ROM drive does not **N O T E** exist. In this case, there are two ways to go: Search for a Linux bootkernel that supports your CD-ROM or use DOS to copy the installation files to a hard-drive partition. The first option was discussed earlier in this chapter; the second option will be discussed later in this chapter.

The **setup** program then gives you a set of choices about the CD-ROM you're installing from. The choices are straightforward; if you're using a Sony or SoundBlaster CD-ROM interface, you certainly would have known about it before now (you would have needed the proper bootdisk to get to this point), so there are no surprises on this menu.

Choosing the Disk Sets to Install

Now comes the fun part: choosing the software you want to install.

True to its roots as a diskette-based operating system, Linux divides software into *disk sets*. Each disk set is uniquely named and corresponds to a specific part of the operating system. For example, the *A* series contains the core of Linux, and its installation is mandatory.

The **setup** program divides disk sets and the software within into mandatory and optional installations. Some of the elements of Linux, such as the aforementioned *A* series, are mandatory. Other installations, such as terminal packages, are optional. During the installation process, Linux will automatically install the mandatory packages, while prompting you before installing the optional packages.

There is a way to override this, which will be explained later in this section.

N O T E

During the initial menu entitled *Series Selection*, you'll be presented with a list of the disk sets and a short explanation of what is contained on them. Generally speaking, you won't want to install *all* the disk sets; there are some disk sets that overlap, and their coexistence on the hard drive is not a wise thing (particularly when it comes to development tools). In addition, you don't want to waste the hard-disk space needed for a full installation—will you really need three or four text editors, multiple text-formatting packages, and a slew of fonts you will never use? Choose the software you think you're likely to use. You can always run the **setup** program again and install additional disk sets in the future.

Technically speaking, all that's needed for a minimal installation of Linux is the *A* disk set.

N O T E

The disk sets are listed in Table 1.6.

Table 1.6 A full list of the Linux disk sets.

Series	Purpose
A	The base system. If you install only this disk set, you'll have enough to get up and running and have **elvis** and comm programs available.
AP	Various applications and add-ons, such as the online manual (**man**) pages, **groff**, **ispell**, **joe**, **jed**, **jove**, **ghostscript**, **sc**, **bc**, **ftape** support, and the **quota** utilities.
D	Program development. GCC/G++/Objective C 2.7.2, **make** (GNU and BSD), **byacc** and GNU **bison**, **flex**, the 5.3.12 C libraries, **gdb**, kernel source for Linux 2.0.x. **SVGAlib**, **ncurses**, **clisp**, **f2c**, **p2c**, **m4**, **perl**, **rcs**, and **dll** tools.
E	GNU **emacs** 19.31.
F	A collection of FAQs and other documentation.
K	Source code for the Linux 2.0.x kernel.
N	Networking. TCP/IP, UUCP, **mailx**, **dip**, PPP, **deliver**, **elm**, **pine**, BSD **sendmail**, **cnews**, **nn**, **tin**, **trn**, and **inn**.
T	teTeX version 0.4. teTeX is Thomas Esser's Tex typesetting system for Linux.
TCL	Tcl, Tk, TclX. A port of the major Tcl packages to Linux, including shared library support.
X	The base XFree86 3.1.2 system, with **libXpm**, **fvwm** 1.23b, and **xlock** added.
XAP	X applications: X11 **ghostscript**, **libgr13**, **seyon**, **workman**, **xfilemanager**, **xv** 3.1.0, GNU **chess** and **xboard**, **xfm** 1.3.2, **ghostview**, **gnuplot**, **xpaint**, **xfractint**, **fvwm-95-2**, and various X games.
XD	X11 server link kit, static libraries, and PEX support.
XV	Xview 3.2p1-X11R6. XView libraries and the Open Look virtual and nonvirtual window managers for XFree86 3.1.2.
Y	Games. The BSD games collection, Tetris for terminals, and Sasteroids.

Mark the disk sets you want to install by pressing the space bar.

You'll be asked whether you want to use the default tagfiles or create your own. When a piece of software is installed, it's said to be *tagged*. By using the default tagfiles, you are installing software deemed to be mandatory, while the system prompts you before installing packages that aren't mandatory. Again, your best move is to go with the default, unless you've had experience with custom tagfiles and know exactly what you want to install.

At this point there's an option to install *everything*. Don't do this, unless you've designated a small group of disk sets to be installed and know that you do indeed want to install everything.

WARNING

Installing Linux

Linux will begin the installation. It will tell you what's being installed, including mandatory packages. When it comes to a nonmandatory piece of software, it will stop and ask if you do indeed want to install the software. (It further differentiates between software, noting if the installation is recommended—which means you really should install it—or merely optional.) An added bonus during this process is that **setup** will tell you how much disk space the nonmandatory software will use (alas, there's no overall reckoning of how much space the entire installation will use). Use the cursor keys to move between the **Yes** and **No** choices, and use **Enter** to move on.

We're not going to list every piece of software that can be installed; you can make most of these decisions on your own. However, there are some things to note as the disk sets are installed:

- Linux will install a kernel best suited for your PC configuration; most of the precompiled kernels should meet the needs of most users. However, during the installation process, you'll be asked about installing various kernels that are not applicable to your PC configuration. In fact, one of the first disk sets includes support for a Linux kernel lacking SCSI support. Since the **setup** program doesn't know anything about your hardware, it will ask if you want to install this kernel. In most cases, you'll want to install the kernel from your bootdisk—**setup** gives you this option once all the packages are installed.

- During the installation process you'll be asked whether you want to install a package called **gpm**, which manages the mouse for Linux running in character mode. This package can cause conflicts with the X Window System and its mouse control, so if you plan to use X, you shouldn't install this software. (However, if you don't plan on using X, you should install **gpm**, because it allows you to better use the Midnight Commander, a useful text-based disk utility.)

- There are many text editors available in the Linux disk sets, including **emacs** and **vi** clones called **elvis** and **vim**. These should meet your needs; if you're tight on space, you can avoid the other text editors, such as **jove** and **joe**. (Not that we're saying anything pejorative about **jove** or **joe**, mind you.)

- You'll be asked about alternate shells, including **zsh**, **ash**, and **tcsh**. The default Linux shell is **bash** (Bourne Again SHell), and most users—especially beginners—will find that it works well. However, you may find that one of the alternate shells better fits your needs or works more like a shell you've used in the past. Because the shells don't take up much disk space, go ahead and install them all.

- If you install the GNU C compiler, you also need to install **binutils**, **libc**, and the **linuxinc** package (this contains the include file from the Linux kernel source). Some of these packages are tagged as mandatory by the Linux **setup** program; the warning applies if you use your own tagfiles.

- The version of **emacs** that's initially installed from the CD-ROM was compiled with the assumption that it would be running under the X Window System. If you don't plan on using X, be sure to install the **emac_nox** package, which doesn't contain the X Window support and can be run in character mode. It's also smaller and will save you some disk space.

- If you install the **x** series of disk sets, you'll be asked about the chipset used in your graphics card, as there are some X Window servers tailored to specific chipsets. If you're not sure which chipset you have, don't respond to any specific chipsets and install the SuperVGA or VGA X server; you can always change this when you install XFree86 (as described later in this chapter).

- Some of the older applications require some older libraries to run, and at some point you'll be asked about including those libraries. You should install the older libraries.

- Generally speaking, you should install as many fonts as possible.

Being a Good Linux Citizen

As you install the disk sets, you'll occasionally see a message pointing out that Linux is installing unregistered software. This means that the UNIX freeware is being included as a service, and it's up to you to pay a registration fee. (The best example of this is **XV**, an outstanding graphics program from John Bradley.) As a good Linux citizen, you'll want to check through the online-manual pages or **README** documents associated with these programs and register the software.

Dealing with Errors

Though this is a very infrequent occurrence, you may experience an error message or two when installing Linux from the disk sets. One of the errors may be *Device Full*, which means that you've filled your hard drive. Slackware96, however, will continue to attempt to install software, even if the disk is full.

To end the installation program, you can either hit the **Esc** key a few times or type **Ctrl-C**.

Configuring the Installed Software

There are two main tasks involved after the Linux disk sets are installed: configuring XFree86 and setting up boot options. Here, we'll discuss boot options.

Installing a Kernel

The first Linux configuration task is to install a Linux kernel on your hard drive. It's possible that you've already installed a kernel from the A series (there are two kernels on the A series, an IDE and a SCSI generic kernel), but in most cases it will be preferable to replace this kernel with the one you used to install. That way, there won't be any surprises when you reboot—you've installed a kernel that you know works on your machine.

To do this, select the **bootdisk** option on the kernel installation menu. You'll be asked to reinsert your installation bootdisk, and the kernel will be copied from it onto your hard drive. Other options on this menu include installing a kernel from a DOS floppy or from the Slackware CD-ROM drive. If you know exactly which kernel you need, you can try one of these options. You should be aware that installing the wrong kernel here can leave Linux unbootable, requiring you to use your bootdisk or **Loadlin** to start the system.

When you install a kernel from this menu, all it does is put the kernel file onto your root Linux partition as **/vmlinuz**. Until you make a system bootdisk from it or install LILO, your system is not ready to boot. So, you'll want to make a system bootdisk from the next menu.

Creating a Boot Floppy

Linux will boot from either a floppy drive or a hard drive. However, it's recommended that you set up the means to boot either way—if you have hardware problems, you can always boot the system from a floppy drive. Hence, the request from the **setup** program to create a boot floppy. This floppy can be used to boot Linux at any time. This will be handy if you experience some hard disk problems or screw up your hard disk so severely that the system won't load.

Configuring the Modem

If you're planning on using a modem to connect to online systems or a TCP/IP network via SLIP or PPP, you need to configure the modem. Essentially, this merely involves telling Linux exactly what serial port the modem is connected to. The first serial port on a PC is called *com1*, and under Linux parlance this becomes *cua0*; the second serial port on a PC is called *com2*, and under Linux parlance this becomes *cua1*; and so on. (Note the numbering difference; UNIX likes to start things at 0; PCs prefer to start at 1.)

After you set up the modem, you'll be asked to set the speed for the modem. The choices (**38400**, **19200**, et al.) are pretty clear.

If you're using a modem and the speed isn't represented on the menu, use the next-fastest speed. For example, to properly configure a 28800-bps modem, you'd choose **38400**.

Configuring the Mouse

You'll want to use a mouse if you're using the X Window System, and this menu allows you to set up the proper mouse. For newer PCs, setting up a mouse isn't a hassle at all, since they usually contain a serial port for that purpose. All you need to do is tell Linux what kind of mouse you're using, its location (if you're using a serial mouse, you'll need to specify where the mouse is connected), and move on from there.

Configuring LILO

LILO is the *LInux LOader,* and it's used to boot Linux from the hard disk. Additionally, it can be used to boot additional operating systems (like OS/2 and MS-DOS) from the hard disk.

NOTE LILO is a tool best left to Linux veterans. If you've used LILO before, go ahead and follow these directions to install it. However, if you're a Linux newbie and don't feel up to the task of a challenging configuration, it's best to skip LILO.

LILO works with a configuration file that's generated automatically through this **setup** program. Your first move will be to start the process and then mark any operating systems you want to appear in this configuration file. Because you want Linux to be able to boot, begin with specifying **Linux**. After that, you can designate another operating system (**MS-DOS** or **OS/2**) as a possible boot option. Specify Linux first, however, so it appears first in the configuration file. When you're finished running through these queries, you'll end up with a file that looks like this:

```
# LILO configuration file
# generated by 'liloconfig'
#
# Start LILO global section
boot = /dev/hda
#compact          # faster, but won't work on all systems.
delay = 50
vga = normal      # force sane state
ramdisk = 0       # paranoia setting
```

```
# End LILO global section
# Linux bootable partition config begins
image = /vmlinuz
   root = /dev/hda2
   label = Linux
   read-only # Non-UMSDOS filesystems should be mounted read-only for
checking
# Linux bootable partition config ends
# DOS bootable partition config begins
other = /dev/hda1
   label = DOS
   table = /dev/hda
# DOS bootable partition config ends
```

This file is stored as **/etc/lilo.conf**.

You'll also be asked about how long to wait before loading Linux. LILO is pretty handy in that it lets you specify a period of time (5 or 30 seconds for example) between when LILO loads and the first operating system is loaded. (In the **/etc/lilo.conf** file, this appears as the numeral *50* if you chose 5 seconds, and *300* if you chose 30 seconds.) This gives you time to specify another operating system to boot, should you want to boot DOS or OS/2 instead of Linux. This is done by pressing the left **Shift** key after LILO loads, which gives you the prompt:

```
boot:
```

If you specify DOS, DOS will boot from the DOS partition (provided, of course, you've marked it as a boot partition). Pressing the **Tab** key gives you a list of options.

If you're using OS/2's Boot Manager, you may want to use that for the primary boot loader, and use LILO to boot Linux.

N O T E

There might be other configuration options presented to you, depending on what you installed (for example, if you installed **sendmail**, there will be a query regarding its installation). These tend to be advanced topics, so you'll need to check out a more advanced Linux installation and configuration guide (such as *Linux Installation and Configuration* from MIS:Press).

Now that the installation is finished, it's time to run Linux. Before we get to that point, however, we'll discuss some alternate installation methods.

Other Installation Methods

You may run into situations where you can access a CD-ROM drive from DOS but not from Linux's installation process. (This will happen if a SCSI card is not supported by Linux but there are drivers available for DOS or OS/2.) If this occurs, you can still use the accompanying CD-ROM for installation; but you'll need to copy the files to your hard drive, floppy disks, or a tape drive. All three types of installation are explained here.

Installing from Hard Drive

This installation method involves moving installation files from the CD-ROM to a DOS hard-disk partition and installing from there. This must be a straight DOS partition and not one altered via a disk-doubling technology, such as the disk doubler in MS-DOS 6.x or Stacker.

You'll need to replicate the file structure from the CD-ROM on the DOS partition, keeping intact the many subdirectories (**A1**, **A2**, and so on).

When you run the **setup** program and specify the source of the installation files, you'll choose a hard-disk partition instead of a CD-ROM.

Installing from 3.25-Inch Floppy Disk

The disk sets contained on the CD-ROM can be copied directly to a DOS-formatted diskette. (You'll end up with a slew of diskettes, of course.) For each disk, make an MS-DOS format disk and copy the proper files to it. Then, when you run the **setup** program, you can specify that you're installing from diskettes and not from another source.

The **00index.txt** files are added by the FTP server; you don't need those.

Installing from 5.25-Inch Floppy Drive

Linux prefers to be installed from a 3.5-inch disk drive. However, it is possible to install on a machine that has only a 5.25-inch drive. This isn't as easy as installing from a 3.5-inch drive, but if you install off of your hard drive it may actually be easier.

The first three disks of Slackware Linux, the A disks, should all fit within a 1.2-MB diskette. To install them, you'll need a boot-kernel and a rootdisk. To make the boot-kernel disk, copy the boot-kernel of your choice to a floppy using the UNIX command **dd** or **RAWRITE.EXE**. To make the rootdisk, write **color.gz**, **text.gz**, **umsdos.gz**, or **tape.gz** to a floppy in the same way. (These are in **/ROOTDSKS**.)

Use the boot-kernel disk to boot the rootdisk, and install from there. This will load the ramdisk. Once you have the *slackware:* prompt you can remove the disk from your machine and continue with the installation.

Once you've got the base system installed, you can install the rest of the disks by downloading them on to your hard drive and installing them from there. Disk series other than A won't fit onto 1.2-MB disks.

Installing from Tape

The **TAPE.GZ** rootdisk file can be used to install Slackware96 from tape. This has been tested on a Colorado Jumbo 250, but it should work for most floppy tape and SCSI tape drives. To do this, you'll need to know a little about UNIX and its filesystem.

Any of the bootkernel disks will work for floppy tape support. If you're installing from a SCSI drive, make sure you use a bootkernel with SCSI support.

You need to have a blank MS-DOS formatted disk ready to store the install scripts and installation defaults. The installation uses two tape passes—one to read these files from the tape, and the second to do the actual installation. Once you've written the files from the first tape pass to your floppy, you won't need to scan those files again if you install from the same tape in the future.

The tape must be written in GNU **tar** format (or a compatible block size with some other **tar**). This is the command that would write out the tape, assuming you're sitting in a directory set up like **/pub/linux/slackware** on **ftp.cdrom.com**:

```
tar cv {a?,ap?,d?,d1?,e?,f?,k?,n?,t?,tcl?,x?,x1?,xap?,xd?,xv?,y?}/*
```

This ensures that the files are written to the tape in the proper order.

You must set your TAPE variable first, like these lines in the **.profile** file under **bash**:

```
TAPE=/dev/nrft0
export TAPE
```

Unlike installing from floppy disks, you don't need to install all the *.tgz** files, or even all the directories. The only requirement is that **base.tgz** be the first package (***tgz** file) written to the tape.

This method isn't guaranteed to work.

Installing When RAM is Very Tight

Installation can be tricky on a machine with 4 megabytes or less of RAM. Here are a few tricks that can be helpful if you run into problems. (Some of the symptoms of low memory might include system hangs while booting the bootdisk; root password required on the rootdisk; inability to run **fdisk** or **mkswap**; and so on.)

It's still possible to install Linux in this situation by avoiding the use of a ramdisk during installation. Normally the entire rootdisk image is loaded into memory before installation begins—this uses 1440K of RAM, a sizable chunk on a machine with only 4096K (and probably fewer available) in the first place. To save this memory for Linux, you'll need to prepare a decompressed rootdisk and use it to install.

First, you'll want to prepare a directory for the various files you'll need to decompress the rootdisk image and write it to a floppy. Under DOS, create a directory with the **MKDIR** command. The name of the directory doesn't matter; in the following examples we've arbitrarily chosen **SLACK** as the name of the directory:

```
C:> MKDIR SLACK
```

You'll then want to copy the appropriate files from the CD-ROM to the **SLACK** directory. We'll start with **GZIP.EXE** (needed to decompress the image file) and **RAWRITE.EXE** (needed to write the decompressed image to floppy disk). In the following example, we assume the CD-ROM drive is represented by the drive letter **E:**. If your drive uses a different letter, use that instead.

```
C:> COPY E:\INSTALL\GZIP.EXE C:\SLACK
C:> COPY E:\INSTALL\RAWRITE.EXE C:\SLACK
```

Next, select an appropriate rootdisk image from the **E:\ROOTDSKS** directory on the CD-ROM and copy it to the **C:\SLACK** directory. In this example we'll use the **COLOR.GZ** image:

```
C:> COPY E:\ROOTDSKS\COLOR.GZ C:\SLACK
```

Now we need to use **GZIP.EXE** to decompress the image. Execute these commands to change into the **SLACK** directory and decompress the rootdisk image:

```
C:> CD \SLACK
C:\SLACK> GZIP -D COLOR.GZ
```

Once **GZIP** has done its thing, the **COLOR.GZ** file will be replaced in the **C:\SLACK** directory by the uncompressed version, named **COLOR**. To write this to a diskette, insert a formatted 3.5-inch floppy disk in your **A:** drive and use the **RAWRITE** command to dump the image to disk:

```
C:\SLACK> RAWRITE COLOR A:
```

If your 3.5-inch drive is on **B:**, use this command instead:

```
C:\SLACK> RAWRITE COLOR B:
```

Now you're ready to boot the install disk. Assuming you've selected and created a bootdisk already (if not, see the previous section explaining this), put the bootdisk in your **A:** drive and reboot. When the disk starts, you'll see a welcome message and a screenful of information, as well as a

```
boot:
```

prompt at the bottom of the screen. You'll need to enter some information at this prompt to tell the kernel where to mount your rootdisk. If you have a 3.5-inch floppy drive on **B:**, great—you'll want to use that for the rootdisk. If not, you'll have to use the rootdisk in your boot drive. With the rootdisk in the boot drive you won't be able to install from floppy disks or make a bootdisk at the end of the installation process, because the disk will be "mounted" in the boot drive and cannot be removed (no matter what the screen tells you) until the machine is rebooted. Here's the command to enter on the *boot:* prompt to use an uncompressed rootdisk in your **A:** drive:

```
boot: mount root=/dev/fd0 ramdisk=0
```

If you have the rootdisk in your **B:** drive, enter this command instead:

```
boot: mount root=/dev/fd1 ramdisk=0
```

The kernel will now boot. If you're using drive **A:** for your rootdisk, you'll be prompted to exchange the disks and hit **Enter**. Once you've done this, the rootdisk will start loading, eventually giving you a login prompt. From here, you can install Linux. A word of caution: If you're using this method to install with the rootdisk in drive **A:**, you cannot remove the rootdisk from your drive until the machine has been shut down. As a result, you'll be unable to install your bootdisk kernel or make a system bootdisk when configuring your system and will need to have a different method of initially starting your machine. A simple way to boot your machine is to use the installation bootdisk with a slightly different command on the boot prompt. If, for example, you installed Linux on **/dev/hda2**, you can start Linux with this command on the bootdisk's *boot:* prompt:

```
boot: mount root=/dev/hda2 ramdisk=0 ro
```

This will boot Linux on **/dev/hda2**, with no ramdisk, read-only. If you use UMSDOS, you'll want to boot your system in read-write mode instead, like this:

```
boot: mount root=/dev/hda2 ramdisk=0 rw
```

Once your machine is up and running, you can switch to a different kernel if you like, using one of the choices in the **\KERNELS** directory on the CD-ROM or compiling your own from the kernel source in **/usr/src/linux**. This will provide optimal performance, because it won't contain any unnecessary drivers.

Booting Linux from DOS Using Loadlin

Loadlin is a handy utility for Linux users who also run MS-DOS or Windows 95. Using **Loadlin**, you can start Linux from a DOS prompt or set up an icon in Windows 95 that allows you to switch to Linux. **Loadlin** is also probably the safest way to launch Linux from your hard drive, because it doesn't require messing with the partition table at all; you just boot DOS normally and then use the **LOADLIN.EXE** command to start Linux when you need it.

To use **Loadlin**, you need to install it on your DOS drive. To do this, you'll need to use an unzip program, such as **UNZIP.EXE** or **PKUNZIP.EXE**. Most DOS users will already have copies of these. Assuming your Slackware CD is on drive **E:** and you want to put **Loadlin** on drive **C:**, unzip the file like this:

```
C:\> PKUNZIP -d E:\KERNELS\LODLIN16.ZIP
```

The **-d** flag tells the command to preserve the directory structure found in the zip archive. This will create a **C:\LOADLIN** directory on your machine containing a number of files.

The next step is to pick an appropriate kernel from a subdirectory under **\KERNELS** on the CD-ROM. The **\BOOTDSKS.144\WHICH.ONE** document might help you select. The actual kernel file will be named **ZIMAGE** or **BZIMAGE**—this is what you'll want to copy into your **C:\LOADLIN** directory.

For this example, we'll use the kernel in the **E:\KERNELS\BARE.I** directory:

```
C:\> CD LOADLIN
C:\LOADLIN> COPY E:\KERNELS\BARE.I\ZIMAGE .
```

Now we have everything we need to start a Linux system. To do that, you need to know the following things:

- The device name of the Linux partition you intend to boot (such as **/dev/hda2**).
- The path and filename of the Linux kernel you plan to use (such as **C:\LOADLIN\ZIMAGE**).
- Whether the partition should be mounted read-only (as in the case of a native Linux partition, so it can do safe filesystem checking at boot time) or read-write (needed by UMSDOS, which does not check filesystems at boot).

This information is fed to the **LOADLIN.EXE** program, which in turn loads Linux into memory and boots it. Here's an example:

```
C:\LOADLIN> LOADLIN C:\LOADLIN\ZIMAGE ROOT=/dev/hda2 RO
```

This loads the Linux kernel and boots the **/dev/hda2** partition in read-only (RO) mode. If you're using UMSDOS, you'd replace the *RO* with *RW* to use read-write mode instead.

NOTE Some DOS drivers interfere with **Loadlin**, in particular the emm386 driver for expanded memory. If this happens, you'll have to remove the driver from your **CONFIG.SYS** file and try again. Also, **Loadlin** will not run directly under Windows 95, although you can still set up an icon for it that first switches your computer into DOS mode. (In other words, the process is to start a DOS session under Windows 95 and then launch **Loadlin**. We explain it further in the next section.)

If all goes well, your machine should switch to Linux. If you'd like to automate the process further, edit the **LINUX.BAT** file in your **C:\LOADLIN** directory. Then copy **LINUX.BAT** into your **C:\DOS** directory and you'll be able to switch to Linux from DOS by simply typing **LINUX** at a prompt.

Adding a Linux Icon to Windows 95

For users running Windows 95, it can be handy to set up a shortcut to start Linux from the Windows desktop. Once you've installed **Loadlin** and configured your **LINUX.BAT** file, it's a simple matter to add an icon that starts **LINUX.BAT**. Here's how it's done:

1. Click on the Windows Desktop with your right mouse button. Under New, select **Shortcut**.
2. Windows 95 will display a Create Shortcut dialog box, asking for the command line used to start the program. Type the location of your **LINUX.BAT** file into the box and hit **Enter**. For example:

    ```
    C:\LOADLIN\LINUX.BAT
    ```

3. Next, Windows will want a title for the program. The default of *Linux* should be just fine, or you can enter whatever you like.
4. Now you need to select an icon. Again, you can pick whatever you like. (We use the first-aid kit icon—Linux to the rescue!)

The new Linux icon will appear on the desktop. It's not quite ready to go yet, though; as you recall, **Loadlin** will not run directly under Windows 95, so we need to adjust the properties to force the program to run in real MS-DOS mode:

1. Click on the **Linux** icon with your right mouse button and select **Properties** from the menu.

2. Click the **Program** tab.

3. Click the **Advanced...** button.

4. Select the checkbox for **MS-DOS mode**, and then hit the **OK** button.

5. Hit the main dialog box's **OK** button, and your Linux icon is ready to use.

Using Loadlin to Install Linux without Floppies

It's rare, but in some cases (especially with laptops, it seems) a machine's floppy controller doesn't work correctly with Linux and the boot/rootdisks don't load correctly. If that happens on your machine, you'll be happy to know that **Loadlin** has a new feature that allows you to use it to load an installation rootdisk.

First, you'll need to install **Loadlin** as described before, unzipping the **lodlin16.zip** file on your **C:** drive:

```
C:\> PKUNZIP -d E:\KERNELS\LODLIN16.ZIP
```

Next, choose a kernel from under the CD-ROM's **\KERNELS** directory and install it in your **C:\LOADLIN** directory. In this example we'll use a kernel from the **E:\KERNELS\BARE.I** directory:

```
C:\> COPY E:\KERNELS\BARE.I\ZIMAGE C:\LOADLIN
```

Now you'll need to copy a rootdisk image such as **COLOR.GZ** into your **LOADLIN** directory:

```
C:\> COPY E:\ROOTDSKS\COLOR.GZ C:\LOADLIN
```

Now you're all set to use **Loadlin** to start the installation process. Change into the **LOADLIN** directory and use **Loadlin** to load the Linux kernel and your rootdisk image:

```
C:\> CD LOADLIN
C:\LOADLIN> LOADLIN ZIMAGE ROOT=/dev/ram RW INITRD=COLOR.GZ
```

 This will boot Linux and give you a login prompt. From here you can login and install Linux as usual.

Recompiling a Kernel

Most Linux users will find that the precompiled kernels that come on the accompanying CD-ROM work for them. However, in the remote chance you need to recompile your kernel (whether directed to in a Linux HOW-TO or through the advice from an expert on the Usenet; these will happen if you're using an nonsupported SCSI CD-ROM, bus mouse, or sound card), here's how to do so:

0 If you haven't installed the C compiler and kernel source, do that.

1 Use the bootkernel disk you installed with to start your machine. At the *LILO* prompt, enter:

```
LILO: mount root=/dev/hda1
```

 assuming that **/dev/hda1** is your Linux partition. (This is the assumption made in the rest of this section.) If not, enter your Linux partition instead. After this, ignore any error messages as the system starts up.

2 Log in as **root**, and recompile the kernel with these steps:
```
cd /usr/src/linux
make config
```

At this point you'll choose your drivers. Repeat this step until you are satisfied with your choices.

 If you are using LILO, the following will build and install the new kernel:

```
make dep ; make clean ; make zlilo
rdev -R /vmlinuz 1
```

If you are using a bootdisk, the following commands will build the kernel and create a new bootdisk for your machine:

```
make dep ; make clean ; make zImage
rdev -R zImage 1
rdev -v zImage -1
rdev zImage /dev/hda1
fdformat /dev/fd0u1440
cat zImage > /dev/fd0
```

You'll need to place a clean floppy disk into your drive before the **fdformat** command.

You should now have a Linux kernel that can fully use all supported hardware installed in your machine. Reboot and try it.

Upgrading from a Previous Version of Linux

If you're using an older version of Slackware and want to upgrade to the version on the accompanying CD-ROM, you can do so without going through the agony of a full installation.

The new versions of **pkgtool** (a package maintenance tool developed for the Slackware distribution) should have a clean upgrade path from earlier versions of Slackware. Because it can now remove packages from your hard drive while running on a self-contained Linux filesystem loaded into a ramdisk, it can remove *any* files from your system, including ones that were difficult or impossible to remove while running on the hard drive (such as the shell, shared libraries, **init**, and other crucial system files).

N O T E   Upgrading through this method is probably more trouble than it's worth. For example, several commonly reported bugs are caused by improper upgrading— mixing disks from different versions of the distribution and/or failing to remove old packages first. We need to face the fact that things haven't quite settled down yet, and until they do it may not be possible to foresee differences in filesystem structure, daemons, utilities, and so on that can lead to problems with the system.

The *correct* and best way to upgrade to a new distribution version is to back up everything you want saved and then to reinstall from scratch. This is especially true for the A and N series disks. If you upgrade packages from one of those disk sets, you should seriously consider which packages from the other one might be related somehow and install those too. Again, it can be tricky to know which packages are related, given the overall complexity of the Linux system. That's why unless you really know what you're doing, there is a substantial risk of screwing up a system while attempting to upgrade it.

Here's how you'd upgrade to a newer version of Slackware from any previous version that supports package information files in **/var/adm/packages**. (If your system puts these files elsewhere, you might still be able to do this by creating a symbolic link from the package information directory to **/var/adm/packages**.) The steps are as follows:

1. Back up important files, or take your chances; odds are you'll come through OK. However, there are two important exceptions to this rule. The first (and most obvious) is when a package overwrites a file you meant to keep with a new one. The second, and possibly the more serious situation, is when the system needs to replace an existing file with a symbolic link. It will replace the file, whether it's a simple file, a file with a file permission of 444, or a directory filled with other subdirectories, each containing part of your doctoral dissertation. So, be careful.

2. Make a list of the packages you plan to replace.

3. Use a bootkernel disk to boot one of the root/install disks. Login as root.

4. Mount your root Linux partitions under **/mnt** while logged into the install disk. The method used here differs depending on what filesystem you're using for Linux. Here are some examples:

   To mount an *ext2fs* partition:

   ```
   mount /dev/hda1 /mnt -t ext2
   ```

   Replace **/dev/hda1** with the name of your root partition.

If you're using UMSDOS (the system that allows you to install onto an existing MS-DOS filesystem), you would use the following command:

```
mount /dev/hda1 /mnt -t umsdos
```

If you have other partitions that are part of your Linux filesystem, mount them after you've mounted that root partition. The method is the same—for example, here's how you'd mount an ext2fs /usr partition:

```
mount /dev/hda2 /mnt/usr -t ext2
```

5. Once the partition has been mounted, we need to activate swap space if the system has fewer than 8 megabytes of RAM. (If you have 8 or more megabytes of RAM, you may go on to step 6.)

   You may use either a swap partition or a swapfile. To get a quick list of your partition information, you can always type **fdisk -l**. Doing this on a typical machine provides the following information:

```
Disk /dev/hda: 15 heads, 17 sectors, 1001 cylinders
Units = cylinders of 255 * 512 bytes
    Device Boot  Begin   Start    End  Blocks   Id  System
   /dev/hda1            10      10     90  10327+    1  DOS 12-bit FAT
   /dev/hda2            91      91   1000  116025    5  Extended
   /dev/hda3     *       1       1      9    1139    a  OPUS
   /dev/hda5     *      91      91   1000  116016+   6  DOS 16-bit >=32M

Disk /dev/hdb: 16 heads, 31 sectors, 967 cylinders
Units = cylinders of 496 * 512 bytes

    Device Boot  Begin   Start    End  Blocks   Id  System
   /dev/hdb1     *       1       1    921  228392+   6  DOS 16-bit >=32M
   /dev/hdb2           922     922    966   11160   82  Linux swap
```

From this display, you can see that **/dev/hdb2** has been designated as the Linux swap partition. If the partition was not previously prepared with **mkswap**, here's how that would be done:

```
mkswap /dev/hdb2 11160
```

To activate the swap partition, you would type:

```
swapon /dev/hdb2
```

6. Remove the packages. To do this, type **pkgtool** and select the option **remove installed packages**. You'll be given a list of packages that you've installed—just select those you plan to replace.

   If you're using one of the full-color versions of **pkgtool**, you select the packages to remove by moving up and down through the list with **+** and **-** and selecting packages to remove with the **Spacebar**. Once you've selected all the packages you want to remove, hit **Enter** to remove them.

   If you're using one of the tty-based versions of **pkgtool**, you'll have to type in the names of the packages you wish to remove. Separate each name with a space. Don't worry about how long the line is; just keep typing the names until you've entered them all and then hit **Enter** to remove them.

That's it! Now you've cleaned up the old packages and you're ready to install the new ones. Type **setup** at a command line and install the new packages as usual.

   Although it never hurts to play it safe and remove all packages from the bootdisk, almost all of them can be removed using **pkgtool** from your hard drive. The *A* series is the important exception here.

Booting the System

After Linux has been installed, go ahead and reboot. If you've installed LILO, you'll see it appear after the PC runs through its BIOS check. As Linux boots, you'll see a long Linux-related diagnostic, as Linux checks the system and makes sure everything is where it's supposed to be. For the most part, you can ignore any errors messages you see here (such as a proclamation that the name of the machine *darkstar* does not appear to

be supported). After all the diagnostics, you'll finally be presented with
a command prompt:

```
Welcome to Linux 2.0.0.
darkstar login:
```

If you're installed networking capabilities when you installed Slackware96, you were
asked the name of your machine. This name should appear in the place of *darkstar*.

Because there are no users on the system, you'll login as the root user.
Go ahead and type **root** as the login. There will be no prompting for a
password.

A *root user* is the supreme being on a UNIX system. Most of the traditional security
tools within the UNIX operating system don't apply to the root user—when logged
in as root, you can do just about anything. It's generally not a good idea to use the
UNIX system as the root user, however; the proscribed practice is to set up your
own account and then save the root login only for those times when you're
performing system administration.

After you're logged in, you'll see the following command prompt:

```
darkstar:~#
```

A *command prompt* is where you enter commands in the UNIX system.
Your first commands will be to set up a user account for yourself and
change your machine name.

Adding Users

Your first action as the Linux supreme being is to set up an account for
your daily use. To do this, type the following at the command prompt:

```
darkstar:~# adduser
```

```
Adding a new user. The username should not exceed 8 characters
in length, or you may run into problems later.
Enter login name for new account (^C to quit): kevinr
```

The **adduser** command does exactly what it says: adds a new user to the system. In the previous example, the user *kevinr* has been added to the system. After specifying the username, you'll be asked additional information about the preferences of the user. Unless you're familiar with Linux, stick with the defaults for now. (The defaults will be listed in brackets. Wherever there's a default, you can hit the **Enter** key instead of typing in the selection. In our example, we'll type in the defaults.) The entire sequence will look something like this:

```
Editing information for new user [kevinr]:

Full name: Kevin Reichard
GID[100]:100

Checking for an available UID after 500

First unused uid is 501

UID [501]: 501

Home Directory [/home/kevinr]: /home/kevinr

Shell [/bin/bash]: /bin/bash

Password [kevinr]: newpassword1

Information for newuser [kevinr]:
Home Directory: [/home/kevinr] Shell: [/bin/bash]
Password: [newpassword1] gid: [100] uid: [501]

Is this correct? [y/n]:

Adding login [kevinr] and making directory [/home/kevinr]

Adding the files from the /etc/skel directory:
./.kermrc -> /home/kevin/./.kermrc
```

```
./.less -> /home/kevin/././.less
./.lessrc -> /home/kevin/././.lessrc
./.term -> /home/kevin/././.term
./.term/termrc -> /home/kevin/././.term/termrc
./.emacs -> /home/kevin/././.emacs
```

If you're not planning on using Linux for anything but a single-user operating system, you don't need to worry about things like GID (which is short for group ID) and UID (which is short for user ID). And if you do plan on using Linux on a network, you can always change these parameters later.

Additionally, you probably noticed that the name *darkstar* appears as the name of your machine. You probably don't want to leave this as the name of your machine so change it. This name is contained in the file **/etc/HOSTNAME**: the default is **darkstar.frop.org**. To change it, you'll use a text editor (in the example, we'll use **vi**) to edit this file. To load the **vi** text editor and the **/etc/HOSTNAME** file, use the following command line:

```
darkstar:~# vi /etc/HOSTNAME
```

You may have to make further changes if you're on a TCP/IP network. For now, you can change the name to anything you'd like.

N O T E

You'll want to edit this file, changing *darkstar.frop.org* to whatever you'd like. If your system is configured properly, you should have the following directories in your root directory:

bin/	dev/	home/	mnt/	sbin/	var/
boot/	dos/	lib/	proc/	tmp/	
cdrom/	etc/	lost+found/	root/	usr/	

If you installed Slackware96 from the CD-ROM and the system refuses to see the drive when you reboot, you'll need to install a new kernel or add the support through loadable kernel modules.

Using Kernel Modules

The kernels used in Slackware96 are designed to support the hardware needed to get Linux installed. Once you've installed and rebooted your system, you may find that your kernel lacks support for some of your hardware, such as a CD-ROM drive or Ethernet card. In this case, there are a couple of ways you can add this support. The traditional way would be to compile a custom Linux kernel that includes drivers for all your hardware. This requires that you have the Linux source code and C compiler installed and that you know exactly which options need to be compiled into your kernel. In short, compiling a custom kernel can be a rather difficult task for Linux beginners.

Kernel modules to the rescue! If you've installed device drivers before on MS-DOS, you'll probably find this a familiar way of adding support—just think of the module configuration file **/etc/rc.d/rc.modules** as being the Linux counterpart of DOS's **CONFIG.SYS** file. To add support for new hardware, you need to edit the file and uncomment the lines that load the needed support. As an example, let's look at the section of the file used to load CD-ROM support, as shown in Figure 1.4.

```
# These modules add CD-ROM drive support. Most of these drivers will probe
# for the I/O address and IRQ of the drive automatically if the parameters
# to configure them are omitted. Typically the I/O address will be specified
# in hexadecimal, e.g.: cm206=0x300,11
#
#/sbin/modprobe aztcd aztcd=<I/O address>
#/sbin/modprobe cdu31a cdu31a_port=<I/O address> cdu31a_irq=<interrupt>
#/sbin/modprobe cm206 cm206=<I/O address>,<IRQ>
#/sbin/modprobe gscd gscd=<I/O address>
#/sbin/modprobe mcd mcd=<I/O address>,<IRQ>
#/sbin/modprobe mcdx mcdx=<I/O address>,<IRQ>
#/sbin/modprobe optcd optcd=<I/O address>
# Below, this last number is "1" for SoundBlaster Pro card, or "0" for a
clone.
#/sbin/modprobe sbpcd sbpcd=<I/O address>,1
#/sbin/modprobe sonycd535 sonycd535=<I/O address>

#/sbin/modprobe sjcd sjcd=<I/O address>
```

Figure 1.4 A section of the **/etc/rc.d/rc.modules** file.

You'll notice that each line starts with #. In most Linux configuration files, any line beginning with # is ignored, much like lines in DOS configuration files that begin with *REM*. To activate support for one of these devices, you need to remove the # from the beginning of the line and then edit the line to include any extra information about your hardware needed by the kernel module. For example, if your machine needs support for a SoundBlaster CD-ROM drive on port 0x300, you'd need to edit the line for **sbpcd** support so that it looks like this:

```
/sbin/modprobe sbpcd sbpcd=0x300,1
```

Then, the next time you boot your machine, the **sbpcd** module will be loaded and you'll be able to use your drive. Drivers for nearly every device supported by Linux can be added in a similar fashion.

N O T E   If you use kernel modules and decide later to upgrade your kernel, you'll need to upgrade your kernel modules as well. When configuring the kernel, select **M** instead of **Y** to build selected drivers as kernel modules instead of building them into the kernel. Once you've compiled your kernel with:

```
make dep ; make clean ; make zImage
```

you can compile and install the kernel modules with the command:

```
make modules ; make modules_install
```

The modules will be installed in a directory named for the running kernel. For example, if you're running Linux 2.0.0, you'll find them under **/lib/modules/2.0.0**.

Looking for Help

Most UNIX systems have an online-manual-page system, and Linux is no exception. You can use the **man** command to summon information about specific commands:

```
darkstar:~# man man
```

Online-manual pages aren't organized by topic; they're organized by command.

Shutting Linux Down

Like any good UNIX, Linux responds to the **shutdown** command. You'll need to provide it with a command-line parameter and the amount of time to wait before actually shutting down the system. This may seem odd if you're used to working alone on a PC, but the **shutdown** command is usually saved for serious shutdowns; most UNIX installations support many users and rarely shut down. Use the following command line:

```
$ shutdown -r now
```

This shuts down the system immediately.

Don't just turn off the power to turn off a Linux system. This can damage important files.

An alternative method of shutting down Linux is the old tried-and-true PC **Ctrl-Alt-Del** sequence, which is used to reboot a system. When running Linux, this sequence performs the same functions as **shutdown -r now**. When the PC cycles to reboot, simply turn it off. Despite what others claim, this is a perfectly acceptable way to shut down a Linux system.

What to Do If Things Go Wrong

For the most part, installation of Linux from the accompanying CD-ROM is a pretty straightforward proposition, and you shouldn't have many problems. However, you may run into problems when you reboot the Linux system after installation. These problems may include:

- You're told that the system is out of memory. You'll probably run into this problem if you're operating with 4 megabytes or less of RAM.

- Your system hangs when you first run Linux. In these situations, you'll want to watch the screen closely for any error messages. Sometimes Linux will be seeking a device at a specific address (say, a CD-ROM drive) and instead it finds a network card. In these situations, Linux will hang. You need to tell Linux to look for the device at the address on your system, which requires that you send an option line to Linux upon bootup. This situation is covered in the many documents included in the CD-ROM.

Other Configuration Procedures

Now that you've got Linux basically installed and running, you can take the time to set up some system peripherals. These include printers, sound cards, and (for laptop users) PCMCIA devices.

Setting Up a Printer

When you installed Slackware96, you were asked about the location of your printer. This information was translated into the UNIX equivalent; a printer on the first parallel port is assigned a device name of **/dev/lp0**. Similarly, if you're using a serial printer (which, thank goodness, is getting rarer and rarer), it will probably be assigned a device name of **/dev/ttyS1**.

This simple configuration means that you can immediately print ASCII characters, with the Linux system treating your printer like a simple line printer. Printing is actually a more involved process that you might think. Printing in Linux involves the following steps:

- When your computer boots, the **lpd** daemon runs, looking at the **/etc/printcap** to see what printer you're using; the process continues to run throughout your Linux computing session.
- When you print a document with **lpr**, the **lpd** command actually handles the print job.

- To change anything in the printing process (like if you want to kill or suspend print jobs), the **lpc** and **lprm** commands are used to talk with the **lpd** daemon.

Obviously, you'll want to make sure that **/etc/printcap** contains correct information about your printer. When you look at it in a text editor like **elvis** or **emacs**, you'll see that all the lines are commented out with # characters. Most popular printers are listed in this file (such as HP LaserJets), and if you uncomment the lines specific to your printer, you should be able to use it.

It's important to get this information correct, because Linux printers that aren't configured properly have a tendency to suffer from the "staircase effect," where lines are staggered at the beginning:

```
We hate the staircase effect.
            It makes our documents look really stupid.
                    And it makes it hard for us to do our work properly.
                        In fact, we find that we don't print things out
when our printer is misconfigured.
```

Working with PCMCIA Devices

The Slackware96 installation prompts you for the installation of PCMCIA devices with Card Services. This will save you many steps that are best avoided, such as the recompilation of a kernel.

In fact, one of the nicest things about Card Services is that it's relatively painless (thanks to David Hinds for all his work on this) after you've installed a kernel. During the boot process, Card Services will avoid hardware conflicts and work with a wide range of PCMCIA devices automatically. The trick, of course, is to use a PCMCIA device that generally conforms to PCMCIA standards. In our experience, most new hardware conforms to these standards, but some older laptops were rather liberal in their interpretation of PCMCIA support.

Working with a UPS

Slackware96 supports uninterruptible power supplies, or UPSes. This support is rather easy to implement. First you get a UPS, hook it up to your PC, and then run a Linux daemon called **powerd** that monitors the power situation and shuts down the system if necessary. (It will also halt the shutdown if the power appears in time.)

For more information, check out the **man** page for the **powerd** command.

The X Window System

Simply put, the X Window System, or just X, provides graphics on UNIX. (It's never called X Windows; to call it X Windows is a sign of ignorance.) Although X runs on many more operating systems than UNIX, such as Windows NT, Windows, MacOS, and DOS, X is by far the *de facto* graphics system on UNIX. As such, X tends to be confusing for anyone with more experience in the personal-computer world.

Since X tends to confuse, this section starts with an overview of both the X Window System and X on Linux. If you're experienced with X in general, jump ahead to the part covering X on Linux for a rundown of how X differs on Linux. After that, we tackle the toughest part of X: installing and configuring X for your hardware. We've all been lulled by the ubiquitous PC hardware and assume that because Microsoft Windows runs with just about every graphics card, so should Linux. Linux does to an extent, but you pay a price in added complexity.

The X Window System began life as an academic exercise at the Massachusetts Institute of Technology's Project Athena. The goal was to link a motley crew of disparate workstations from various vendors. Instead of providing the link at the operating-system level, the decision was made to create a C-based graphical windowing layer that could exist with any operating system. And so the X Window System was born.

Now under the supervision of the not-for-profit X Consortium Inc., (though plans were underfoot to transfer X to the Open Group in 1997), the X Window System is made available to the computing public at large, which has engendered its widespread adoption in the UNIX world. Virtually every UNIX vendor supports X on some level. The popular interfaces CDE/Motif and OpenWindows, as well as the Common Desktop Environment (CDE), are based directly on X.

X on the Network

True to its UNIX roots, the X Window System runs graphics with multiple processes. The main process, simply called **X**, is the X server itself. The server deals with local requests (thus its usage on a single-user Linux workstation) and TCP/IP-based network requests. Because of this networking capability, it's possible to run an X application on one workstation and display the results on another workstation. You could, for example, save your local computing resources for something important while running Doom on your boss's workstation and displaying the game on yours. You get to play the game; your boss's system provides the CPU horsepower.

The X server controls the monitor, keyboard, and mouse and allows graphics applications—called *X clients*—to create windows and draw into them. On the face of it, this seems so basic that it shouldn't require any explanation. But, as is true of most of UNIX, X takes a simple concept and makes it difficult. You benefit a lot from the complexity of X, but it can make things tough to get started.

The X server process is the only process allowed to draw dots on the screen or track the mouse. X application programs then connect to the X server via an interprocess communication link, usually some form of TCP/IP network socket. Because it uses a network link, programs running on other machines connected by a network can display on your workstation.

Many programs can connect to the same X server at the same time, allowing you to run multiple applications on the same screen—again, a basic fact you've probably taken for granted. One thing you cannot take for granted is that one of these X applications you run must be a window manager. (Technically, you don't *have* to run a window manager, but it makes things a lot more difficult if you don't.)

The Window Manager

Unlike the Macintosh and Windows environments, X makes the window manager a separate process. In fact, a window manager is merely a special X application program. By separating the windowing system from the window manager, you are free to run any of a variety of window managers, whichever suits your needs best. The main purpose of a window manager is to control how you move and resize windows on your Linux display. The window manager also creates the title bar at the top of your application windows.

X also provides the means to do neat things—the *mechanism*—without making any decisions about what is good for the user—the *policy*. This mechanism with policy approach has led to a great deal of innovation in the X and UNIX worlds, but at a general level of difficult-to-configure, poorly done interfaces across the board. Slackware Linux comes with a number of window managers, including those listed in Table 1.7. You're free to choose the window manager you want and change any time you see fit.

Table 1.7 Linux window managers.

Window Manager	Description
fvwm	The most common window manager, presenting a Motif-like look
fvwm-95	An adaptation of **fvwm** that mimics Windows 95
twm	The bared-boned Tab Window Manager
olwm	Open Look Window Manager, from Sun Microsystems
olvwm	A virtual-screen version of **olwm**

Most commercial UNIX systems run **mwm**, the Motif window manager, or a close variant. You'll find this on workstations from Hewlett-Packard, SCO, IBM, Silicon Graphics, and even Sun Microsystems (with the

Common Desktop Environment). Since **mwm** (and the rest of Motif, including the programming libraries) is a commercial product, you won't see **mwm** on Linux unless you purchase it separately (see Appendix V for details). Because something so fundamental to most UNIX systems remains different on Linux, this may make getting used to Linux harder, especially if you work on other UNIX systems. Because of this common problem, we'll show you how to configure **fvwm**, the default window manager on Linux, to look and act more like the Motif window manager, to help make you feel right at home on Linux. See the section on "Toward a Motif-Like Look and Feel" later in this chapter for details.

X on Linux

X is very hardware-dependent. In the UNIX workstation world, you don't see many problems with this, because UNIX vendors maintain a tight control over the hardware and do the hard work of supporting X for that hardware.

The PC realm, though, is different. You have zillions of vendors and a huge number of combinations of graphics cards, monitors, buses, and even lowly mice. So, as we'll repeat again and again, you need to know the intimate details of your hardware to get the X Window System up and running. If you're used to the UNIX workstation world, this will come as a rude surprise.

X on Linux is actually in the form of XFree86, a public project devoted to bringing X Window to PC-based Unices. While there are some changes between a straight X Window System installation on a workstation and XFree86, you probably won't notice these differences.

How XFree86 Works

Remember that X is both the X server (also named *X*) and a number of X application programs (also called *clients*). To get X going, you must first start the X server and then start a number of X applications. Almost always, one of these X applications is a window manager.

Once you login and get the Linux shell prompt, you can start X with the **startx** script:

```
yonsen~#: startx
```

This assumes that XFree86 has been configured correctly for your Linux installation, a process we'll go over soon.

The **startx** script runs a program called **xinit**, which starts up the X server, **/usr/X11R6/bin/X** (you may be more familiar with **/usr/bin/X** on most other UNIX systems), and looks for a file named **.xinitrc** (note the leading dot) in your home directory. The **.xinitrc** file is a shell script that launches all the X applications you want. For example, our **.xinitrc** file launches a number of instances of the **xterm** program, which provides a shell window, and the rounded clock called **oclock**, as shown in Figure 1.5.

Figure 1.5 A typical X environment started from the **.xinitrc** file.

Before any of these programs is launched, however, the X server must be started, a task also handled by **xinit**.

The X server looks for the XFree86 configuration file, the most critical file for X on your system. This file, usually named **XF86Config** and stored in **/usr/X11R6/lib/X11** (symbolically linked to **/var/X11R6/lib**), is a specially formatted file that tells XFree86 about your system's hardware.

The hardest part about installing XFree86 on your system will be fleshing out this file. There are tools that help, but the process is still dangerous and fraught with error.

The **XF86Config** file contains sevenx sections, each of which describes some part of your system to the X server. We list these sections in Table 1.8.

Table 1.8 Sections in the XF86Config file.

Section	Usage
Files	Tells where font and RGB files are located
ServerFlags	Special X server flags like DontZap, which turns off the **Ctrl-Alt-Backspace** sequence that aborts the X server
Keyboard	What kind of keyboard you have
Pointer	Information on your mouse
Monitor	Excruciating details about your monitor
Device	Graphics card
Screen	Combined card and monitor

Installing XFree86

To install and properly set up XFree86, a scary task under the best of conditions, you need to go through the following steps:

- Determine your system configuration.
- Set up the proper X server for your graphics card.
- Fill out the infamous **XF86Config** file.

- Test that you can run X at all.
- Tune your **XF86Config** file.

Virtually all of XFree86—including the version included with the Slackware Linux on the accompanying CD-ROM—installs into the **/usr/X11R6** directory. Note that many other directories, such as **/usr/bin/X11** and **/usr/lib/X11**, will be symbolic links into locations in **/usr/X11R6**.

If you installed Linux and XFree86 from the accompanying CD-ROM, all the files are in the right place.

If you picked up an update to XFree86 from the Internet, you'll likely need to unpack the collected files. Check the **README** file that was in the same directory as the XFree86 files you grabbed. Most likely, the files are compressed **tar** archives. For example, if you see a file like **X312bin.tar.gz**, you know that this file was compressed with GNU **zip** (**.gz**) from a **tar** file (**.tar**). To extract this file, use the following commands:

```
mv X312bin.tar.gz /usr/X11R6
cd /usr/X11R6
gunzip X312bin.tar.gz
tar xvof X312bin.tar
```

The first two commands move the XFree86 file (and your current working directory) to the **/usr/X11R6** directory, where Linux expects X files to be located.

Especially if you acquired XFree86 over the Internet, you must **untar** any XFree86 archives as the root user. Otherwise, XFree86 does not install properly.

If you load XFree86 from the Slackware CD-ROM and use Slackware's installation program, you shouldn't have any problems.

Setting Up XFree86

Because there's so much variety in PC graphics hardware and because doing something wrong can destroy your hardware (in theory, anyway; we're rather credulous of tales of exploding monitors and such), XFree86 ships in a mode that prevents you from running X. This fact strikes us as bizarre, but setting up X is probably the hardest thing you have to do to get Linux up and running.

Before you start setting up XFree86, track down every piece of documentation that came with your monitor and graphics card. You'll need to know some obscure values about your monitor, such as the horizontal and vertical frequency ranges.

If you can't find any of this information, you may want to pop open the machine and check the text written on your graphics card—there's often a lot of useful information there. If even this fails and you can't find out anything about your graphics card, you still have a chance to run X. If your graphics card can support standard Super VGA, you should be able to use the example **XF86Config** file that comes with XFree86.

To see which chipset your graphics card uses, you'll need to look in the documentation that came with your graphics card.

You'll need about 50 megabytes of disk space for XFree86, and you should have at least 16 megabytes of RAM to run X effectively. You can launch X and perform some basic functions with 8 megabytes of RAM, but you'll soon run into performance problems with limited RAM. To compound matters, you won't be told that you're running low on RAM; your chosen X window manager will simply fail to respond to your commands.

Once you've determined your system configuration, the next step is to set up the proper X server for your graphics card. XFree86 ships with a number of X servers, each compiled with drivers for a certain type of graphics card or chipset. Each of these X server executables usually starts with *XF86_* and ends with the type of cards supported. For example, the **XF86_SVGA** X server is built with support for standard Super VGA chipsets. **XF86_S3** is the X server for S3-based graphics cards.

You'll need to know which chipset your graphics card has and then figure out which X server to use. We list the X servers in Table 1.9.

Table 1.9 XFree86 X servers.

Filename	For Chipsets
XF86_8514	8514/A and true clones
XF86_AGX	IIT AGX-014, AGX-015, AGX-016
XF86_Mach8	ATI Mach8
XF86_Mach32	ATI Mach32
XF86_Mach64	ATI Mach64
XF86_Mono	Monochrome VGA; also Hercules, Hyundai HGC1280, Sigma LaserView, Visa, Apollo monochrome cards
XF86_P9000	Weitek P9000
XF86_S3	S3-based cards
XF86_SVGA	Super VGA
XF86_VGA16	16-color VGA server
XF86_W32	Tseng ET4000/W32, ET4000/W32i, ET4000/W32p

The reason you have to know which X server to use is that the wrong server at best won't work and at worst may damage your system.

XFree86 is set up to run only one X server, the program named **X** stored in **/usr/X11R6/bin**. Because of this, you need to link the X server you chose to the file named **X**. The following command, when run by the root user, links the S3 X server we use to the standard named X:

```
ln -sf /usr/X11R6/bin/XF86_S3 /usr/X11R6/bin/X
```

All the XFree86 files are stored in **/usr/X11R6**, but there are many links to other parts of the filesystem. For example, **/usr/bin/X1** is linked to **/usr/X11R6/bin**, where the X binaries really reside. The Slackware installation should have taken care of these links for you.

Now you have the proper X server set up to run when you start X. The next step is to tell XFree86 about your hardware in even more detail by filling out the infamous **XF86Config** file.

Setting Up the XF86Config File

The **XF86Config** file, located in **/usr/lib/X11** (really a link to **/usr/X11R6/lib/X11**), is read when the X server starts up; it describes your graphics hardware and other configuration options for XFree86.

When you've gotten to this step, there are two routes you can take. You can set up a generic **XF86Config** file for Super VGA graphics, or you can tune the **XF86Config** file for your particular card. We'll cover both routes. We strongly advise you to configure the **XF86Config** file for your graphics card. Unfortunately, this has proven (in our experience) to be the most daunting task under Linux; nothing else has been this difficult. So be warned—dangerous waters lie ahead.

The main reason this is a difficult task is that virtually all graphics-card vendors write device drivers for Microsoft Windows, but virtually none write drivers for Linux. Because of this, you're left with the task of setting up your system to run with the graphics card.

Hardware, Hardware, Hardware

We keep repeating the mantra that you need to know your system's hardware inside and out. If you know your hardware, you can get the most out of X. If you don't, you run the danger of destroying your system.

Yes, we'll repeat that: Making a mistake in your X configuration can result in damaged hardware.

WARNING

Unless you're independently wealthy, this should cause you to pause for a moment. Take advantage of the time and go dig up all the documentation on your mouse, monitor, and graphics card. This can be hard. On a system that's a few years old, you may not be able to find everything. On a new system, your computer case may be full of no-name off-brand hardware, and the documentation may tell you nothing of value.

We've found that some newer systems just tell you the amount of video RAM and how to run DOS terminate-and-stay-resident (TSR) programs to configure the card, which is not very useful for a non-BIOS operating system like Linux. Let's face it: most PC users run DOS and Microsoft Windows, not Linux. As one of the few pioneers, your task is harder. One hint that served us well is to examine the original boxes the system came in. On at least one of our prepackaged systems, we found more technical information about the graphics card (especially the chipset) than we did in all the printed manuals that came with the system.

Laptops and X

If your hardware includes a laptop computer, you just may be able to run X on it. Many others have taken the time to configure X on a wide range of laptops. If you have a ThinkPad laptop, for example, there's a wealth of information specific to Linux on the World Wide Web at URL *http://peipa.essex.ac.uk/tp-linux/tp-linux.html*. This Web page also contains a number of X configuration files for various ThinkPad models.

You are likely to have problems with the ThinkPad 700, 720, and any other MCA-architecture machines, as Linux does not yet support MCA.

WARNING If you have a model 760, you may have problems with the latest editions of XFree86. See the Linux Notebook Web page at URL *http://www.castle.net/X-notebook/index_linux.html*. Because versions of X change rapidly, this problem may already be fixed.

Some of the key bits of information you want to discover about your system are listed in Table 1.10.

Table 1.10 Information you need to know about your system.

Aspect	What You Need to Know
Card	Vendor and model
Card	Chipset, such as S3
Card	Amount of video RAM, such as 1 or 2 megabytes

continued...

Aspect	What You Need to Know
Card	RAMDAC, if one is used, such as ATT20C490
Monitor	Bandwidth in megahertz (MHz), such as 25.2
Monitor	Horizontal Sync range, such as 31.5–64.3 kilohertz (kHz)
Monitor	Vertical refresh range, such as 55–120 Hertz (Hz)
Mouse	Serial or parallel? If serial, which serial port it's connected to
Mouse	Vendor and model, such as Logitech Firstmouse

Note that some of the more obscure details, such as the RAMDAC, may be described in the XFree86 documentation. XFree86 comes with a description of a number of graphics cards and monitors. If you're lucky, you can pull some of these values directly from the XFree86 documentation and into your **XF86Config** file, the master file that describes your hardware to X.

Normally located in **/usr/X11R6/lib/X11**, the **XF86Config** file is an ASCII text file, formatted in a special way that the XFree86 X server understands. By default, XFree86 searches for this file in a number of directories, in order:

> **/etc/XF86Config**
>
> *<Xroot>***/lib/X11/XF86Config.hostname**
>
> *<Xroot>***/lib/X11/XF86Config**

<Xroot> is shorthand for the top-level X directory. In Slackware Linux, this is **/usr/X11R6**. Previous to release 6 of X11 (hence *X11R6*), XFree86's top directory was **/usr/X386**.

You can create the **XF86Config** file with a text editor such as **vi** or **emacs**. In most cases, though, you'll want to copy an example file to avoid entering the whole thing. Under Slackware, this example file is named **XF86Config.eg**. While this example is not ready to go, you can get a lot of useful information out of it. (See the section on Super VGA later.)

In the **XF86Config** file, each section follows the same basic pattern:

Section "SectionName"

data entry…

...

EndSection

The # acts as a comment character, which is very useful in documenting the odd syntax in the **XF86Config** file.

In the next sections of this chapter, we'll cover these six sections in depth and show how you can automate part of the process by using a program called **xf86config**.

WARNING

Never use someone else's **XF86Config** file. And, don't use the examples we provide verbatim. Always configure X for your hardware. Wrong data in the file may cause X to damage your hardware.

Automating the Configuration Process

For a number of years, various programs have attempted to automate the difficult creation of **XF86Config** files. So far, though, all have failed miserably for us—that is, until the most recent versions and a program called **xf86config**. For the first time, **xf86config** seems to create a workable **XF86Config** file, and we don't even have any odd hardware.

Before running **xf86config**, read each of the following sections which describe the various parts of the **XF86Config** file that the **xf86config** program will be filling in. By having a greater understanding of the **XF86Config** file, your success with the **xf86config** program will be much greater.

Because of this, we'll discuss each of the six sections and then cover using **xf86config**.

Setting Up Paths in the Configuration File

The *Files* section is by far the easiest to set up in your **XF86Config** file. That's because just about everybody has the same paths. In the *Files* section, you need to tell X where the RGB (Red-Green-Blue) color database file is kept and where the fonts are located. Because both should go in standard locations, you can simply use the following section in your **XF86Config** file (in fact, the sample version already comes this way):

```
Section "Files"
    RgbPath        "/usr/X11R6/lib/X11/rgb"
    FontPath       "/usr/X11R6/lib/X11/fonts/misc/"
    FontPath       "/usr/X11R6/lib/X11/fonts/Type1/"
    FontPath       "/usr/X11R6/lib/X11/fonts/Speedo/"
    FontPath       "/usr/X11R6/lib/X11/fonts/75dpi/"
    FontPath       "/usr/X11R6/lib/X11/fonts/100dpi/"
EndSection
```

This *Files* section tells XFree86 that your RGB database is located in **/usr/X11R6/lib/X11/** and the fonts are located in **/usr/X11R6/lib/X11/fonts/**. These are the standard locations for both. One tricky thing to note, though, is that you may not have loaded all the font directories (we recommend you do, though). Because of this, you should check the **/usr/X11R6/lib/X11/fonts/** directory:

```
$ ls /usr/X11R6/lib/X11/fonts/
100dpi/  75dpi/   PEX/     Speedo/  Type1/   misc/
```

On our system, we have all the directories and shown a PEX directory for PEX fonts). What you should do is delete any entries in the **XF86Config** file if you don't have the corresponding font directory. For example, if you did not load the 100 dots-per-inch fonts (the **100dpi**) directory, then your *Files* section should look like:

```
Section "Files"
    RgbPath        "/usr/X11R6/lib/X11/rgb"
    FontPath       "/usr/X11R6/lib/X11/fonts/misc/"
    FontPath       "/usr/X11R6/lib/X11/fonts/Type1/"
    FontPath       "/usr/X11R6/lib/X11/fonts/Speedo/"
    FontPath       "/usr/X11R6/lib/X11/fonts/75dpi/"
EndSection
```

We removed the entry for 100-dpi fonts.

When running **xf86config**, you should say you do not intend to use the X font server, even if you'd like to. If the font server isn't running before you start X, your system may lock up. We found it's much easier to split the problem. First, get X up and running. Then, configure the X font server (which provides scaled fonts). You may have to go back and edit the **XF86Config** file, but that's a lot easier than having your system lock up.

Configuring the Server Flags Section

After the *Files* section comes the *ServerFlags* section. Again, you rarely have to do much with this. In fact, we normally have everything commented out in this section. The main options you can set here are listed in Table 1.11.

Table 1.11 Server flag options.

Option	Meaning
NoTrapSignals	Core dumps X when a signal arrives; useful for debugging
DontZap	Disables **Ctrl-Alt-Backspace**
DontZoom	Disables switching between graphics modes

Most of these flags work backwards. If you uncomment the entry, it turns the feature off. By default, we comment out (leaving on) the two *don't* features. We also comment out (leaving off) the *NoTrapSignals* option.

We like being able to kill an errant X server by simply holding down **Ctrl-Alt-Backspace**, so we always comment out *DontZap*. If you turn on *DontZap*, you are disabling this feature.

DontZoom disables the keyboard sequences that allow you to switch between graphics modes. We find this switching essential in testing our **XF86Config** files, so we always leave this feature on by commenting it out in the **XF86Config** file.

Our *ServerFlags* section, with everything commented out, looks like:

```
Section "ServerFlags"
#    NoTrapSignals
#    DontZap
#    DontZoom
EndSection
```

Just like in UNIX shell scripts, the # character marks a comment line in the **XF86Config** file.

Configuring the Keyboard Section

The *Keyboard* section allows you to set up a number of options about your keyboard, which we list in Table 1.12.

Table 1.12 Options in the Keyboard section.

Option	Usage
Protocol	Standard (the default) or Xqueue
AutoRepeat delay rate	Sets up the keyboard auto-repeat delay and rate
ServerNumLock	Asks X server to handle **NumLock** internally
LeftAlt key	Overrides default for left **Alt** key (**Meta**)
RightAlt key	Overrides default for right **Alt** key (**Meta**)
ScrollLock key	Overrides default for **Scrolllock** key (**Compose**)
RightCtl key	Overrides default for right **Ctrl** key (**Control**)
XLeds	Allows programs to use LEDs, rather than the keyboard
VTSysReq	Uses **Alt-SysRq-Fn** to switch to virtual terminals
VTInit command	Runs command passed to **/bin/sh -c**, when X server starts up and has opened its virtual terminal

You almost never want to run the Xqueue protocol, which uses a UNIX SVR3 or SVR4 event queue driver. With Linux, skip this option.

With X11 Release 6, X finally handles the **NumLock** key properly. You probably don't need to worry about the **ServerNumLock** protocol unless you have older applications that prove to be a problem.

For the key-mapping overrides, you can set each to one of the following values:

- Compose
- Control
- Meta
- ModeShift
- ModeLock
- ScrollLock

This is probably more than you want to know about your keyboard. See the online-manual page for **XF86Config** for more information on this.

Virtual Terminals

Linux supports virtual terminals. A *virtual terminal* is a pseudo-tty UNIX terminal connected to your screen. X uses up one virtual terminal, but you may have many more.

Each virtual terminal takes over your entire display and presents a traditional UNIX textual terminal, much like what you see when you login. A special key sequence allows you to change between virtual terminals. When you do this, the screen gets cleared and you see the next virtual terminal.

The magic key sequence to change to a virtual terminal is **Alt-F*n***, where **F*n*** is one of your keyboard's function keys, such as **F1**. But, watch out; in X, the magic key sequence to change to a virtual terminal is not **Alt-F*n***, but **Ctrl-Alt-F*n***. The discrepancy is because most window managers capture all **Alt-F*n*** keys.

Most laptops have a special **Fn** key that's used to provide a second set of functions to the keyboard function keys. The **Fn** key on a laptop keyboard should not be confused with the **F*n*** notation used here.

N O T E

A virtual terminal is not very worthwhile when you have a whole screen with multiple **xterm** terminal windows. The X environment allows you to use the font of your choice, provides a great many lines, supports a scrollbar, and copies and pastes—none of which the virtual terminals do. So, we rarely use a virtual terminal.

But there's one place where a virtual terminal comes in handy: if your X display gets locked up, you can often switch to another virtual terminal and kill off all the X processes.

The *VTSysReq* option in Table 1.12 allows you to use **Alt-SysReq-F***n* instead of the default **Ctrl-Alt-F***n*.

Putting this all together, our *Keyboard* section follows:

```
Section "Keyboard"
      Protocol     "Standard"
#     Protocol     "Xqueue"
      AutoRepeat   500 5
#     ServerNumLock
#     Xleds        1 2 3
      LeftAlt      Meta
      RightAlt     ModeShift
#     RightCtl     Compose
#     ScrollLock   ModeLock
EndSection
```

Note that we comment out most of it.

Configuring the Pointer Section

The mouse—called *pointer* in X terminology—is rather easy to set up, but you must watch out for some tricks. The main reason for this is that many vendors' mice (e.g., Logitech) are set up to emulate other vendors' mice, most notably Microsoft Mice. Because of this, you may have to lie about your mouse.

For example, one of our test systems uses a serial Logitech Firstmouse. This mouse, though, was designed by Logitech to emulate the Microsoft serial mouse. What's odd is that the Logitech mouse has three buttons (a very good thing for X, as most X programs expect three-button mice), while the Microsoft serial mouse sports only two buttons.

When we configure the **XF86Config** file, we claim our Logitech mouse is really a Microsoft mouse (the other common choice for Logitech mice is to claim that they are Mouseman mice).

The two key things you must specify for your *Pointer* section is what kind of mouse, e.g., Microsoft, and what port if it's a serial mouse.

With this, our *Pointer* section is rather short:

```
Section "Pointer"
    Protocol    "Microsoft"
    Device      "/dev/ttyS0"
EndSection
```

Be sure to put in the type of mouse you have and the device it is connected to, rather than merely copying our configuration.

The protocol must be one of the options listed in Table 1.13.

Table 1.13 Pointer protocols.

Protocol
BusMouse
Logitech
Microsoft
MMSeries
Mouseman
MouseSystems
PS/2
MMHitTab
Xqueue
OSMouse

For Logitech mice, you'll most likely use BusMouse (if a bus mouse) or the Microsoft or Mouseman protocols (for serial mice), rather than the more obvious Logitech protocol. If your mouse is connected to a PS/2 port, use the PS/2 protocol. (If you're using a newer system from a mass merchandiser like Dell, check the mouse port. Many newer systems feature PS/2 mouse ports, but they're not always called PS/2 ports; for example, Dell calls it a *mouse port*.)

The Xqueue protocol is only used if you set that up for the keyboard, too. We don't advise using this. The OSMouse is only for SCO UNIX, not for Linux.

In our case, the mouse is connected to serial-port number one, often called *com1* in the DOS lexicon. In true UNIX tradition, though, Linux starts counting serial ports with 0. To specify our mouse is connected to com1, we use a device name of **/dev/ttyS0**, the Linux device file for this port. We list commonly used ports in Table 1.14.

Table 1.14 Commonly used serial ports in Linux.

Port	Device Filename in Linux
com1	**/dev/ttyS0**
com2	**/dev/ttyS1**
com3	**/dev/ttyS2**
com4	**/dev/ttyS3**

Your system may also have the **/dev/mouse** device file set up for the mouse port. No matter what device file you choose, the device must exist beforehand. (On our system, **/dev/mouse** is a link to **/dev/ttyS0**.)

The bus mouse device files are listed in Table 1.15.

Table 1.15 Bus mouse device names.

Device	Usage
/dev/atibm	ATI bus mouse
/dev/logibm	Logitech bus mouse
/dev/inportbm	Microsoft bus mouse
/dev/psaux	PS/2 or Quickport mice

Note that except for the **/dev/psaux** PS/2 mice, all the bus mice should use a protocol of *busmouse*.

There are a few more options for the *Pointer* section, but you're usually better off leaving them alone. (We know; we were curious and we managed to mess things up.)

We list the other *Pointer* options in Table 1.16.

Table 1.16 Other Pointer section options.

Option	Usage
BaudRate rate	Specifies the baud rate for the serial mouse
Emulate3Buttons	Allows a two-button mouse to act like it has three; the third is emulated by pressing both at once
ChordMiddle	Fixes a problem with some Logitech Mouseman mice
SampleRate rate	Fixes a problem with some Logitech mice
ClearDTR	May be required by dual-protocol mice in MouseSystems protocol mode
ClearRTS	May be required by dual-protocol mice in MouseSystems protocol mode

We generally don't set the baud rate. When we tried to, the mouse didn't work. If you do this, it is one time where the **Ctrl-Alt-Backspace** zapping sequence comes in handy.

For best results in X, you want to have a three-button mouse. Many X programs assume such a mouse.

Configuring the Monitor Section

The *Monitor* section describes your monitor to X. You can define a number of monitors in the **XF86Config** file, as each *Monitor* section is named. The *Screen* section (discussed later) then connects a monitor to a video card. For example, the following abbreviated entry defines our NEC MultiSync XE17 monitor:

```
Section "Monitor"
Identifier   "NEC MultiSync XE17"
VendorName   "NEC"
ModelName    "MultiSync 4FGe"
HorizSync    31.5 - 64.3
```

```
VertRefresh 55-120
# Modes from the NEC MultiSync 4FGe monitor, a close monitor.
ModeLine "640x480"   31  640   680   704   832 480 489 492 520
ModeLine "800x600"   50  800   864   976 1040 600 637 643 666
ModeLine "1024x768"  81 1024 1068 1204 1324 768 776 782 807
EndSection
```

For each monitor, you need to define the items listed in Table 1.17.

Table 1.17 Monitor data.

Item	Usage
Identifier string	Used to identify the monitor later
VendorName string	Used for your reference
ModelName string	Used for your reference
Bandwidth bandwidth	The bandwidth for the monitor, in MHz
HorizSync range	Horizontal sync frequencies, in kHz
VertRefresh range	Vertical refresh range, in Hz
Gamma value	Gamma correction value for your monitor
Modeline values	A single resolution mode

The *identifier* is a string used to refer to the monitor later. You can define more than one monitor in the **XF86Config** file.

The HorizSync range describes the horizontal sync frequencies for your monitor. It can be a set of comma-separated values or a range separated by a dash, such as 42-65, for multisync monitors. You should get this value from your monitor documentation (where you'll find most of the key information needed here).

The format for a Modeline is:

```
Modeline "name" horizontal-values vertical values
```

For example, the following sets up a standard VGA mode:

```
# 640x400 @ 70 Hz, 31.5 kHz hsync
Modeline "640x400"  25.175 640   664   760   800   400 409 411 450
```

There can be a whole set of Modeline values. You can get this from the **probeonly** mode of X (discussed later) or from documentation that comes with XFree86. Some of the relevant documentation is listed in Table 1.18.

Table 1.18 Video-mode documentation with XFree86.

File	Usage
VideoModes.doc	Explains—in excruciating detail—how to calculate modes
modeDB.txt	Database of Modelines for monitors
Monitors	Database of Modelines for monitors

All these files are located in **/usr/X11R6/lib/X11/doc**. An example entry from the **Monitors** file follows:

```
#Date: Sat, 17 Sep 1994 00:50:57 -0400
#From: Erik Nygren <nygren@mit.edu>
Section "Monitor"
  Identifier "NEC MultiSync 4FGe"
  VendorName "NEC"
  ModelName "MultiSync 4FGe"
  BandWidth 80Mhz          #\
  HorizSync 27-62KHz         #> from monitor documentation
  VertRefresh 55-90Hz      #/
  ModeLine "640x480"  31  640  680  704  832 480 489 492 520
  ModeLine "800x600"  50  800  864  976 1040 600 637 643 666
  ModeLine "1024x768" 81 1024 1068 1204 1324 768 776 782 807
EndSection
```

One of the monitors we have, an NEC MultiSync XE17, was not in either the **modeDB.txt** or **Monitors** file. We found the closest monitor in the listing, for a NEC MultiSync 4FGe, and experimented with those Modelines. Calculating the Modelines yourself is a real pain, so you want to find a monitor or a close facsimile in the **Monitors** or **modeDB.txt** file.

WARNING

Having said that, be careful about using Modelines for other monitors. You can destroy your monitor if you're not careful.

Configuring the Graphics-Card Section

The *Device* section describes your graphics card to X. For example, a standard Super VGA device appears as the following:

```
# Standard VGA Device:
Device
     Identifier    "Generic VGA"
     VendorName    "Unknown"
     BoardName     "Unknown"
     Chipset       "generic"
#    VideoRam      256
#    Clocks        25.2 28.3
EndSection
```

A more detailed device section, for an Actix S3 accelerated card, follows:

```
# Device configured by xf86config:
Section "Device"
Identifier  "Actix GE32+ 2MB"
VendorName  "Actix"
BoardName   "GraphicsENGINE Ultra"
#VideoRam    1024
#Option "dac_8_bit"
Ramdac      "att20c490"
Clocks      25 28 40 72 50 77 36 45 90 120 80 32 110 65 75 95
EndSection
```

Of these options, the clocks are the hardest things to fill in. One option is to try X in **probeonly** mode (discussed later) to fill in the details. You can also look in a file called **AccelCards** in **/usr/X11R6/lib/X11/doc** for more information on accelerated chipsets and cards. An entry from the **AccelCards** file follows:

```
Card Vendor              : Actix
Card Model               : GraphicsEngine32 Plus
Card Bus (ISA/EISA/VLB)  : ISA
Chipset                  : S3 86C801
Video Memory             : 2048k
Memory Type (DRAM/VRAM)  : DRAM
Memory Speed             : 45ns
```

```
Clock Chip              : Avasem AV9194-11
Programmable? (Y/N)     : No
Number of clocks        : 16
Clocks                  : 25.175 28.322 40.0 0.0 50.0 77.0 36.0 44.9
Clocks (cont)           : 130.0 120.0 80.0 31.5 110.0 65.0 75.0 95.0
Option Flags            :
RAMDAC                  : AT&T 20C490-11
Submitter               : David E. Wexelblat <dwex@xfree86.org>
Last Edit Date          : Sept 25, 1993
```

You can convert the *Clocks* lines into the proper syntax for the **XF86Config** file by placing the same values in order in a line (or lines) starting with *Clocks* in the *Device* section:

```
Clocks 25.175 28.322 40.0 0.0 50.0 77.0 36.0 44.9
Clocks 130.0 120.0 80.0 31.5 110.0 65.0 75.0 95.0
```

Be sure to put all the clock values in the original order.

Combining the Graphics Card with the Monitor to Make a Working X Setup

The *Screen* section connects a monitor with a graphics card. Your **XF86Config** file may have multiple devices and monitors defined. It is the *Screen* section that connects the two.

A complicated *Screen* section can look something like:

```
Section "Screen"
   Driver       "accel"
   Device       "Actix GE32+ 2MB"
   Monitor      "NEC MultiSync XE17"
   Subsection "Display"
      Depth        8
      Modes        "1024x768" "800x600" "640x480"
      ViewPort     0 0
      Virtual      1024 768
   EndSubsection
```

```
Subsection "Display"
   Depth        16
   Modes        "640x480" "800x600"
   ViewPort     0 0
   Virtual      800 600
EndSubsection
Subsection "Display"
   Depth        32
   Modes        "640x400"
   ViewPort     0 0
   Virtual      640 400
EndSubsection
EndSection
```

Note that the *Screen* section uses the monitor and device identifiers we entered earlier. This is essential to connect the screen to the proper monitor and card.

The driver tells what kind of X server you're using. The choices are Accel, SVGA, VGA16, VGA2, or Mono. In almost all cases, you'll use SVGA for Super VGA cards (and the **XF86_SVGA** X server) or Accel for any accelerated chipset and X server, such as the **XF86_S3** server we mentioned earlier.

Each *Display* subsection covers the modes available at a particular depth. (A depth of eight specifies eight planes for color, or 256 maximum colors.) The modes used refer back to the Modelines for the monitor that we defined earlier.

Virtual Screens

The *Virtual* line allows you to define a virtual screen that is larger than the number of pixels supported by your monitor. The X server will automatically scroll the display when the mouse hits the end. If you like this effect (we don't), set the Virtual resolution to something larger than your monitor allows, such as:

```
Virtual 1152 900
```

This virtual setting creates a traditional Sun Microsystems resolution. This is useful if you need to run older programs that were designed with Sun systems in mind and you want to grab more than the default 1024-by-768 screen areas available on most PCs.

The *ViewPort* line tells where the X server should start up. For example, a ViewPort of 0,0 tells X that when it starts up, it should display position 0,0 in the upper-left corner (which is what you'd expect on X). If you'd rather start in the middle (an unlikely option), you can change this.

WARNING

The **fvwm** window manager also supports a different kind of virtual screen. Don't mix the two types of virtual screen or you'll likely have trouble.

Running the Xf86config Program

Now that we've gone over the contents of the **XF86Config** file, we can run the **xf86config** program, or, if you'd prefer, fill in the file by hand. We recommend using **xf86config** and then checking the **XF86Config** file it builds by hand. The **xf86config** program isn't flawless and needs careful supervision.

When you run **xf86config**, you should not be in the **/usr/X11R6/lib/X11** directory. Instead, put an **XF86Config** file in a directory in your user account and try copying it to **/usr/X11R6/lib/X11**.

As the program starts up, it will ask a lot of questions. The **xf86config** program will prompt you for a lot of the values necessary for the **XF86Config** file, such as type of mouse, your desires for the keyboard, monitor frequencies, and the like. When you're done, **xf86config** will write the data into a file named **XF86Config** in the current directory. (For this reason, you don't want to be in **/usr/lib/X11**, which is a symbolic link to **/usr/X11R6/lib/X11**, when you run this program.)

Once the **xf86config** program finishes, you should carefully examine the **XF86Config** file it generates. This file will be incomplete, because you haven't probed for the clocks yet. Edit the **XF86Config** file. If it looks OK, then, as the root user, copy the file to **/usr/X11R6/lib/X11**. Be sure to back up any existing **XF86Config** file first.

Now you're ready to try X in **probeonly** mode.

Probing for Dot Clocks

The XFree86 X server has a special **probeonly** mode that outputs values from the **XF86Config** file and values it detects. You need to run X in this mode to see if things are going to work and to see if there are any problems it detects.

Run the command line:

```
X -probeonly
```

when your system has no extra load on it. Stop any unneeded programs before running this, as any extra system load may influence the timings X obtains.

The following command runs X in **probeonly** mode and sends the output to the file named **/tmp/x.values**:

```
X -probeonly > /tmp/x.values 2>&1
```

Be sure to run **X** from the console. Don't try to run **X** if you're already running the X Windows System.

If you have some dot clocks in the **XF86Config** file, then **X -probeonly** won't try to detect new ones. Because of this, the first time you run X this way, you should comment out the clocks in your **XF86Config** file. After you run X in **probeonly** mode, you can add in the clocks to the **XF86Config** file and try it again, seeing if things still seem to work.

You can then look at the file **/tmp/x.values**, which should contain something like the following:

```
XFree86 Version 3.1.1 / X Window System
(protocol Version 11, revision 0, vendor release 6000)
Operating System: Linux
Configured drivers:
  S3: accelerated server for S3 graphics adapters (Patchlevel 0)
      mmio_928, s3_generic
(using VT number 7)
```

```
XF86Config: /usr/X11R6/lib/X11/XF86Config
(**) stands for supplied, (—) stands for probed/default values
(**) Mouse: type: Microsoft, device: /dev/ttyS0, baudrate: 1200
(**) S3: Graphics device ID: "Actix GE32+ 2MB"
(**) S3: Monitor ID: "NEC MultiSync XE17"
(**) FontPath set to
"/usr/X11R6/lib/X11/fonts/misc/,/usr/X11R6/lib/X11/fonts/Type1/,/usr/X
11R6/lib/X11/fonts/Speedo/,/usr/X11R6/lib/X11/fonts/75dpi/,/usr/X11R6/
lib/X11/fonts/100dpi/"
(—) S3: card type: ISA
(—) S3: chipset:    928, rev E or above
(—) S3: chipset driver: mmio_928
(**) S3: videoram:   1024k
(**) S3: Ramdac type: att20c490
(—) S3: Ramdac speed: 110
(—) S3: clocks:  25.24   28.32   39.99    0.00  50.13  77.02  37.35
44.89
(—) S3: clocks:  90.11 119.98  80.30  31.50 110.16  65.08  75.17
94.68
(—) S3: Maximum allowed dot-clock: 110.000 MHz
(**) S3: Mode "1024x768": mode clock =  81.000, clock used =  80.300
(**) S3: Mode "800x600": mode clock =  50.000, clock used =  50.130
(**) S3: Mode "640x480": mode clock =  31.000, clock used =  31.500
(—) S3: Using 6 bits per RGB value
(**) S3: Virtual resolution set to 1024x768
```

Note that many of these values come from our **XF86Config** file.

Now, add the clocks to the *Device* section of your **XF86Config** file. Note that each time we ran **X -probeonly**, it returned slightly different clock values. For example, in this run, we got the following clock values (formatted for the **XF86Config** file):

```
Clocks  25.24  28.32  39.99   0.00  50.13  77.02  37.35  44.89
Clocks  90.11 119.98  80.30  31.50 110.16  65.08  75.17  94.68
```

From the **AccelCards** file, we found these clocks—close, but not exact:

```
Clocks 25 28 40 72 50 77 36 45
Clocks 90 120 80 32 110 65 75 95
```

Testing Your Configuration

Now you're ready to start X and see if things work. Type the following command and see if things start up:

```
startx
```

The **startx** shell script is the official way to start X from a user account.

Starting X

The **startx** script runs the **xinit** program, which does two things: **xinit** runs the X server (the program named **X**) and then runs the commands in the **.xinitrc** file in your home directory. These commands should set up the X applications you want launched on startup. If there's no **.xinitrc** file in your home directory, then **xinit** runs a default script. The system default **.xinitrc** file is **/usr/lib/X11/xinit/xinitrc.fvwm** (no dot).

The best way to start with X is—once you verify your **XF86Config** file—to copy the system **.xinitrc** into your home directory and edit this file. Most of the **.xinitrc** file comes from the standard XFree86 installation for Linux; it looks for certain files, few of which will actually exist, and it executes programs using those files it finds. The section at the end is where you'll set up the X applications you want started when X starts.

In our case, we use **xsetroot** to change the screen's background color and then launch **oclock**, a rounded clock, the **fvwm** window manager, and two **xterms**. No matter what, you need a window manager program to control the display. The default window manager on Linux is **fvwm**, and you'll find it highly customizable.

X quits when the last program in the **.xinitrc** (system or local) stops. Often, this last program is preceded by an **exec** statement. When you quit this last program, X stops and you're back at the console. In our case, we use **fvwm** as this last—key—process, because you need a window manager running during your entire X session, making **fvwm** a natural for this last process.

All our customizations to the **.xinitrc** file fit into a few simple lines:

```
# Start X applications
xsetroot -solid bisque3
/usr/bin/X11/oclock -geom 100x100+0+6    &
/usr/bin/X11/xterm -ls -geom 80x24+3+372 &
/usr/bin/X11/xterm -ls -geom 80x48+264+13 &
fvwm
```

The full **.xinitrc** file will look something like the following:

```
#!/bin/sh
userresources=$HOME/.Xresources
usermodmap=$HOME/.Xmodmap
sysresources=/usr/X11R6/lib/X11/xinit/.Xresources
sysmodmap=/usr/X11R6/lib/X11/xinit/.Xmodmap
# merge in defaults and keymaps

if [ -f $sysresources ]; then
    xrdb -merge $sysresources
fi

if [ -f $sysmodmap ]; then
    xmodmap $sysmodmap
fi

if [ -f $userresources ]; then
    xrdb -merge $userresources
fi

if [ -f $usermodmap ]; then
    xmodmap $usermodmap
fi

# start some nice programs
xsetroot -solid SteelBlue

# Changed lines are below.
xterm -geom 80x32+264+0 -ls &
xterm -geom 80x32+0+250 -ls &
oclock -geom -7-7 &
exec fvwm
```

If you don't set up a **.xinitrc** file and there is no system one, the default behavior is to create a single **xterm** window in the top-left corner of the screen. This **xterm** then becomes the key process, even if you later launch a window manager. When this **xterm** exits, X exits.

Chances are you can start with the file just listed and customize it to your needs later.

Stopping X

To stop X in the no **.xinitrc** file configuration, you need to find the **xterm** window that started out in the upper-left corner (you might have moved this window) and exit it. You'll soon be out of X and back to the boring old terminal mode.

If you use a **.xinitrc** file, simply exit the window manager to exit X. Normally, you can exit the window manager from a menu called up by placing the mouse over an empty area of the screen and holding down the leftmost mouse button. If this doesn't work, try any and all mouse buttons.

Tuning Your Modes

It's likely that the default mode in the **XF86Config** file will specify a 640-by-480 resolution. Chances are your hardware supports much higher resolutions. While running X, you can press the **Ctrl-Alt-Keypad-+** keys simultaneously to switch to the next mode in the **XF86Config** file.

This is very useful, because X may not look like a normal screen when it comes up. If this is the case, try switching modes to see if things get better.

You can also change the **XF86Config** file to start up in the best mode. Look for the *Screen* section in your **XF86Config** file. You'll want to change the modes line from something like

```
Modes "640x480" "800x600" "1024x768"
```

to

```
Modes "1024x768" "800x600" "640x480"
```

Note that we merely put the best mode first. This makes XFree86 start up in 1024-by-768-pixel-resolution mode, a much nicer display mode, especially for X. Before doing this, though, make sure that all graphics modes work, using **Ctrl-Alt-keypad+** while X is running. Ensure that each change results in a valid display.

VGA to the Rescue

If all the methods given have failed, you may want to fall back on VGA, just to get X up and running. This is presuming, of course, that you don't have a plain old Super VGA card, for which the Super VGA modes would be most appropriate. Instead, the theory is that if you can't get your super-duper card to run X in its super-duper accelerated mode, maybe you can get it running in plain old VGA. Most PC graphics boards support the VGA modes, so this method, while it won't take advantage of the power of your graphics card, may at least allow you to run X, presuming you can't so far.

In the next section, we'll show how to get a generic VGA file built because this step is usually quicker than getting the file properly built for your graphics hardware.

WARNING   Setting up XFree86 incorrectly can harm your system hardware, so watch out.

Using the Default Super VGA

In this section, we discuss using the sample Super VGA **XF86Config** file that comes with XFree86. You should always set up the **XF86Config** file for your exact hardware configuration. We only mention this technique because setting up X can prove to be nearly impossible. It is always best to set up X for your hardware. Remember, you were warned.

The first thing to do is find the example **XF86Config** file that comes with XFree86. This file, usually named **XF86Config.eg** and stored in

/usr/X11R6/lib/X11, has the default mode for a 640-by-480-pixel Super VGA device. Because most PC graphics boards support this mode, you might be in luck.

Copy the **XF86Config.eg** and edit it. You'll need to add the data about your mouse and monitor. In fact, the more you can fill in, the better. When you're finished, you can copy this file to **XF86Config** and start up X. If you use the Super VGA example file, you must use this X server. (Unless you have an Accel screen section set up, none of the accelerated X servers will work.)

Remember that running X this way may damage your hardware (don't say we didn't warn you). The only reason you want to run in a lower-resolution mode is if all else fails.

Again, it's best to configure X for your hardware. Only try the Super VGA mode if you have a card for which all else fails (unless, of course, your graphics card is a Super VGA card and the **XF86_SVGA** program is the appropriate X server.)

If you're still having problems with X, you may want to look for extra help on the Internet.

Making the Most of X

By now, you should have X up and running. Even so, with only a window manager and a few shell windows (**xterm**s), you haven't seen much of what X can do for you and how to configure X more to your liking.

Setting Up Your X Account

Depending on your preferences, there are a lot of different programs you may want to set up in your X environment. If you're more familiar with UNIX, you'll probably want to run a number of shell windows with the program called **xterm**. Xterm presents a UNIX shell in a window but allows you to specify the number of lines, the fonts, and the colors used. You can also copy and paste between **xterm** windows, a handy feat with long complicated UNIX command lines. (See the section on **xterm** for more on this handy application.)

Configuring the Xterm Program

The **xterm** program is probably the most popular X program. It seems kind of funny to run a shell window program, which is what **xterm** is, in a fancy graphical environment. But we're still running X on top of Linux and we still need access to the UNIX environment.

Figure 1.6 shows **xterm**.

```
VIM - /usr/X11R6/INSTALL
Installation instructions for XFree86[TM] 3.1.1 Linux distribution [1/28/95]
---------------------------------------------------------------------------

Introduction
------------
         This is the Linux binary distribution of XFree86 release 3.1.1.
Please read this document carefully before installation, and the included
doc package for detailed configuration information.

Requirements
------------
        Linux 1.0, 1.1.X, or later
        libc-4.5.26, or newer
        libm-4.5.26, or newer
        ld.so-1.4.3, or newer
        shadow-3.3.2 (if using xdm-shdw)

        This distribution was tested using Linux 1.1.54 and should work
without problems on all versions 1.0, 1.1.X and later. Kernel networking
support is required, although each server will work without TCP support
(using the "partial network" option). In order to use the XShm extension,
kernel shared memory support is required. All serial and bus mice detected
by the 1.1.54 kernel are supported by the servers.

Contents
--------
        The distribution is composed of the following parts:

        name         req/opt description
        X3118514.tgz   R[1]  Server for 8514-based boards.
        X311AGX.tgz    R[1]  Server for AGX-based boards.
        X311Ma32.tgz   R[1]  Server for Mach32-based boards.
        X311Ma64.tgz   R[1]  Server for Mach64-based boards.
        X311Ma8.tgz    R[1]  Server for Mach8-based boards.
        X311Mono.tgz   R[1]  Server for monochrome video modes.
        X311P9K.tgz    R[1]  Server for P9000-based boards.
        X311S3.tgz     R[1]  Server for S3-based boards.
        X311SVGA.tgz   R[1]  Server for Super VGA-based boards.
        X311VGA.tgz    R[1]  Server for VGA/EGA-based boards.
        X311W32.tgz    R[1]  Server for ET4000/W32-based boards.
        X311bin.tgz    R     The rest of the X11R6 binaries.
        X311cfg.tgz    R     Configuration files.
```

Figure 1.6 The **xterm** program.

The neatest things about **xterm** are that you can:

- run multiple shell windows (**xterm**s) at once.
- control the size of each **xterm** window.
- control the fonts and colors used by the **xterm** program.
- copy and paste between **xterm** windows and other X programs.
- use a scrollbar to view program output that has scrolled by.

Even though it's called **xterm**, the program isn't really a terminal emulator. It basically just provides a UNIX shell window.

Controlling the Size of the Xterm Window

The simplest way to control the size of an **xterm** window is through the *-geometry* command-line parameter:

```
gilbert:/$ xterm -geometry WidthxHeight &
```

With this parameter, the *Width* is the number of characters wide, almost always 80, and the *Height* is the number of lines to use. We find that 40 is a good number (the default is 24 lines).

Just about every X program supports the *-geometry* command-line parameter, but virtually every X program treats the *-geometry* command-line parameter differently from **xterm** (**xterm** is the main exception, in other words). While you specify the width and height in terms of characters with **xterm**, just about every other X program treats the *-geometry* as the size in pixels. This is important to note if you create some really small windows.

For example, the command to start **xterm** with 80 columns (the default) and 40 lines is:

```
$ xterm -geometry 80x40 &
```

With the *-geometry* command-line parameter you can also specify the starting location in pixels. The full syntax is:

```
-geometry WidthxHeight+X+Y
```

In this case, *X* and *Y* specify the location of the upper-left corner of the program's window in pixels. In X, the origin is also in the upper-left corner of the screen, so the following command creates an **xterm** window offset 10 pixels (in both *X* and *Y*) from the upper-left corner:

```
gilbert:/$ xterm -geometry 80x40+10+10 &
```

You can skip the size (*width* and *height*) or the location (*x* and *y*). The following are all valid commands:

```
gilbert:/$ xterm -geometry 80x40 &
gilbert:/$ xterm -geometry +10+10 &
gilbert:/$ xterm &
```

X Resource Files

Another topic under X that is different from the Windows and Macintosh environments is *resource files*. You'll find that X resource files are either the savior or the bane of your existence. Like the Windows and Macintosh systems, resource files on X allow you to customize fonts, colors, and even text messages, all without access to the application's source code.

This concept is just great. You can tell an application to use a more readable font, you can get rid of garish colors, you can even write Finnish messages in place of all the English ones, or you can fix the English messages to something more to your liking.

X resource files provide a powerful mechanism to customize just about every X application. There are many options within a resource file. In addition, there are many places to store resource files on disk—there is no default location. Because many options conflict, it's easy to get lost in all the details.

Stripped to its basics, an X resource file is an ASCII text file that specifies some option for a program or programs. Each line of the resource file specifies a resource to set and its value. For example, you can specify in an X resource file that all **xterm** programs should start up with the scrollbar turned on, which we'll show how to do soon. You can also control fonts, colors and a lot of the text displayed by most X programs.

To set up the scrollbar commands for **xterm** in a resource file, create a file named **XTerm** (note the capitalization) in your home directory. Both the file name, **XTerm**, and the location (your home directory) are essential. Put in the following lines:

```
XTerm*scrollBar: True
XTerm*saveLines: 1000
```

These X resource commands tell **xterm** to use a scrollbar and save 1000 lines in its scroll buffer. Save this file and start another **xterm** program. You should see a scrollbar.

For more on X resource files, see the book list in Appendix B.

Controlling Fonts and Colors

Like most options, you can control **xterm**'s choice of fonts and colors from both command-line parameters and X resource files. What we usually do is set up the options we always want in an X resource file and then use the command-line parameters only for options we rarely need.

Normally, we're happy with **xterm**'s color defaults: black text on a white background. It's the font we'd like to change. By default, **xterm** uses the font named *fixed*, a fixed-character-size font (as opposed to a proportional font). We find this font far too small, so we'd like to use a larger one.

To set the font, you can use the *-font* command-line parameter or set the font resource. To do the latter, you can add the following line to your **XTerm** file created earlier:

```
XTerm*font: -*-courier-medium-r-normalÑ14-140-75-75-m-90-*
```

This sets up a much more pleasing (to our eyes at least) and larger font for **xterm**.

To get a list of the available fonts, use the program **xlsfonts**, which will present a huge list. For **xterm**, you want a fixed-width font. The

Courier fonts are typically fixed-width, as are the Lucida typewriter fonts. In the very long font names, the fixed-width fonts should have an *m* or *c* as shown here after the two *75*s:

```
-adobe-courier-medium-r-normalÑ14-140-75-75-m-90-iso8859-1
```

As usual, to test this, save the **XTerm** file and start another **xterm** program.

For our **XTerm** file, we set the following resources:

```
!
!     XTerm resource file
!
XTerm*foreground:  black
XTerm*cursorColor: black
XTerm*background:  white
XTerm*scrollBar:   True
XTerm*saveLines:   1000
XTerm*font: -*-courier-medium-r-normalÑ14-140-75-75-m-90-*
```

Lines beginning with an exclamation mark (*!*) are comments. We list the most-used **xterm** command-line parameters in Table 1.19.

Table 1.19 Commonly used xterm command-line parameters.

Parameter	Meaning
-bg *color*	Sets background color; defaults to white
-cr *color*	Sets color of text cursor; defaults to black
-display *hostname***:0**	Sets name of X display to connect to
-e *program* **[***args***]**	Runs program instead of shell
-fg *color*	Sets foreground color; defaults to black
-fn *fontname*	Uses the given font
-font *fontname*	Uses the given font
-geometry *geom*	Uses given size and location
-ls	Turns shell into login shell
-sb	Turns on scrollbar

Copying and Pasting between Xterm Windows

One of the best benefits of **xterm** over the console terminal is that you can copy and paste text between **xterm** windows. This is very handy if you edit documents. You can view one document in one **xterm** window and edit another in a different **xterm** window, copying and pasting between them.

Xterm is highly configurable, but in the default configuration, you select text by holding down the left mouse button and dragging over the text you want to select. Double-clicking on a word selects just that word. Triple-clicking anywhere in a line selects the entire line.

To paste, press the middle mouse button. The text will be inserted just as if you typed it.

Xterm just presents a shell window. Inside the **xterm** window, you run text-based shell programs, few of which know anything about the mouse and selecting text. Therefore, you have to ensure that the program you run within the **xterm** window is ready for the pasted text. In the **elvis** text editor, for example, you should enter input mode by typing **i** in command mode.

NOTE **elvis** does not support middle-mouse button pastes, which is very annoying. To paste in **elvis**, you must hold down the **Shift** key while you press the middle mouse button.

Our fix is to use a different **vi** clone that comes with Linux, called **vim**. **Vim** fully supports mouse pasting in **xterm** windows without the hassle of **elvis**.

Starting X Automatically at Boot-Up and Creating an X Login Screen

Up to now, we've been running **startx** to begin an X session. You still need to login at the console and start X yourself (or use the automatic method we will describe). In addition to this method, there's a way to set up an X login screen, using XDM. *XDM* stands for the X Display Manager, a means to control an X session. As such, XDM is generally much nicer on the user; it automatically starts the X server and presents a graphical login window.

The X Display Manager is run from a program called **xdm**. While **xdm** takes a little getting used to, we like it better than the **startx/xinit** we've been running so far. This is because **startx** (which runs **xinit**) requires you to login to a text screen and then starts up X (via **startx**). **Xdm** allows you to log directly into an X session.

Xdm also allows one program to control your workstation's console and a number of X terminals. If you're interested in this, look in Appendix B for books that cover **xdm**.

To set up **xdm**, you need to edit at least one system file. This is a key file used when booting Linux, so it is a serious endeavor. Always back up any system file before you edit it.

UNIX Run Levels

Xdm is usually set to trigger what is called a *run-level*. With a few exceptions, a run-level in UNIX is an arbitrary concept that mostly follows ancient UNIX traditions. The run-level *S* implies a single-user stand alone system.

In Linux, run-level 1 and higher is multiuser. This means that more than one user is allowed to login. On many systems, run-level 3 starts up networking. This is also the default Linux run-level. Linux also has special run-levels for power-fail (which shuts down the system) and the Vulcan death-grip (**Ctrl-Alt-Backspace**).

You can get some ideas about run levels by looking in the **/etc/inittab** file. In **/etc/inittab**, one of the first entries will be something like the following:

```
# Default runlevel.
id:3:initdefault:
```

In Slackware 2.3, the Linux default run-level was 5. The default X run level was 6. Now, that has changed to 3 and 4 respectively. Run-level 6 will now reboot the system, a great surprise if you intend it to run X.

N O T E

This states that the default system run-level is level 3. When Linux boots up, it will boot into run-level 3. Later in the **/etc/inittab** file, you'll find something like:

```
x1:4:wait:/etc/rc.d/rc.4
```

This states that on entry to run-level 4, run **/etc/rc.d/rc.4**. This file then starts up the X Display Manager, which will present an X login screen.

On our system, **/etc/rc.d/rc.4** starts the following program:

```
# Tell the viewers what's going to happen...
echo "Starting up the X Window System V.11 R.6..."

# Call the "xdm" program.
exec /usr/X11R6/bin/xdm -nodaemon
```

This is what starts up **xdm**. To get **xdm** up and running, all you should really have to do is edit the **/etc/inittab** as **root** and change the following line:

```
id:3:initdefault:
```

to:

```
id:4:initdefault:
```

That's it. Everything else comes preconfigured. You may want to change the configuration, but you have a good start.

After making these changes, when you next boot Linux, you'll boot into run-level 4 rather than run-level 3. The process of going into run-level 4 will start **xdm**, because of what's in the **/etc/rc.d/rc.4** file.

Before doing this, though, make a copy of /**etc/inittab**. You also should test **xdm** before setting the system to boot into it, because you always want to be able to boot Linux. (Making a mistake in **/etc/inittab** can result in a Linux that won't boot.) To test **xdm**, you can type in the following command as root, to change to run-level 4 now:

```
# init 4
```

This will jump you to run-level 4. Be patient; this command takes a while.

Make sure X is not running when you do this. You should be logged in as root at the console.

If you set up your **.login** or **.profile** file to automatically call **startx** when you login (see "Starting X Automatically on Login" later), you must disable this first. These two methods for starting X conflict. Quit X, then comment out those lines you added to the **.login** or **.profile** file, for example:

```
if ( 'tty' == '/dev/tty1' ) then
#      Commented out.
#      startx
endif
```

After a while, you should see a graphical login screen. It is best to test **xdm** using *init 4* first, to see if everything is set up. Try to login and see what happens. If this works, you're in business and you can confidently modify the **/etc/inittab** file.

The **xdm** configuration files are in **/usr/lib/X11/xdm**. If you want to change the background color for the login screen, look in **Xsetup_0** in that directory. You probably won't have to edit much in **/usr/lib/X11/xdm**, especially for a standalone Linux system without X terminals on the network. (If your needs are more demanding, you'll need to look into a book specifically on X, such as *The UNIX System Administrator's Guide to X*; see Appendix B for more on this.)

User Accounts Under Xdm

While you probably won't have to edit any of the **xdm** system files in **/usr/lib/X11/xdm**, you'll probably have to edit files in your home directory. By default, **xdm** runs a file named **.xsession** from your home directory, instead of the **.xinitrc** that is run by **startx** (and **xinit**).

To create the **.xsession** file, you can start by copying your **.xinitrc** file to **.xsession** in your home directory. (Remember to put in the leading period on the filename in your home directory.) Then, modify this file like you changed the **.xinitrc** file earlier.

Here's a copy of our **.xsession** file:

```
#!/bin/sh
userresources=$HOME/.Xresources
usermodmap=$HOME/.Xmodmap
sysresources=/usr/X11R6/lib/X11/xinit/.Xresources
sysmodmap=/usr/X11R6/lib/X11/xinit/.Xmodmap

# merge in defaults and keymaps

if [ -f $sysresources ]; then
    xrdb -merge $sysresources
fi

if [ -f $sysmodmap ]; then
    xmodmap $sysmodmap
fi

if [ -f $userresources ]; then
    xrdb -merge $userresources
fi

if [ -f $usermodmap ]; then
    xmodmap $usermodmap
fi

# start some nice programs
xsetroot -solid SteelBlue

xterm -geom 80x32+264+0 -ls &
xterm -geom 80x32+0+250 -ls &
oclock -geom -7-7 &
exec fvwm
```

If you don't want to start up X at boot time, you may want to start X every time you login.

Starting X Automatically on Login

If you don't set up **xdm**, you'll need to type in **startx** after you login to get X and all these applications in your **.xinitrc** file started. If you don't like to type **startx** every time you log in and you're sure that you really want to run X all the time when you login, you can put the **startx** command in your **.login** or **.profile** file (depending on the shell you use, **csh** or **bash**). If you do, be sure you're running from the console only. Otherwise, the **.login** or **.profile** files will error out if they get run from elsewhere (such as when you login over a serial line or from another virtual terminal).

The way to check for this is to check the result of the **tty** program. The **tty** program returns the current device file used for your terminal. When run from an **xterm** shell window, **tty** will print something like **/dev/ttyp1** (for the first pseudo-terminal device). But when run from the console (from the first virtual terminal), **tty** will print **/dev/tty1**. When run from the second virtual terminal, **tty** prints **/dev/tty2**. So, we can check for **/dev/tty1**.

To do this, we can enter **tty** at the console (before starting X):

```
$ tty
/dev/tty1
```

Use the value **tty** returns for you, not necessarily the value we received.

Armed with this information, you can edit your **.login** file (presuming you use the C shell, **csh**, as your shell) to add the following lines:

```
if ( 'tty' == '/dev/tty1' ) then
    startx
endif
```

This will start up X when you login at the console. You can also set up your account to log you out when you quit X. Most of the time, we begin X at login and quit X when we want to log out. If this fits your pattern, you can change the **.login** file to contain the following:

```
if ( 'tty' == '/dev/tty1' ) then
    startx
    logout
endif
```

The X Font Server

The X font server is a special program that can scale fonts. This ability dramatically increases the already-prolific set of X fonts available on your system (use the **xlsfonts** command to list these fonts). To get the font server up and running, you must:

- Configure the font server and tell it where to get fonts
- Configure the font server to start up before X does
- Configure the X server to communicate with the font server

To configure the font server, we need to tell it where to find the scalable fonts. Luckily, Linux comes with a workable preconfigured file, **/usr/X11R6/lib/X11/fs/config**.

To start the font server, use the **xfs** (short for X font server) command. Enter the following command as root:

```
# xfs -port 7000 &
```

This uses the default configuration file, **/usr/X11R6/lib/X11/fs/config**, and runs on TCP/IP port 7000 (an arbitrary port to which the X font server defaults).

Once started, we can verify that the font server is running by using the **fsinfo** command:

```
gilbert:/$ fsinfo -server hostname:port
```

You need to fill in the hostname and port number. For example, with a hostname of *eric* and the default port number of *7000*, the command would be:

```
gilbert:/$ fsinfo -server eric:7000
```

You should see output like the following:

```
name of server: eric:7000
version number: 2
vendor string:  X Consortium
vendor release number:  6000
maximum request size:    16384 longwords (65536 bytes)
number of catalogues:    1
        all
Number of alternate servers: 0
number of extensions:    0
```

Once you verify that the font server is running, you can set up XFree86 to communicate with the font server. This is necessary so that X applications can take advantage of the font server's fonts.

To get the X server ready to accept the font server, you need to adjust its font path, or **fp** for short. Enter the following commands:

```
gilbert:/$ xset +fp tcp/eric:7000
gilbert:/$ xset fp rehash
```

In your case, you need to replace *eric* with your system's hostname. The first command tells the X server to use a TCP/IP port as a sort of font directory. The *tcp/hostname:port* syntax is the standard way to do this. The second command tells the X server to query again for all the available fonts.

If you're running **xdm** (see "Starting X at Boot-Up," earlier), you should stop that, verify that things work manually, and then set up **xdm** again. Problems with the font server may cause X to quit. If X quits, this may prevent an X-based login, leaving you in an unhappy situation.

The Fvwm Window Manager

The window manager is one of the most important applications you'll run, as it sits around each and every application window on the screen and can influence how the windows work. The de facto window manager for Linux is called **fvwm**.

This window manager provides a great deal of control over the way you interact with X, especially because **fvwm** supports a host of configuration options. While you can run any window manager you want, **fvwm** seems to be the most popular in the Linux world.

You can run only one window manager at a time.

Configuring Fvwm

Most window managers under X support a configuration file. Usually, this file is located in a dot file in your home directory. Most window managers also follow a naming convention for their configuration file. For the **mwm** window manager, the file is named **.mwmrc**. For **twm**, it's **.twmrc**. For **fvwm**, it's **.fvwmrc**.

At startup, **fvwm** will look for your customizations in a file named **.fvwmrc** in your home directory. If you have no **.fvwmrc** file (which is likely when you start), **fvwm** will look for a system file named **/usr/lib/X11/fvwm/system.fvwmrc**. If that file, too, is missing, **fvwm** will exit.

Because **fvwm** is a very complex window manager, you should copy the **system.fvwmrc** file or one of the example files to your home directory and name this file **.fvwmrc**. If you start from a working example, you'll find it a lot easier than creating a **.fvwmrc** file from scratch.

Once you find the **fvwm** system directory, you'll see a number of sample configurations in the **sample_configs** directory. It's easiest to configure **fvwm** from a working model. You can either copy the **system.fvwmrc** or one of the files in the **sample_configs** directory.

Once you have copied a working configuration file into your home directory, the next step is to start customizing. The **.fvwmrc** file is very long, so we'll provide an overview of the areas you're most likely to customize and then we'll provide an example **.fvwmrc** file—a very long example—that you can use. Just browsing this example should give you plenty of ideas. In addition to our example, you may want to look at the **fvwm** example files mentioned earlier and look at **fvwm**'s online-manual page.

In the **.fvwmrc** file, the order of items is very important. It's best to start with a working example and then search for the items we mention. Change the item's value, but leave the item itself in the same relative position in the **.fvwmrc** file.

Configuring Fonts and Colors

The foremost area you'll likely customize in the **.fvwmrc** file is fonts and colors.

Each window manager, **fvwm** included, allows only one application at a time to get keyboard input. This window, usually called the *active window* or the *keyboard focus window*, is usually highlighted by the window manager. In the **.fvwmrc** file, *HiForeColor* sets the text foreground color for the active window's title. *HiBackColor* sets the active title bar color. *StdForeColor* and *StdBackColor* work similarly for nonactive windows.

We use the following colors (copied from the default **.fvwmrc** file):

```
StdForeColor        Black
StdBackColor        #60a0c0

# this is used for the selected window
HiForeColor         Black
HiBackColor         #c06077
```

Window managers usually support two policies for selecting which window is made active: click-to-focus and focus-follows-mouse. Few people agree on which is better (Microsoft has decided click-to-focus). Choose the mode you want.

If you want focus-follows-mouse, make sure the following line is commented out:

```
#ClickToFocus
```

If you want click-to-focus, then uncomment (remove the # character) the same line:

```
ClickToFocus
```

For fonts, you can control a number of the fonts used by **fvwm**:

```
Font        -adobe-helvetica-medium-r-*-*-14-*-*-*-*-*-*-*
#Font       -*-times-medium-i-*-*-*-140-*-*-*-*-*-*
WindowFont  -adobe-helvetica-bold-r-*-*-12-*-*-*-*-*-*-*
#IconFont   -adobe-helvetica-medium-r-*-*-11-*-*-*-*-*-*-*
IconFont    fixed
```

The asterisks (*) in the font names are wildcards. We only specify the minimum amount of data necessary to get Helvetica fonts at 10 and 12 point. A few fonts are commented out. You can uncomment these lines (and comment out the corresponding line) to try these other fonts, or type in your own font names.

By default, **fvwm** asks you to place each new window that appears on the screen. This can be a real pain, so we usually ask **fvwm** to place windows for us—you can always move them later—by setting the oddly named *RandomPlacement* option. Uncomment the following line to get this effect:

```
RandomPlacement
```

You also need to comment out the following line:

```
#NoPPosition
```

By default, **fvwm** places no border around dialog windows (called *transient windows* in X terminology). To make **fvwm** act more like the Motif window manager, uncomment the following line:

```
# If you want decorated transient windows,
# uncomment this:
```

```
# Ensure that a title bar appears on dialog boxes.
DecorateTransients
```

Testing Your Fvwm Configuration

Now that we've made a change to our **.fvwmrc** file, it's time to test our new configuration. To do this, you need to restart **fvwm**. You can either quit X and restart everything or call up **fvwm**'s root window menu, where hopefully you'll find a **Restart Fvwm** menu choice. (This choice may be on a submenu.) You can access **fvwm**'s root menu by holding down the left mouse button over the screen background.

Turning Off the Virtual Desktop

Both XFree86 and **fvwm** provide the ability to use *virtual screen space*, screen space beyond the confines of your monitor's resolution. XFree86 calls this a *virtual screen*, and **fvwm** calls this a *virtual desktop*.

These two methods tend to conflict, and frankly we don't have much use for either kind of virtual screen space, as we don't run that many X applications at once and we can iconify windows to get them out of the way. Furthermore, it's easy to accidentally warp to one of **fvwm**'s virtual desktop spaces, which tends to get annoying.

Because of all this, we turn off **fvwm**'s virtual desktop in our **.fvwmrc** file with the following:

```
DeskTopSize 1x1
```

You specify the desktop value in units of the screen size; *1x1* means no virtual desktop.

Placing Icons

Fvwm's defaults result in bizarrely placed icons, with hidden icons strewn throughout the screen. We want to change this. To do so, use the **IconBox** command in the **.fvwmrc** file. We like our icons to go across the top of the screen but start from an offset of about 130 pixels to leave room for the round **oclock** window we place in the upper-left corner of the screen. (See our **.xinitrc** file.)

IconBox specifies a rectangular area where you want the icons to appear. Here's our area:

```
IconBox 130 5 600 15
```

Exiting X from Fvwm

To exit from **fvwm** and usually quit X (if **fvwm** is the last X application in your **.xinitrc** or **.xsession** file), you usually call up the **fvwm** root menu and quit. The default choices are **Exit Fvwm**, which invokes a submenu to confirm, and **Yes, Really Quit**.

Summary

Installing Linux can be a detail-oriented procedure that tries your patience, as you learned in this long chapter.

This chapter also dealt with one of the most tedious, nonintuitive, and uninspiring aspects of Linux installation and configuration—messing around with XFree86. You learned about all the mundane details that go into a typical XFree86 configuration process, including mucking around with various files and settings.

The **fvwm** window manager is advertised as being Motif-like, and it is—on the surface, anyway. After you use it for a while, you'll learn that it doesn't respond to the same commands as the Motif window manager (**mwm**), and all in all, it works differently than **mwm**.

In the next chapter we will cover C and C++ Linux tools.

C Programming Tools
and Linux

This chapter covers:

- C programming tools in Linux
- GNU CC
- C++ and GNU CC
- ELF files
- Linking in the right libraries
- Creating your own libraries with **ar**
- Parsers and lexers
- Other related Linux tools
- Using **make**
- Objective-C

C Programming Tools in Linux

Now that you've got Linux up and running on your PC, it's time to begin your programming education.

It's no surprise that we're beginning our programming coverage with a discussion of the C and C++ tools available on Slackware Linux. As you'll recall from the Introduction, Linux is a UNIX workalike. UNIX relies heavily on the C programming language, for both its structure (UNIX was originally developed in C) and its programming environment.

We're not going to teach basic C programming here; indeed, there are a host of C programming books (including some recommended tomes in Appendix B) that should introduce you to the joys of C. Instead, we'll spend our time detailing the C and C++ tools available under Linux.

For the programmer, Linux offers all the freeware utilities and compilers you'd expect for software that relies heavily on offerings from the Free Software Foundation. Starting with the GNU C compiler, you can develop C, C++, Fortran (via **g77**), and Objective-C programs on your Linux system.

Your main worry is whether you've installed the proper disk sets for your compiler and associated tools. (If you haven't heard of one before, a *compiler* is a tool that converts a program in text form into an executable Linux command.) Being programmers ourselves, we always recommend this; if you haven't, you can always go back and use the **setup** program to reinstall the proper disk sets, as we detailed in Chapter 1.

If you're not a programmer, chances are that you'll be lost in much of this chapter—and the rest of the book. Even so, you'll find some interesting Linux utilities mentioned here. In addition, many free Linux programs come in source-code-form only; you'll need to learn to compile them, so it might be important to know about the process of compiling and linking C programs.

Basically, there are five types of tools you'll need to create C (and X Window) applications on Linux:

- An *editor* for creating source-code files. Linux includes a set of text editors, including **elvis** (the Linux version of **vi**), **emacs**, and others. Because you'll need to use a text editor to create applications (well, most of the time, anyway), we'll cover how to use these text editors in Appendix C.

- A *compiler* for compiling and linking source-code files. In Linux, this is GNU **gcc**.

- A *utility* for building the software—essentially, a program that combines all the disparate parts of the software-development process. Slackware Linux includes both **make** and **imake**. This chapter will cover **make**; Chapter 3 will delve into **imake**.

- A *debugger* for debugging applications. There are two debuggers with Slackware Linux: the text-based **gdb** and the X Window–based **xxgdb**.

- A *version-control system* to monitor changes of source code and how they apply to a current application. Slackware Linux includes Revision Control System, or RCS.

These tools were installed if you followed the standard installation procedures outlined in Chapter 1.

The Linux C Compiler: GNU cc

The main C and C++ compiler on Linux is the GNU **gcc**. It is an all-encompassing program that can compile a number of programming languages: C, C++, and Objective-C. **Gcc**, or **cc**, which is linked to **gcc**, compiles C and C++ programs just like you'd expect. The command-line parameters are all standard **cc** parameters and the traditional **gcc** parameters. If you're used to programming on UNIX, you'll find Linux works as you'd expect.

In the GNU/Slackware Linux documentation, you'll run into references to G++. G++ and **gcc** are the same thing; G++ refers to the compiler under the auspices of C++ programming, while **gcc** refers to the compiler under the auspices of C and Objective-C programming.

C Programming

C programs—and in fact, most programs in general—usually start in plain old text files. (Linux makes extensive use of simple text files, as you've seen throughout this book.) These text files are created with text editors like **vi** or **emacs**. Once created, C programs must be compiled with a C compiler, **cc** or **gcc** (which are the same on Linux). This C compiler converts the text file, which the programmer wrote, into object or machine code for the Intel platform. Then, object modules (files of object code) are linked together to make an executable program, a brand new Linux command. Once the process is successfully completed, you can execute this program like any other command you type at the command line. Being able to create your own command is a neat thing.

The first step is identifying what types of files you're dealing with. Table 2.1 lists the most common Linux file types and their common file extensions.

Table 2.1 Program file types.

File Suffix	Meaning
.a	Library
.c	C program
.C	C++ file (note the uppercase *C*)
.cc	C++ file
.cpp	C++ file
.cxx	C++ file
.c++	C++ file
.f	Fortran program
.for	Fortran program
.h	C or C++ include file
.hxx	C++ include file
.o	Object module (compiled from a **.c** file)
.pl	Perl script

continued...

File Suffix	Meaning
.pm	Perl module script
.s	Assembly code
.sa	Shared library stubs linked with your program
.so.*n*	Run-time shared library, version number is *n*
.tcl	Tcl script
.tk	Tcl script

Most C programs are stored in one or more files that end with **.c**, for example, **neatstuff.c** and **myprog.c**. When you compile a C file, the C compiler, **cc**, creates an object file, usually ending with **.o**. The linker (called *linkage editor* in Linux parlance), **ld**, then links the **.o** files to make an executable program. The default name for this program is **a.out**, although no one uses **a.out** for their program names. Instead, programs have names like **ls**, **cp**, and **mv**. All of this is controlled by the **cc** command.

The Cc Command

The **cc** command executes the C compiler, which can compile and link C programs into executable commands. To test your Linux C compiler, we'll use the following short program:

```
/*
 * Example C program for Chapter 2,
 * Linux Programming.
 */
#include <stdio.h>

int main(int argc, char** argv)

{
    /* This is a comment. */
    printf("Linux is my favorite operating system!\n");

    return 0;
```

```
}

/* chap2.c */
```

Enter this code into a text file named **chap2.c**, using your favorite Linux text editor.

It's a good idea to always name C program files with a **.c** extension. This isn't required, but following conventions like this make Linux easier to use.

After you type in this short program, you can do the following simple steps to create a working executable program from this C file.

The program you typed in was simply a text file. There's nothing in it to make it an executable command. To do so, we need to compile and link the program. Both steps are accomplished by the following **cc** command:

```
$ cc -o chap2 chap2.c
```

This command runs the C compiler, **cc**. The *-o* option tells **cc** to build a program named **chap2** (the default name without the *-o* option is the awkward **a.out**). The **chap2.c** part of the command tells **cc** to compile the file named **chap2.c**. The **cc** command both compiles and links the program.

You should now have an executable program named **chap2**. You can execute this program by typing **chap2** at the command line. When you do, you'll see the following output: .

```
$ chap2
Linux is my favorite operating system!
```

Now you're a real C programmer, ready for a lucrative new career.

Compiling the Long Way

When we just used the **cc** command, **cc** first compiled the program into an object module. Then **cc** linked the object module to create an executable program, the file named **chap2**. This is very important if you have more than one file to compile into your program. Most C programs require a number of **.c** files, all of which must be compiled and linked together to form one program. One of the main reasons for separating C programs into multiple files is sanity: reading a 1MB program in one file is ludicrous. And yes, C programs get to this size, and even much bigger than 1 megabyte. Some C programs we've worked on include more than a million lines of C code. You need to know how to compile multiple **.c** files into one executable command because the vast majority of Linux freeware comes in this fashion.

To use the long method of compiling and linking, we split the tasks into two steps. First, you compile all the **.c** files you require. Then you link the resulting **.o** files (we'll get into this later) into your executable program. Because we have a very small C program typed in already (you did type it in, didn't you?), we'll start with that.

Compile **chap2.c** into an object module, an **.o** file, with the following command:

```
$ cc -c chap2.c
```

If successful, you should see a file named **chap2.o** in your directory. The **.o** file is called the *object file* (or *object module*), and it contains unlinked machine code.

The next step is to link the object files (usually there's more than one) into an executable file. To do this, we again use the *-o* option to **cc**, but this time we pass a **.o** file at the end of the command line rather than the **.c** file we used earlier:

```
$ cc -o chap2 chap2.o
```

This command links the file **chap2.o** into the executable program **chap2**. You can place more than one object filename on the command line, as in the following example:

```
$ cc -o chap2 chap2_a.o chap2_b.o chap2_c.o
```

Normally, you'll want to pick more descriptive filenames than the ones we've used.

Working with Cc

In normal operation, the **cc** command executes a number of other commands under the hood. One such command is **cpp**. The **cpp** command is the C preprocessor. This reads a C program file, a **.c** file, and expands any # directives. In the short program listed earlier, the *#include* directive means to include the file **stdio.h**. That is, **cpp** reads in **stdio.h** and inserts the contents right at the *#include* directive. Most C programs use one or more include files.

These include files are normally stored in **/usr/include**. If you use the angle brackets (< and >) around an include filename, like **<stdio.h>**, this means that **cpp** looks for a file named **stdio.h** in the standard places, of which **/usr/include** is the default (the *-I* command-line parameter can add more directories to the include file search path; see Table 2.2 later). You can also use quotation marks (") around the filename.

All C programs are built around the section labeled *main()*. The *main()* section (called a *function* in C parlance) is executed when the program starts. Our *main()* function simply calls the *printf()* function, which prints the text between the quotation marks to your screen. As you can tell, this is not a sophisticated program.

The \n character passed to *printf()* in the program means that a new-line character is printed. This starts a new line. If you're used to a DOS machine, then you'll note that UNIX uses a new-line character where DOS uses a carriage return and then a new line. The backslash, \, is used as a special character in C programs. Usually, a backslash is combined with another character to make a nonprintable character, such as \n for a new line, \t for a tab, or \a for a bell.

Using the Cc Command

The **cc** command uses a number of command-line parameters to tell it what to do and to allow you to fine-tune the process of building executable programs from C language text files. Table 2.2 lists commonly used **cc** command-line parameters.

Table 2.2 Cc command-line parameters.

Parameter	Meaning
-Idirectory	Searches the given directory and **/usr/include** for include files.
-c filename.c	Compiles the file ***filename.c*** and builds the object module ***filename.o***. This does not create an executable command.
-o progname	Names the executable program *progname*. The default name is **a.out**.
-g	Compiles with debugging information.
-O	Optimizes the program for best performance.
-llibrary	Link in the named *library*.

Most UNIX compilers don't allow you to mix the *g* (include debugging information) and *O* (optimize) options, but the GNU C compiler used by Linux does. (Nevertheless, it's not recommended.)

Linking with Libraries

For C programs, a *library* is a collection of commonly used routines that you can reuse in your programs. Most C programs require more than the standard C library. If you look in **/usr/lib**, you'll see most of the libraries supported by Linux. Table 2.3 lists the major locations for Linux libraries.

Table 2.3 Locations for Linux libraries.

Directory	Libraries
/usr/lib	Main system libraries
/usr/openwin/lib	Open Look libraries like the Xview library
/usr/X11R6/lib	Most X Window libraries

To link with a given library, you use the *-l* command-line option to **cc**. To link with the X11 library, use *-lX11*. This is shorthand notion for linking in the library named **libX11.a** (or its shared-library equivalent, **libX11.so**).

ELF Files

This version of Linux uses a new object module format called *ELF*, short for Executable and Linking Format. Programs compiled with ELF differ from ones compiled in the older **a.out** format. ELF provides better support for shared libraries, the primary reason for this migration. Shared libraries save on memory usage when you run more than one program at a time, especially more than one X Window program.

Normally, you won't have to pay attention to ELF or **a.out** issues at all, except for one thing: the **a.out** libraries are not compatible with the ELF libraries. This is especially true for shared libraries.

Thus, you need to be careful about any Linux binary programs you acquire. If you compile everything from source code, you're OK; Linux will use the libraries you have on your system.

But if you pick up applications in precompiled binary format, such as Netscape Navigator or NCSA Mosaic, you have to ensure that you have the proper shared libraries expected by the application, or the program won't run.

When you install Linux (or later if you run the **setup** program), you can install both the **a.out** and the ELF libraries. If you have the disk space, you should load both. If you need to choose one or the other, go with ELF, as everything in the Linux world is migrating to ELF.

To see what systems your linker, **ld**, is configured for, try the following command:

```
ld -V
```

You should see output like the following:

```
ld version cygnus-2.6 (with BFD 2.6.0.10)
  Supported emulations:
   elf_i386
   i386linux
   i386coff
   m68kelf
   m68klinux
   sun4
   elf32_sparc
```

The *sparc*, *sun4*, and *m68k* (Motorola 68000) are for cross-compiling. Chances are you won't use these options.

By default, **gcc** will compile to ELF format. To verify, use the **file** command on any executable file, such as the **chap2** file created earlier:

```
file chap2
```

You should see output like the following:

```
chap2: ELF 32-bit LSB executable i386 (386 and up) Version 1
```

This indicates that the default object file format on Linux is now ELF, as expected.

The term **a.out**, unfortunately, means different things in different contexts. If you compile a C program with **gcc**, the default output filename remains **a.out**. Even so, this **a.out** file will appear in ELF object file format, not the older object file format, called **a.out** format. This is another confusing part of Linux.

If for some reason you need to force **gcc** to compile in **a.out** format, you can use the following command in place of **gcc**:

```
gcc -b i486-linuxaout -c foo.c -o foo
```

This command requires the **a.out** libraries. If you did not load them, this command will fail.

Linux Libraries

There are a number of other libraries that you'll find useful; they are listed in Table 2.4.

Table 2.4 GNU libraries included with Slackware Linux.

Library	Purpose
glibc	The standard C run-time library
iostream	The GNU C++ iostream library
gmp	The GNU MP arbitrary precision arithmetic library
regex	The GNU regular expression library
termcap	The termcap library, which allows applications to handle character-display terminals

These libraries are stored in **/usr/lib**.

NOTE There are other libraries for X Window application development. These will be covered in Chapter 3.

Creating Your Own Libraries with ar

The **ar** command creates, extracts, and modifies information from archives. In some ways, it's a cousin to the **tar** command you've probably run across if you've used UNIX or Linux at all.

In this situation, you'll use **ar** to create libraries of C and C++ routines. There's really nothing magical about this—all you need to do is use the **ar** command with the relevant options and the target name of the archive, followed by the names of the object files to be archived:

```
$ ar options archive.a files.o
```

The relevant options to **ar** are listed in Table 2.5.

Table 2.5 Options to the ar command.

Option	Purpose
r	Replaces old files in the archive with new files.

continued...

Option	Purpose
s	Updates the symbol table used in the archive.
t	Table of contents is printed.
v	Verbose mode; tells you what's happening.

Most of the time you'll use the *r* and *v* options to **ar**. For example, the following command creates an archive called **newlib.a** that incorporates the **file1.o**, **file2.o**, and **file3.o** object files:

```
$ ar rv newlib.a file1.o file2.o file3.o
```

Building Programs with Make

Most C programs require more than one **.c** file of source code. When one of these files change, at least one (and maybe more) of the files must be recompiled to have the executable program reflect the changes. Programmers, who tend to be lazy, don't want to recompile all the files if just one changed. Furthermore, these lazy programmers don't want to have to keep track of all the files that changed. This is where the tool called **make** comes in.

Make is a command that helps build or "make" UNIX programs from the C language source-code files. **Make** uses a set of rules, stored in a file called **Makefile**, to tell it the most efficient way to rebuild a program. You keep a **Makefile** in each directory where you develop C programs.

The **Makefile** contains a set of rules, using a rigid syntax, that describe how to build the program. Most of the rules declare what parts of the program depend on other parts. Using these dependency rules, **make** determines what has changed (based on the file-modified date) and what other things depend on the file or files that changed. Then, **make** executes the commands in the **Makefile** to build each thing that needs to be rebuilt.

The basic **Makefile** syntax is deceptively simple. (Linux includes the GNU **make** program, which accepts a number of rule shortcuts. For this chapter, we'll just cover the basics. Use the **man make** command to find out more about **make**.)

You start with a so-called *target*. The target is something you want to build, such as our program **chap2** from the earlier example.

To create a target in the **Makefile**, begin with a new line. You name the target—what you want to build—then place a colon (:), a tab, and then list the files the target depends on. On the next line, begin with a tab, then place the UNIX command used to build the target. You can have multiple commands, each of which should go on its own line, and every command line must start with a tab.

In the abstract, the **Makefile** rules look like the following:

what_to_build: *what_it_depends_on*

> *command1_to_build_it*

> *command2_to_build_it*

> *command3_to_build_it*

> ...

> *lastcommand_to_build_it*

In the abstract, this looks confusing. Here's a more concrete example, using the **chap2** program.

The target we want to build is the **chap2** program, which depends on the object module **chap2.o**. Once we have the object module **chap2.o**, the command line to create the **chap2** program is:

```
chap2:    chap2.o
cc -o chap2 chap2.o
```

This **make** rule states that if **chap2.o** has a more recent date, then execute the **cc** command to build the **chap2** program from the object module **chap2.o**.

This is just part of the task; we still have to compile **chap2.c** to create the object module **chap2.o**. That is, the file **chap2.o** is said to depend on the file **chap2.c**. You build **chap2.o** from **chap2.c**. To do this, we use another **make** rule.

This time, the object module **chap2.o** depends on the text file **chap2.c**. The command to build the object module is:

```
chap2.o:   chap2.c
cc -c chap2.c
```

With this **make** rule, if you edit **chap2.c**, you'll make the file **chap2.c** have a more recent date/time than the object module **chap2.o**. This causes **make** to trigger the **cc** command to compile **chap2.c** into **chap2.o**.

You've discovered the secret to **make**'s rules. Everything depends on the date/time of the files, a very simple—but clever—idea. The idea is that if the text of the program **.c** file is modified, you better rebuild the program with **cc**. Because most users are impatient, if the **.c** file hasn't been changed, there's no reason (at least in our example) to rebuild the program with **cc**.

A Make Example

To try **make**, enter the following text into a file named **Makefile**:

```
#
# Test Makefile
#
# The program chap2 depends on chap2.o.
chap2:   chap2.o
   cc -o chap2 chap2.o

# The object module chap2.o depends on chap2.c.
chap2.o:   chap2.c
   cc -c chap2.c
```

This **Makefile** should be in the same directory as your sample C program file, **chap2.c**. To use **make**, we need to tell it what to make, that is, what target we want to build. In our case, we want **make** to build the program **chap2**. The following command will build this program:

```
$ make chap2
        cc -c chap2.c
        cc -o chap2 chap2.o
```

We should now have the **chap2** program ready to run. If we try **make** again, it—being very lazy—tells us there's no new work to do:

```
$ make chap2
chap2 is up to date.
```

Why? Because the **chap2** program was built and nothing has changed. Now, edit the **chap2.c** file again, or use the **touch** command to bump up the date/time associated with the file:

```
$ touch chap2.c
```

When you call **make** again, it knows it needs to rebuild the **chap2** program, because presumably the **chap2.c** file has changed since the last time **chap2.c** was compiled with **cc**. Because **touch** only updates the date/time associated with the file and not the internals of the file in any way, we've fooled **make**. **Make** doesn't bother checking if a file is different; it merely checks the time the file was last written to, blindly assuming that no one would ever write to a file without modifying its contents. Normally, though, you don't want fool **make**, but use its simple rules to make your life easier.

Make supports a number of useful command-line parameters, as shown in Table 2.6.

Table 2.6 Make command-line parameters.

Parameter	Meaning
-f *makefile*	Uses the named file instead of **Makefile** for the rules.
-n	Runs in no-execute mode—only prints the commands, doesn't execute them.
-s	Runs in silent mode; doesn't print any commands **make** executes.

As you compile Linux freeware, you'll notice that there are a lot of conventions with **make** and **Makefile**s. For example, most **Makefile**s contain a target called **all**, which rebuilds the entire program when you execute:

```
$ make all
```

For this command to work, the **Makefile** must have a target named *all* that tells **make** what to do to rebuild everything. In addition, most **Makefile**s contain a clean target that removes all **.o** files and other files created by the compiler and an install target that copies the built executable file to an installation directory, such as **/usr/local/bin**.

> **N O T E** In addition to **make**, there's a tool called **imake**. **Imake** is used to generate **Makefile**s on a variety of systems. **imake** uses an **Imakefile** for its rules. These rules then help generate a **Makefile**. This **Makefile** is then used by **make** to build the program. Sound convoluted? You bet it is. That's why we'll spend a lot of time on it in Chapter 3.

There are a host of options to the **make** command, which you can look through by either using the following command line:

```
$ make -h
```

or viewing the help files under **info**.

Debuggers

Because Linux remains firmly in the GNU program-development world, it provides the **gdb** debugger and the X Window front end, **xxgdb**.

Basically, a debugger is a simple beast: it allows you to find errors in applications. Before it can do so, you need to tell **gcc** to generate information within the program that the debugger can use. This is a matter of using the *-g* option to **gcc**, which can be done within a **Makefile** with the following line:

```
CFLAGS= -g
```

It can also be done at the command line by using the *-g* option to **gcc**.

The GNU **gdb** debugger is also quite flexible. You can use it to launch an application to be debugged when running or you can launch the program and then turn **gdb** loose on it.

For more information about **gdb**, see Chapter 9.

Parsers and Lexers

If you're used to building your own parsers, you'll find the GNU **bison** (a port of UNIX **yacc**—Yet Another Compiler Compiler) and **flex** (a fast **lex**). Linux even includes **flex++** for developing C++ scanners.

Other Tools

We list some more useful tools for programmers in Table 2.7.

Table 2.7 More useful programming tools.

Tool	Usage
ar	Collects object files into libraries.
diff	Compares differences between files.
gprof	Gathers timing statistics about your programs for performance tuning.
hexdump	Displays ASCII, decimal, hexadecimal, or octal dump of a file.
objdump	Displays information on object files.
ranlib	Generates an index in an **ar**-created archive (library).
rcs	Source-code Revision Control System.
strace	Displays system calls from your program.

There's even a tool called **ansi2knr** that converts ANSI C to old-style Kernighan and Ritchie-style C (without function prototypes). With Linux, you don't really need this, as **gcc** fully supports ANSI C.

Other Programming Languages

C is by and large the programming *lingua franca* on UNIX and Linux, with C++ (an object-oriented extension to C) fast gaining in popularity. In addition to these languages, Linux provides a host of other opportunities to program.

First, the GNU C compiler also supports the Objective-C extension to the C programming language. Objective-C is very popular under the Nextstep environment. The GNU C compiler also supports a Fortran 77 front end called **g77**.

Summary

C programming is the basis of programming in Linux. In this chapter, we introduced the tools you'll need to program your C applications. However, we don't spend much time on actual C programming. C programming is a very involved subject, and many long books have been devoted to the subject.

In this chapter, you were introduced to the five types of tools needed to create C applications:

- An *editor* for creating source-code files. Linux includes a set of text editors, including **elvis** (the Linux version of **vi**), **emacs**, and others. Because you'll need to use a text editor to create applications (most of the time), we'll cover how to use these text editors in Appendix C.

- A *compiler* for compiling and linking source-code files. In Linux, this is GNU **gcc**.

- A *utility* for building the software—essentially, a program that combines all the disparate parts of the software-development process. Slackware Linux includes both **make** and **imake**. This chapter covered **make**; Chapter 3 will delve into **imake**.

- A *debugger* for debugging applications. There are two debuggers with Slackware Linux: the text-based **gdb** and the X Window–based **xxgdb**.

- A *version-control system* to monitor changes of source code and how they apply to a current application. Slackware Linux includes RCS.

X Window Programming

This chapter covers:

- X and window managers
- XFree86
- **Imake**
- Xt Intrinsics
- LessTif
- Motif
- Athena
- Xaw
- XForms
- Fresco

What is X?

The X Window System provides graphics on Linux. From that simple statement, you can delve into incredibly complex subjects. That's because like in all things, Linux provides many choices but makes you pay a corresponding price in flexibility.

This chapter covers X Window APIs—and there are many—for creating graphical programs on Linux. You'll find out how to compile and link, as well as what APIs are available. You'll also learn some background on what X is and why it's so popular.

Why X?

A long time ago, in an operating system many revisions away, UNIX never had any standardized graphics system. Sun workstations ran SunView, Hewlett-Packard workstations ran HPWindows; everything was a mess.

Then, along came X, originally developed at the Massachusetts Institute of Technology. X started life as a project supported by multiple UNIX vendors, most notably Digital Equipment and IBM, which aimed at providing a common windowing system on all platforms. Strangely enough, the folks who developed X wanted to give the source code away for free, leading to many implementations on every conceivable system.

They certainly succeeded on UNIX, where X dominates.

While X runs on Windows and Macintosh systems, the original goal has only partially succeeded, because X is not the native system on most non-UNIX platforms.

X on the Network

True to its UNIX roots, the X Window System runs graphics with multiple processes. The main process, simply called **X**, is the X server itself. The server deals with local requests (thus its usage on a single-user Linux workstation) and TCP/IP-based network requests. Because of this networking capability, it's possible to run an X application on one workstation and display the results of the application on another workstation. You could, for example, save your local computing resources for something important while running Doom on your boss's workstation and displaying the game on yours. You get to play the game; your boss's system provides the CPU horsepower.

The X server controls the monitor, keyboard, and mouse, and it allows graphics applications—called *X clients*—to create windows and draw into them. On the face of it, this seems so basic that it shouldn't require any explanation. But, as is true of most of UNIX, X takes a simple concept and makes it difficult. You benefit a lot from the complexity of X, but it can make things tough getting going.

The X server process is the only process allowed to draw dots on the screen or track the mouse. X application programs then connect to the X server via an interprocess communication link, usually some form of TCP/IP network sockets. Because it uses a network link, programs running on other machines connected by a network can display on your workstation.

Many programs can connect to the same X server at the same time, allowing you to run multiple applications on the same screen—again, a basic fact you've probably taken for granted. One thing you cannot take for granted is that one of these X applications you run must be a window manager. (Technically, you don't have to run a window manager, but it makes things a lot more difficult if you don't.)

The Window Manager

Unlike the Macintosh and Windows environments, X makes the window manager a separate process. In fact, a window manager is merely a special X application program. By separating the windowing system from the window manager, you are free to run whichever window manager suits your needs best. The main purpose of a window manager is to control how you move and resize windows on your Linux display. The window manager also creates the title bar at the top of your application windows.

The key concept if you're new to X is that the window manager—not the application—owns the window's title bar. This is odd if you come from the Windows or Macintosh worlds. One of the most frustrating programming tasks is trying to get the window manager to do what you want. Your programs can ask the window manager for things, but you'll likely get frustrated if you want to do anything fancy, like display graphics in a title bar. The window manager simply won't cooperate.

Fvwm, the de facto window manager on Linux, provides good emulation of the main features of the Open Look and Motif window managers, at least from a programmer's point of view. Because of this, any code you've developed to interact with the window manager should port well to Linux.

X on Linux

X is very hardware-dependent. In the UNIX workstation world, you don't see many problems with this, because the UNIX vendors maintain tight control over the hardware and do the hard work of supporting X for that hardware.

The PC realm, though, is different. You have zillions of vendors and a huge number of combinations of various graphics cards, monitors, buses, and even lowly mice. So, as we'll repeat again and again, you need to know the intimate details of your hardware to get the X Window System up and running. If you're used to the UNIX workstation world, this will come as a rude surprise.

X on Linux is actually in the form of XFree86, a public project devoted to bringing X Window to PC-based Unices. While there are some changes between the straight X Window System on a workstation and XFree86, you probably won't notice these differences.

In fact, on Linux you get the advantage of all sorts of X Window extras that have been added to Slackware Linux.

X Resource Files

Another topic under X that is different from the Windows and Macintosh environments is resource files. You'll find that X resource files are either the savior or bane of your existence. Like the Windows and Macintosh systems, resource files on X allow you to customize fonts, colors, and even text messages, all without access to the application's source code. From within your applications, you can use resource files if you program with the toolkits that support them to allow a great degree of user customization or even to translate your program's interface into another language.

This concept is just great. You can tell an application to use a more readable font, you can get rid of garish colors, you can even write Finnish messages in place of English ones, or you can fix the English messages to something more to your liking.

X resource files provide a powerful mechanism to customize just about every X application. There are a lot of options within a resource file and on disk in which you can place these resources files. Because many options conflict, it's easy to get lost in the details.

Stripped to its basics, an X resource file is an ASCII text file that specifies some option for a program or programs. Each line of the resource file specifies a resource to set and its value. For example, you can specify in an X resource file that all **xterm** programs should start up with the scrollbar turned on, which we'll show you how to do soon. You can also control fonts, colors, and a lot of the text displayed by most X programs.

For example, to set up the scrollbar commands for **xterm** in a resource file, create a file named **XTerm** (note the capitalization) in your home directory. Both the filename, **XTerm**, and the location (your home directory) are essential. Put in the following lines:

```
XTerm*scrollBar: True
XTerm*saveLines: 1000
```

These X resource commands tell **xterm** to use a scrollbar and to save 1000 lines in its scroll buffer. Save this file and start another **xterm** program. You should see a scrollbar.

For more on X resource files, see the book list in Appendix B.

Imake

In the last chapter, we mentioned that there was an X Window tool named **imake**, which is used to generate Makefiles on a variety of systems. This probably doesn't seem very useful on Linux, unless you're trying to do one of two things:

- Create an X Window program that runs on a variety of UNIX platforms, including LessTif.
- Compile and link a freeware application that just happens to come with an **Imakefile** and not a **Makefile**.

The **imake** command uses an **Imakefile** for its rules. These rules then help generate a **Makefile**. This **Makefile** is used by **make** to build the program. Sound convoluted? You bet it is. The main reason **imake** exists is because of radically different system configurations, especially where the X Window System is concerned.

You'll find **imake** especially popular with programs for X Window. The problem with X is that there are so many options that every UNIX platform is configured slightly differently. There's simply no way you could write a portable **Makefile** that could work on all platforms. The **imake** command uses an **Imakefile** and configuration files that are local to your system. Together, the **Imakefile** and the local configuration files generate a **Makefile** that should work on your system. (In addition to **imake**, there's an even handier package called GNU **Configure**. Unfortunately, **imake** is very common among X Window programs and **Configure** is not. Ironically, the Motif clone called LessTif, which we'll cover later, uses **Configure** and not **imake** to set things up for compiling on different platforms.)

If you need to compile programs for the X Window System and you see an **Imakefile**, here's what you should do. First, run the **xmkmf** shell script. This script is merely a simple front end to **imake**:

```
$ xmkmf
mv Makefile Makefile.bak
imake -DUseInstalled -I/usr/lib/X11/config
```

These commands should make a backup of any **Makefile** you have (to **Makefile.bak**) and then create a new **Makefile** based on the commands in an **Imakefile**.

imake then builds a **Makefile**, which should be customized for your system by looking at rules in the following places:

- **Imake.tmpl**, which includes information on what kind of operating system you have.
- **Linux.cf**, which contains information specific to Linux as opposed to Solaris, HP-UX, and other versions of UNIX.
- **Site.def**, a place for you to edit your own site-specific configurations.
- **Project.tmpl**, a file used mostly by the XFree86 team for building the X Window System in the first place.
- **Imake.rules**, which contains a set of generic rules for building X programs.
- **Imakefile**, in your current directory, which should contain rules, like a **Makefile**, for what source-code files need to be recompiled.

All but the **Imakefile** are located in **/usr/X11R65/lib/X11/config**. The files in **/usr/X11R65/lib/X11/config** should be set up properly for XFree86 and Linux. You may want to make a few changes, though.

In the **linux.cf** file, you'll see a number of Linux-specific flags that you can control. The most important are the flags that indicate whether your system uses extended linking format (ELF) libraries. (See Chapter 2 for more on ELF.) Among these flags are the ones shown here:

```
#ifndef LinuxElfDefault
#define LinuxElfDefault        YES
#endif

#ifndef UseElfFormat
#define UseElfFormat           YES
#endif
```

The **linux.cf** file also includes the files **lnxLib.rules** and **xfree86.cf**. **LnxLib.rules** then includes **lnxLib.tmpl**, while **xfree86.cf** includes **xf86.rules**. You may want to look in all these files.

The **site.def** file includes **xf86site.def**. The **xf86site.def** file is mostly used when rebuilding your X server. It defines, for example, which X server to build. This choice depends on your type of graphics card, such as S3.

Normally, you don't want to edit any of the other Linux-specific **imake** configuration files. You can place special configuration options, though, in the **site.def** file, which you can customize for your site.

Debuggers

Because Linux remains firmly in the GNU program-development world, it provides the **gdb** debugger and the X Window front end, **xxgdb**.

X Window Tools

If you're developing X Window applications, a few extra utilities may help. The **xman** program provides a graphical front end and nice formatting for UNIX online-manual pages.

For critical X programs, you'll find **xcmap** very useful. This simple X application displays the current color map. For color-intensive X applications, this can help you track down obscure X problems.

Similarly, the **xev** application helps you see what events the keyboard keys are really sending to the X server.

For selecting fonts, **xfd** and **xfontsel** both help you choose a good-looking font for your applications.

Enough about tools to help you program; it's time to delve into some X programming APIs.

Programming for X on Linux

Unlike the Win32 API on Windows or QuickDraw on the Macintosh, X gives you a plethora of API choices when creating graphical applications. Most of these choices are called *toolkits*, such as Motif,

Fresco, or XView. Each toolkit provides its own API, its own look and feel, and its own programming conventions, which differ radically.

In true UNIX fashion, X layers APIs on top of other APIs. For example, just about every X API depends on the lowest layer in the X API hierarchy: the X library. The X library, or Xlib, provides low-level routines to create windows and draw in them. Virtually no one programs to Xlib directly unless you're creating a new X toolkit. Instead, most programmers avail themselves of the higher layers of X APIs.

For example, the X Toolkit Intrinsics, or Xt, layer, provides the concepts of widgets and a pseudo–object-oriented programming model. Xt is an official API in the same light as Xlib, as this API is endorsed by the X Consortium and should be available on all X platforms.

Xt introduces the concept of a widget, encapsulating user interface elements such as menus, push buttons, and scrollbars. Even so, Xt provides no look and feel. This is left for even higher-level libraries. Motif, LessTif, and the Athena widgets use Xt.

Other APIs avoid Xt with all its idiosyncrasies. The XView API, for example, provides an Open Look style of interface with a programmer's API based on the old SunView API. Originally designed to help SunView applications migrate to X, this library has now been abandoned by Sun, with its mission accomplished. Even though it has been officially abandoned, XView has become increasingly popular on Linux, because it is one of the few free APIs that provide a good look and feel.

Two other toolkits stand out, for different reasons. Fresco is a long-awaited C++ toolkit built as a follow-on to an earlier toolkit called InterViews. Fresco follows an object-oriented programming model with the ability to distribute objects over the network, using a CORBA object broker. Regrettably, this technology is still incomplete. The CD-ROM contains the latest snapshot as of this writing.

An easy-to-use simple library for creating user interface applications, XForms sacrifices some flexibility for simplicity but makes X applications very easy to create. XForms is free for noncommercial, nonprofit use. (We'll cover it later in this chapter.)

Programming with Toolkits

In the next few sections, we'll delve a little deeper into these toolkits and provide some simple programming examples. Be warned though: there's a lot you need to know to create full-fledged X Window applications. See Appendix B for a list of X Window programming books that can help you along the way.

The most commonly available toolkits are based on the X Toolkit Intrinsics, an official toolkit layer provided by the X Consortium.

Xt-Based Toolkits

The two most popular Xt-based toolkits are Motif, because it provides a Windows look and feel, and the Athena widgets, notable for a wretched look and feel but free availability. Another toolkit, the Open Look Intrinsics Toolkit, or OLIT, was popular for a while on Sun and UnixWare systems. As the commercial UNIX community has adopted Motif, OLIT has been fading away.

LessTif and Motif

By far the most popular X toolkit, Motif is a lot of things, which tends to confuse people. Motif is a window manager, a user interface style, and a programmer's library that sits on top of the X Window System.

If you program using the Motif programmer's libraries, your applications will follow the Motif style guide (unless you do something truly bizarre).

One common point of confusion lies with the use of window managers. Yes, you can easily run a Motif application under an Open Look window manager, like **olwm** or **olvwm**. You can consider the resulting combination a Motif or an Open Look style—it doesn't really matter. You can also run Motif applications under the Motif window manager, **mwm**, although this window manager is rare on Linux. Far more popular is the **fvwm** window manager, which provides a Motif look with a highly configurable feel.

Motif is a commercial product. That means you won't find it on Linux unless you purchase a separate Motif package. But, there's also a freeware set of Motif-like APIs called *LessTif*. The LessTif team is trying to create a set of office applications using LessTif, including XWord, a word processor.

We provide LessTif on the CD-ROM that comes with this book. You can do a lot of Motif programming with LessTif, but beware, LessTif is not yet ready for serious applications. Even so, you can still do a lot with LessTif.

The LessTif team aims at creating a set of Motif API libraries that are 100 percent compatible with Motif 1.2. This means that everything you can do with Motif 1.2 should carry over to LessTif. This is great because there is a lot of programming information available on Motif (see Appendix B), and that information carries over to LessTif.

The next sections cover installing LessTif, dealing with incompatibilities, compiling a sample Motif program, and delving into some Motif background for those unfamiliar with this toolkit.

Installing LessTif

The first step is to copy LessTif from the Slackware CD-ROM. You'll see a GNU zip file, **lesstif-current.tar.gz**, in the **LessTif** directory on the CD-ROM. This represents the latest version of LessTif as of this writing.

Copy the **lesstif-current.tar.gz** file into the directory where you want to build LessTif, such as **/usr/local/src**.

Uncompress the zip file with **gunzip**:

```
$ gunzip lesstif-current.tar.gz
```

Then expand the tar file with **tar**:

```
$ tar xvof lesstif-current.tar
```

This command creates a subdirectory called **lesstif-current** and places all the LessTif source code underneath the **lesstif-current** directory.

Change to this **lesstif-current** directory and run the **configure** script, which automatically detects where Linux places the X Window include files (**/usr/X11R6/include**) and libraries (**/usr/X11R6/lib**). Use the following commands:

```
$ cd lesstif-current
$ ./configure
```

The **configure** script should detect everything it needs to know about your Linux system. If it does not, then you have not installed the Linux C development system and need to run the **setup** program to take care of this task first.

Once **configure** finishes, build LessTif with the **make** command:

```
$ make
```

This will take quite a while even on a fast modern system, as **make** travels to each subdirectory and builds the large LessTif libraries. Each file compiled will generate the following warning, which you can safely ignore:

```
warning: 'rcsid' defined but not used
```

If you get an error that the **clients/uil/uil** does not exist, this is because the LessTif **Makefile** isn't set up properly. You can stop compiling at this point and start the installation. The **uil** program won't build until you have installed the shared libraries for LessTif.

After **make** completes, you can install LessTif with the following command:

```
$ make install
```

You need to be superuser to install LessTif.

The *install* **make** target will copy the LessTif library files to **/usr/local/lib**. You then need to use the **su** command to become super user and run the **/sbin/ldconfig** program to reset the system's ideas of shared libraries. However, you can set the **LD_LIBRARY_PATH** environment variable to include **/usr/local/lib** instead of executing **ldconfig**.

The next step is to copy the include files, in the **include/Xm** and **include/Mrm** to **/usr/X11R6/include**, the standard location for Linux include files. Copy the whole directories, for example:

```
$ cp -r include/Xm /usr/X11R6/include
$ cp -r include/Mrm /usr/X11R6/include
```

This should be enough to create Motif programs. If you want to run some of the Motif clients, such as **mwm**, that come with this version of LessTif, you're in for a bit more work.

We don't recommend you run this version of **mwm**; it isn't ready yet, nor does it compile without source modifications.

NOTE

Once you've built, installed, and run **ldconfig** for the shared libraries, you're ready to start creating Motif programs. There are a few problems, though.

Differences from Motif

LessTif aims to create a freeware version of Motif, but LessTif still has some problems.

Here are some problems we found (in other words, consider yourself warned):

- Do not try to compile any code that sets up a tear-off menu.

- Code to create simple menus, created by routines such as *XmVaCreateSimplePulldownMenu*, will not work. You need to use the older, more tedious routines to create your menus.

- The *XmText* widget will not allow you to select text, but the single-line *XmTextField* will.

- Many widgets size themselves incorrectly.

- Option menus display incorrectly and may dump core.

- The clipboard functions don't seem to work.

- If the first radio button isn't the one that starts on, you'll see an extra rectangle surrounding the first radio button that turns on. You can get rid of this by clicking that radio button again.

- Label and push-button widgets do not seem to be able to display pixmaps.

As you can see, there are many problems to solve before LessTif becomes a true Motif clone. But LessTif is free, and you have the source on the accompanying CD-ROM. With it, you can build and run some Motif programs.

Compiling and Linking with LessTif

To build a Motif program, you need the Xm, Xt, and Xll libraries. You'll also need to tell the compiler where to find the library and include files, normally with the **-L/usr/X11R6/lib** and **-I/usr/X11R6/include** options, respectively. For example:

```
$ cc exmotif.c -o exmotif \
   -I/usr/X11R6/include \
   -L/usr/X11R6/lib -lXm -lXt -lX11
```

If you're unfamiliar with Motif, the next section provides a brief overview of this very large X programming API. If you're an old hand with Motif, you can skip ahead to the section on Athena widgets.

The Xt Intrinsics and Motif

The Motif toolkit sits on top of the Xt Intrinsics library. That means Motif uses many of the Xt features and functions. Motif does have a set of functions of its own, and Motif has its own widget set with its own look and feel. The Xt Intrinsics provide some basic mechanism for many widget sets (you'll find a lot of this mechanism stuff as you read about X).

By layering on top of the Intrinsics, the Motif code has less work to do. This also means that all Motif applications pay for the added complexity and difficulty (and massive program size) of all Xt-based applications. If you've worked with other Xt-based APIs, like the Athena widgets or the OLIT toolkit, your Xt knowledge will be a great help as you learn Motif. And, because LessTif aims at Motif compatibility, learning Motif will also teach you LessTif.

What Is a Widget?

A *widget* is a generic abstraction for user-interface components. Widgets are used for scrollbars, push buttons, dialog boxes, and just about everything else in the Motif or other toolkits. Most widgets have an associated window on the X display that holds the user-interface elements of the widget. This makes Motif programs create a great many windows on your X server.

Each widget has a C data structure that is dynamically allocated via *malloc* at creation time. This structure, which is supposed to be treated as an opaque data type, contains the widget's data attributes, called *resources*, and pointers to the functions, such as callbacks, that widgets may have. Each widget is of a certain class, such as *XmText* for scrolled text widgets, and the class defines a set of functions and resources that apply to every widget of that class.

If this looks suspiciously like object-oriented programming done in C, you're catching on.

Some widgets display graphics on the screen. Others serve as container widgets grouping other widgets.

Widget Hierarchies

When you create widgets, you create them in a hierarchy. At the top sits a form of shell widget (which has no relation to the concept of a Linux shell like **bash**). Inside this shell sits the main widget of your main window, usually of type *XmMainWindow*.

The main window then holds the menu bar, any toolbar, status area, and other parts of your main application window.

You then nest widgets going deeper and deeper. Inside the menu bar, for example, you place menus. Inside menus come menu choices. At each level in the hierarchy, the parent widget, such as the menu or menu bar, controls the layout of its child widgets. Such container widgets are often called *parent widgets*.

Each widget has a parent widget, except for the very top-level shell widget returned by *XtAppInitialize*. (You must start somewhere.)

This parent widget controls the layout (called the *geometry* in widget terminology) of its child widgets. Following this simple rule, there are a number of geometry-managing widgets that exist for the sole purpose of laying out child widgets. The *XmPanedWindow* widget, for example, lays out child widgets vertically, in panes. The *XmForm* widget, on the other hand, allows precise control over the placement of child widgets.

Part of the key to Motif application development is understanding the top-down approach to creating interface elements. Not only are widgets arranged in a hierarchy, they must also be created in the hierarchical order. When you're planning your applications, you'll need to choose how many and what kind of widgets you want to use. We've found it's best to start at the top and plan the widget hierarchy, working from the top down. That makes it easier to test and debug Motif applications.

The Basic Format of Motif Programs

Diving right in, we'll create a simple Motif program to give you more of a flavor of the API. Motif programs usually follow six basic steps:

- Initialize the Xt Intrinsics (which also sets up connection to the X server).
- Create widgets.
- Set up any needed callback functions.
- Realize the widget hierarchy with *XtRealizeWidget*.
- Enter the event-handling loop.
- Loop forever—yes, forever.

The *loop-forever* part is serious. Because of this, you'll need to set up at least one callback function to exit your program.

Motif Header Files

All Motif programs require the header file **<Xm/Xm.h>**. In addition, every Motif widget has its own header file, such as **<Xm/PushB.h>**.

XtAppInitialize

The first step in any Motif program is to initialize the Xt Intrinsics. The function *XtAppInitialize* does this:

```
Widget XtAppInitialize(
    XtAppContext* appcontext,  /* RETURN */
    String app_class_name,
    XrmOptionDescList xrm_options,
    int number_xrm_options,
    int* argc,       /* input/output */
    String* argv,    /* input/output */
    String* fallback_resources,
    ArgList args,    /* hard-coded resources */
    int number_args)
```

The application context is set up by *XtAppInitialize*. You use the application context, *appcontext*, in the call to *XtAppMainLoop*. The application-class name specifies a name used for looking up X resource values (see the earlier section on "X Resource Files" for more on this).

For most of the parameters, you can safely pass *NULL* or zero because *XtAppInitialize* offers many more options than most Motif programs need.

Creating Widgets

There are two main ways to create Motif widgets. First, you can use the Xt-provided functions *XtCreateWidget* (and a host of variants, including *XtCreateManagedWidget* and *XtVaCreateManagedWidget*). Second, you can use the Motif-provided functions, one for each widget type, to create widgets. In most cases, this is a matter of your preferred coding style; LessTif supports both methods.

There are a few exceptions, though, where it pays to use the Motif-specific functions. Menus, dialog boxes, scrolled text widgets, and other combinations have Motif front ends to a complex set of code hidden under the hood. If you use the Xt functions, you must mimic this code on your own. In those cases, we strongly urge you to use the Motif *Xm* convenience functions.

Among the built-in Motif functions is *XmCreatePushButton*.

XmCreatePushButton

XmCreatePushButton creates a push-button widget. You'll find all Motif *XmCreateType* functions take the same parameters:

```
#include <Xm/PushB.h>

Widget XmCreatePushButton(Widget parent,
    char* widget_name,
    ArgList args
    Cardinal number_args)
```

When creating a push-button widget, you must pass the parent widget (remember that every widget—except for top-level widgets—must have a parent). The parent controls the size and location of the child widget, created by *XmCreatePushButton*. You also must pass the widget's name; every widget can be identified by its name. This name is important for resource-setting commands. The *args* and *number_args* parameters are the list of hard-coded resource values you want to set for the widget.

 The *XmCreate* functions create, but do not manage, widgets. Therefore, you must later call *XtManageChild*. An unmanaged widget does not appear in a window on the screen. When you manage a widget, the widget is placed under control of its parent. Usually, managed widgets are visible, but sometimes the parent sets the size and location of a managed child widget to something that you cannot see. In addition, if the parent widget isn't managed, the child widget also won't be visible, even if the child widget is managed. While this may seem odd, it's very useful for working with dialog windows.

The main purpose of a push-button widget is to call a function (a callback) when activated. A push-button is activated when the user presses and releases the leftmost mouse button (*Button1* in X terminology) over the widget.

Xt Event Handling

Xt and Motif intercept and handle most X events, freeing your code from this responsibility. If you wish to be notified of an event, though, you can set up an event-handling *callback function* to handle an event. Motif makes heavy use of these callback functions to notify your application code when a high-level event occurs. For example, a push-button widget generates an *activate callback* when the user presses and releases the leftmost mouse button over it. When this happens, your function is called back (executed).

Setting Up Callback Functions

The Xt function *XtAddCallback* registers a function as a callback for a widget:

```
void XtAddCallback(Widget widget,
      String which_callback,
      XtCallbackProc callback_function,
      XtPointer client_data)
```

The *client_data* is a pointer to any extra data you want to pass to the callback function.

XtAddCallback adds your function to the list of callbacks for a particular widget. Every widget supports a number of callbacks, and each callback type is named. For the push-button widget, we use *activateCallback*.

XmNactivateCallback is defined as the text string *"activateCallback"*. Each of the callbacks supported by a widget has a text name and a defined symbol that begins with *XmN*. These symbols are defined in the Motif include file **<Xm/Xm.h>**.

Callback-Function Parameters

All basic callback functions set up with *XtAddCallback* take the same parameters:

- The widget ID of the widget the callback was set up on.
- A pointer (normally *XtPointer* is an alias for *caddr_t* or *void**) to your data, which is termed the *client data*. Xt keeps a copy of this pointer, so it's up to you to maintain the data that is pointed at. This data was originally passed to *XtAddCallback*. Passing data to a callback can be tricky.
- A pointer to a Motif structure that includes specific information about the callback.

Here's an example callback function:

```
void CallbackFunction(Widget widget,
    XtPointer client_data,
    XtPointer call_data)
```

```
{     /* CallbackFunction */

      /* Your code goes here... */

}     /* CallbackFunction */
```

Container Widgets and Complex Programs

Most Motif applications have a menu bar covering the top of the application's window, with pull-down menus on the menu bar. The main part of the application goes underneath the menu bar. The widget that controls the placement of the menu bar and your main data area is considered a *container widget*. Container widgets hold other (child) widgets and control the layout of these child widgets. Container widgets are used extensively in just about every Motif program.

Parent and Child Relationships

Every widget has a parent widget (except for the top-level shells, such as the one returned by *XtAppInitialize*). This parent widget is passed to *XtCreateManagedWidget* or *XmCreate* functions.

Only certain widgets, container widgets, and shell widgets can be parent widgets. This parent widget controls the geometry (size and location) of child widgets. Examples of container widgets include *XmMainWindow*, *XmPanedWindow*, and *XmRowColumn*.

The paned-window widget places its child widgets from top to bottom in vertical *panes*—hence the name *XmPanedWindow*. Between each child, there is an optional *sash*—a line with a control box. The user can use the mouse pointer to move the sash up and down, controlling the size of each pane. You can also specify minimum and maximum sizes for panes, which the paned-window widget will enforce.

The include file for the paned-window class is **<Xm/PanedW.h>**. You can create one with *XmCreatePanedWindow*:

```
#include <Xm/PanedW.h>

Widget XmCreatePanedWindow(Widget parent,
            char* name,
            ArgList args,
            Cardinal number_args)
```

We'll use the paned-window widget returned by *XmCreatePanedWindow* as the parent widget for primitive widgets like *XmPushButton* and *XmLabel*.

Label Widgets

The label widget provides a static text message in a window. (LessTif does not support pixmaps in label widgets yet.) This doesn't sound very interesting, but most programs need to display some sort of text information to the user. Create a label widget with *XmCreateLabel*:

```
#include <Xm/Label.h>

Widget XmCreateLabel(Widget parent,
            char* name,
            ArgList args,
            Cardinal number_args)
```

Managing Widgets

Managing a widget makes that widget visible. Technically, managing a widget places that widget under control of its parent's geometry management. If a widget is unmanaged, it will not be visible at all. If you manage a widget, that widget will be made visible if the parent allows it. If you manage a child widget but the child's parent is still unmanaged, both widgets will remain invisible until you manage the parent.

Dialog widgets, for example, are usually left unmanaged. You do manage all the children of the dialog widgets, though. To show a dialog box, you simply manage the dialog-shell widget. To hide a dialog box, unmanage the dialog-shell widget. (See *Power Programming Motif*, as described in Appendix B, for more on dialog widgets.)

XtManageChild manages a widget. By default, all Motif-created widgets are created unmanaged, unless you use the *XtCreateManagedWidget* function. An unmanaged widget will not be made visible when your application calls *XtRealizeWidget*, so you must manage most widgets after you create them—that is, if you want those widgets to become visible in your application's interface, which you normally do.

XtManageChild takes one parameter, the widget to manage:

```
void XtManageChild(Widget widget)
```

For most widgets, call the *XmCreateType* function to create the widget, set up any callbacks or customizations to the widget, and then call *XtManageChild* to manage the widget.

XtRealizeWidget

XtRealizeWidget realizes a widget and all its child widgets. Normally you must realize all top-level shell widgets, except for pop-up windows like dialog boxes and menus. For simple programs, you call *XtRealizeWidget* on the top-level shell widget returned by *XtAppInitialize*. *XtRealizeWidget* creates the actual window IDs used under the hood by Motif widgets. If you ever want to do advanced operations on the windows associated with Motif widgets, you must realize the widgets first. This forms a common stumbling block when programming Motif applications.

After you've set up all your widgets, and managed them, it is time to make them real. *XtRealizeWidget* takes care of all the initializations necessary for a widget and all its managed children. *XtRealizeWidget* takes one parameter, a high-level widget to be realized. Normally this is the widget returned from *XtAppInitialize*:

```
void XtRealizeWidget(Widget parent)
```

Sometimes *XtRealizeWidget* takes a long time to execute, because it must create a great many windows on the X display. Expect this.

After calling *XtRealizeWidget*, most applications let the Xt Intrinsics take over and loop awaiting events.

XtAppMainLoop

XtAppMainLoop executes the main event-handling loop of a Motif application. This function executes forever, so you must set up at least one callback function that will exit your program.

Looping forever doesn't seem very much fun, but it lets the Xt Intrinsics handle most of the work of an X application for you. With *XtAppMainLoop*, the Xt Intrinsics essentially take over your application. That's one of the prices you pay for using an Xt-based toolkit: the toolkit takes over. *XtAppMainLoop* loops checking for things the toolkit needs to do, including handling timeouts, work procedures, and handling input from the X server (including user input).

When an event arrives, *XtAppMainLoop* determines which widget in your application should get the event and passes the event on to the widget. The widget then determines whether to execute a callback function or handle the event on its own. Usually, the more events a widget can handle means less work your application code has to do.

We won't regain control until the user does something to execute a callback function, such as clicking a mouse button (usually Button 1, or the leftmost button) in a push-button widget. When this happens, the widget executes its *activateCallback* function. At this point, your code regains control from Motif.

In your callback function, you can do what you want. Sometimes your callbacks will need to execute completely in a very short amount of time (in the millisecond range). For now, we can do what we want.

One of the things we want to do is create a callback function that will exit our program. To do so, we can call the C function *exit*, as we do in the *exitCB* callback function, in "A First Motif Program," later in this chapter. Before any callbacks are called, though, your program must cede control to the Xt Intrinsics main event-handling loop by calling *XtAppMainLoop*:

```
void XtAppMainLoop(XtAppContext appcontext)
```

You pass *XtAppMainLoop* one parameter: the application context originally passed to *XtAppInitialize*.

To pull all this together and get a flavor of Motif, look at the following example program:

```
/*
 *   exmotif.c
 *   A first Motif program.
 */

#include <Xm/Xm.h>
#include <Xm/Label.h>    /* XmLabel */
#include <Xm/PushB.h>    /* XmPushButton */
#include <Xm/PanedW.h>   /* XmPanedWindow */

/*
 * exitCB() is a callback for the
 * push-button widget we create below.
 */

void exitCB(Widget widget,
    XtPointer client_data,
    XtPointer call_data)

{   /* exitCB */

    exit(0);

}   /* exitCB */

int main(int argc, char** argv)
```

```
{   /* main */
    Widget          parent;
    XtAppContext    app_context;
    Widget          pane, push, label;
    Arg             args[20];
    int             n;

    /*
     * Initialize the X Toolkit
     * Intrinsics.
     */
    n = 0;
    parent = XtAppInitialize(&app_context,
            "LinuxProgramming",          /* app class */
            (XrmOptionDescList) NULL,     /* options */
            0,                            /* num options */
            &argc,                        /* num cmd-line */
            argv,                         /* cmd-line opts */
            (String*) NULL,               /* fallback rsc */
            args, 0);

    /*
     * Create a paned window
     * widget to contain all
     * the child widgets. Note that
     * the paned window is a child
     * of the top-level parent.
     */
    n = 0;
    pane = XmCreatePanedWindow(parent,
        "pane", args, n);

    /* We manage the pane below. */

    /*
     * Create a push-button widget,
     * as a child of the paned window.
     */
    n = 0;
    push = XmCreatePushButton(pane,
            "quit", args, n);

    /*
     * Set up a callback for the
```

```
 * push-button widget.
 */
XtAddCallback(push,            /* widget */
    XmNactivateCallback,       /* which callback */
    (XtCallbackProc) exitCB,   /* callback function */
    (XtPointer) NULL);         /* extra data to pass */

/*
 * Manage the push-button widget.
 */
XtManageChild(push);

/*
 * Create a Label widget, as
 * a child of the paned window.
 */
n = 0;
label = XmCreateLabel(pane,
        "label", args, n);

XtManageChild(label);

/*
 * Note that we manage the paned window
 * container *after* we fill in the
 * child widgets of the pane.
 */
XtManageChild(pane);

/*
 * Realize widget hierarchy, which
 * brings the top-level widget
 * (and all its children) to
 * reality. That is, create windows
 * for the widgets and then map
 * the windows.
 */
XtRealizeWidget(parent);

/*
 * Process events forever.
 */
XtAppMainLoop(app_context);
```

```
    return 0;

}   /* main */

/* end of file exmotif.c */
```

This program should compile and link under both Motif and LessTif. You can use a command like the following to compile and link on your Linux system:

```
$ cc exmotif.c -o exmotif \
   -I/usr/X11R6/include \
   -L/usr/X11R6/lib -lXm -lXt -lX11
```

The **exmotif.c** program uses the following X resource file:

```
! Resource file
!
! Global Resources
!
! Set font.
*fontList:   lucidasans-12

! Set program background color.
*background:  lightgrey

! Set up window title.
*title: Motif

! Widget-Specific Resources
!
! Set up quit message.
*quit.labelString:    Push here to exit

*label.labelString:   Motif Example

! end of resource file
```

Name this file **LinuxProgramming** and place the file in your home directory. Then run the Motif program just listed.

Using Make with the Exmotif.c File

In Chapter 2 we briefly discussed **make** but didn't spend much time on examples. Here's your chance to see **make** in action, as applied to the **exmotif.c** file.

The target we want to build is the **exmotif** program. The **exmotif** program (the target) depends on the object module **exmotif.o**. Once we have the object module **exmotif.o**, the command line to create the **exmotif** program is:

```
exmotif:   exmotif.o
     cc -o exmotif exmotif.o -L/usr/X11R6/lib \
        -lXm -lXt -lX11
```

The preceding **make** rule states that if **exmotif.o** has a more recent date, then execute the **cc** command to build the **exmotif** program from the object module **exmotif.o**.

This is just part of the task; we still have to compile **exmotif.c** to create the object module **exmotif.o**. That is, the file **exmotif.o** is said to depend on the file **exmotif.c**. You build **exmotif.o** from **exmotif.c**. To do this, we use another **make** rule.

This time, the object module **exmotif.o** depends on the text file **exmotif.c**. The command to build the object module is:

```
exmotif.o:   exmotif.c
  cc -c exmotif.c
```

With this **make** rule, if you edit **exmotif.c**, you'll make the file **exmotif.c** have a more recent date/time than the object module **exmotif.o**. This causes **make** to trigger the **cc** command to compile **exmotif.c** into **exmotif.o**.

You've discovered the secret to **make**'s rules. Everything depends on the date/time of the files, a very simple—but clever—idea. The idea is that if the text of the program **.c** file is modified, you better rebuild the program with **cc**. Because most users are impatient, if the **.c** file hasn't been changed, there's no reason (at least in our example) to rebuild the program with **cc**.

A Make Example

To try **make**, enter the following text into a file named **Makefile**:

```
#
# Test Makefile
#
# The program exmotif depends on exmotif.o.
exmotif:    exmotif.o
   cc -o exmotif exmotif.o -L/usr/X11R6/lib \
              -lXm -lXt -lX11

# The object module exmotif.o depends on exmotif.c.
exmotif.o:    exmotif.c
   cc -c exmotif.c
```

This **Makefile** should be in the same directory as your sample C program file, **exmotif.c**. To use **make**, we need to tell it what to **make**, that is, what target we want to build. In our case, we want **make** to build the program **exmotif**. The following command will build this program:

```
$ make exmotif
        cc -c exmotif.c
        cc -o exmotif exmotif.o -L/usr/X11R6/lib \
              -lXm -lXt -lX11
```

We should now have the **exmotif** program ready to run. If we try **make** again, it—being very lazy—tells us there's no new work to do:

```
$ make exmotif
exmotif is up to date.
```

Why? Because the **exmotif** program was built and nothing has changed. Now edit the **exmotif.c** file again, or use the **touch** command to bump up the date/time associated with the file:

```
$ touch exmotif.c
```

When you call **make** again, it knows it needs to rebuild the **exmotif** program, because presumably the **exmotif.c** file has changed since the last time **exmotif.c** was compiled with **cc**. Because **touch** only updates the date/time associated with the file and doesn't change the internals of the file in any way, we've just fooled **make**. The **make** command doesn't bother checking if a file is different; it merely checks the time the file was last written to, blindly assuming that no one would ever write to a file without modifying its contents. Normally, though, you don't want fool **make**, but to use its simple rules to make your life easier.

Athena

The Athena widgets were the first API that came with the X Window System. Chances are you still use the Athena-based **xterm** application, the world's most popular X Window application.

The Athena widget set, or Xaw library as it is known, doesn't provide the best look and feel, but the toolkit is free. In addition, there have been two major enhancements to the Athena widget set, both of which add look and feel enhancements.

The Xaw3D library adds a 3D beveled look to the Athena widgets, making your applications look snazzier.

The Xaw95 library builds on Xaw3D but changes the look to that of the famous Windows 95. Developed by Eddie Hiu-Fung Lau, the Xaw95 library is generally compatible with the original Athena widget set, so you can recompile Athena applications and link with Xaw95 to get the new look. In addition, because Xaw95 comes as a shared library for Linux, once you install Xaw95 in place of Xaw, normal Athena applications like **xterm** get a new look, as shown in Figure 3.1.

To get a taste for the Athena widget set, you can try the following program, **exaw.c**:

```
/*
 * exaw.c
 * Athena widget example program.
 */
#include <X11/Intrinsic.h>
#include <X11/StringDefs.h>
#include <X11/Xaw3d/Box.h>
#include <X11/Xaw3d/Command.h>   /* Button */
#include <X11/Xaw3d/Label.h>
```

```
/*
 * exitCB() is a callback for the
 * push-button widget we create below.
 */

void exitCB(Widget widget,
    XtPointer client_data,
    XtPointer call_data)

{   /* exitCB */

    exit(0);

}   /* exitCB */

int main(int argc, char** argv)

{   /* main */
    Widget          parent, push, box, label;
    XtAppContext    app_context;
    Arg             args[20];
    int             n;

    parent = XtAppInitialize(&app_context,
            "LinuxProgramming",         /* app class */
            (XrmOptionDescList) NULL,   /* options */
            0,                          /* num options */
            &argc,                      /* num cmd-line */
            argv,                       /* cmd-line opts */
            (String*) NULL,             /* fallback rsc */
            args, 0);

    /* Create widgets. */
    n = 0;
    box = XtCreateManagedWidget("pane",
        boxWidgetClass,
        parent, args, n);

    n = 0;
    XtSetArg(args[n], XtNx, 10); n++;
    XtSetArg(args[n], XtNy, 10); n++;
    XtSetArg(args[n], XtNlabel, "Xaw95 Example"); n++;
```

```
label = XtCreateManagedWidget("label",
    labelWidgetClass,
    box, args, n);

n = 0;
XtSetArg(args[n], XtNx, 10); n++;
XtSetArg(args[n], XtNy, 40); n++;
XtSetArg(args[n], XtNlabel, "Exit"); n++;

push = XtCreateManagedWidget("push",
    commandWidgetClass,
    box, args, n);

XtAddCallback(push,
    XtNcallback,
    (XtCallbackProc) exitCB,
    (XtPointer) NULL);

XtRealizeWidget(parent);

XtAppMainLoop(app_context);

return 0;

}   /* main */

/* end of file exaw.c */
```

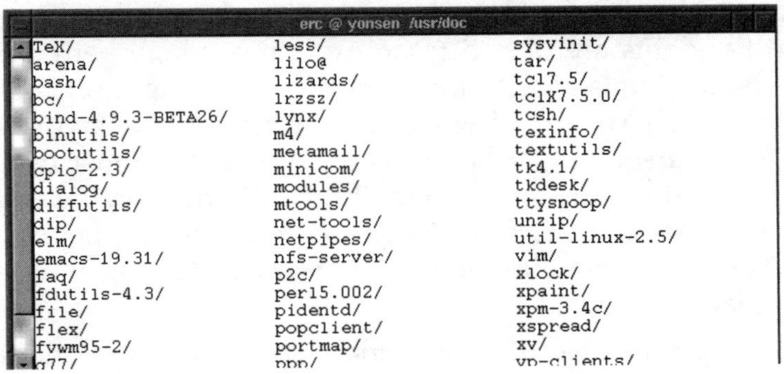

Figure 3.1 Xterm with a Windows 95–style scrollbar.

Note the use of the *XtSetArg* macro. This is how you pass attribute values to Xt-based widgets. The use of multiple commands (the *n*++) on one line avoids errors if you delete one of the *XtSetArg* lines.

To compile this program on Linux, you can use the following command:

```
$ cc -o exaw exaw.c -L/usr/X11R6/lib -lXaw -lXt -lX11
```

Programming with Xt-based toolkits leads to some odd convoluted code. If you're looking for something easier, then perhaps XForms is for you.

XForms

XForms is an X API designed to dramatically simplify the work you need to do to create X programs. As you saw earlier, even the simplest Motif or Athena widget programs require a lot of coding and some strange-looking code.

XForms attempts to make this easier by simplifying the options and coming up with a good set of default values. Because of this philosophy, XForms reduces a lot of the complexity in creating X applications. You pay a price in reduced flexibility, but for many application needs, XForms will be the right fit.

One of the areas of reduced freedom and complexity is widget layout. All widgets are placed to an exact position, whether in pixels, millimeters, or points (1/72 of an inch). Other widget sets, like Motif, provide an extensive set of widgets that control the layout of other widgets. Of course, widget layout is one of Motif's most troublesome aspects for programmers new to the library. XForms, on the other hand, eliminates most of these options and confusion by placing widgets directly. This has severe limitations if you translate your programs into other languages.

For languages like German or French, you should assume that your text messages will gain about 30 percent in size. Because of this, you'll need to mess with the exact placement required by XForms for each language translation—a big pain.

Filling Out Forms

The basic task in XForms is creating *forms*, XForms terminology for panels, windows, or dialog boxes. A form is really a top-level window containing a number of widgets.

XForms allows you to populate your forms with widgets such as buttons, sliders, and text-entry fields. Some of the more innovative widgets include dials, clocks, and X-Y data plots. The latter will appeal to those in the university community who want to display data graphically.

Should the XForms base widget set be too confining for your needs, you can create "free" objects, something like the Motif drawing-area widget, where your application gets a blank canvas to draw in and callbacks to handle all events. This allows a way to extend the base widget set. XForms includes an extensive API for adding new widgets.

The look and feel of XForms applications vary. You can create a variety of push-button styles, including beveled push buttons and rounded-corner buttons, so your interface can look like Motif, Open Look, or almost anything else. We advise sticking to the Motif look and feel, because that's the de facto standard for modern Linux applications, whether or not the applications use the Motif API. (If you're unsure of the Motif style guide, just follow the basics of the Microsoft Windows style guide and you'll do fine. The style guides are quite similar, with both being based on IBM's Common User Access guidelines.)

XForms supports a number of text styles and fonts, which is great for those who don't know a lot about the long X font names. With smart use of the font styles, your XForms programs will look much better than most Motif programs, with much less coding.

Coding is one area where XForms excels. You can generally create a working application in a very short amount of time, with very little code.

A Sample XForms Program

To get a flavor of XForms, look at the following sample program:

```c
/* Sample XForms program. */

#include <stdio.h>
#include <stdlib.h>
#include <forms.h>

/* Callback for push button. */
void
exit_cb(FL_OBJECT* widget,
    long user_data)

{
    /* Clean up. */
    fl_finish();

    printf("Form done.\n");
    exit(0);
}

/*
 * Callback for text-entry.
 */
void
text_cb(FL_OBJECT* widget,
    long user_data)

{
    printf("You entered: %s\n",
        fl_get_input(widget) );
}

int main(int argc, char** argv)

{
    FL_FORM*    form;
    FL_OBJECT*  button;
    FL_OBJECT*  text;

    /* Initialize library and
     * open X connection.
```

```
     */
    fl_initialize(&argc, argv,
        "LinuxProgramming",
        0, 0);

    /*
     * Create a form.
     */
    form = fl_bgn_form(FL_UP_BOX,
            424, 500);

    /*
     * Create text-entry field.
     */
    text = fl_add_input(
        FL_NORMAL_INPUT,
        50, 30, 230, 40,
        "Name: ");

    /* Set up callback. */
    fl_set_object_callback(text,
        text_cb, 0);

    /*
     * Create push button.
     */
    button = fl_add_button(
            FL_NORMAL_BUTTON,
            40, 180, 80, 30,
            "Exit");

    /* Set up callback. */
    fl_set_object_callback(button,
        exit_cb, 0);

    /* Done with form. */
    fl_end_form();

    /* Make things appear. */
    fl_set_app_mainform(form);

    fl_show_form(form, FL_PLACE_CENTER,
        FL_FULLBORDER, "XForms Example");

    /* Event loop. */
```

```
        fl_do_forms();

}

/* xform.c */
```

This program creates a form and populates it with an input (text-entry) and push-button widgets.

The callback on the text-entry widget extracts the text from the widget and prints it. The callback for the button exits the program.

To start things, the *fl_initialize* function connects to the X server and initializes the XForms toolkit. The *fl_bgn_form* function, paired with a call to *fl_end_form*, controls the creation of a form.

All widgets created between the calls to *fl_bgn_form* and *fl_end_form* go inside that form.

All *fl_add* functions create widgets in a form. The *fl_add_input* function creates a text-entry widget, while *fl_add_button* creates a push-button widget.

To make a form appear, call *fl_show_form*. To handle events, call *fl_do_forms*, which acts oddly if you're used to other toolkits. The *fl_do_forms* function returns when a widget changes state, unless you set up a callback function on all widgets, in which case *fl_do_forms* loops forever. You can set up callbacks on only some widgets, in which case *fl_do_forms* returns when a widget without a callback changes state. This tends to be confusing.

The program should give you a good flavor of the toolkit. Once you've created your program, the next step is to build it.

Building XForms Programs

The following command builds the sample XForms program listed earlier:

```
$ cc -o xform xform.c -lforms -L/usr/X11R6/lib -lX11 -lm
```

Interface Builder

One of the best parts of XForms is the bundled interface builder, called **fdesign**.

You can launch **fdesign** with a simple command like the following:

```
$ fdesign -name appname filename
```

You can create any of the base widget types and set attributes on the widgets. The basic way to create widgets is to use the mouse to place and size the widgets. Because few of us are very accurate with a mouse, **fdesign** has an alignment feature that allows you to align widgets together.

Unfortunately, this feature works in a counterintuitive manner, so we ended up aligning our widgets all on top of each other many times.

To change attributes of a widget, you need to select the widget and press **F1** (or click on the push button in the **fdesign** window). You can then specify widget names, color, border, and font attributes, as well as the name of the callback function.

When **fdesign** saves your forms, it generates the C code necessary to create the forms. It's then up to you to call the creation function for each form from your main function—a fairly simple task.

Another handy feature of XForms is the extensive manual that comes with the library. This manual contains a lot of information on the functions in the XForms library. The library comes with about 70 example programs to demonstrate aspects of the library.

XForms appears on the CD-ROM in the **XForms** directory. A simple **make install** and **make demo** got the whole thing up and running. You also need to run **ldconfig** as root user.

If your needs aren't too demanding, XForms could become a very easy way to create X applications without all the headaches involved in learning a complicated library such as Motif. The copyright restrictions may be daunting to those working for profit-making companies, though, as your UNIX systems are likely to come with Motif, and you have to balance the restrictions of XForms against all the competing toolkits.

XForms is a copyrighted product that is freely available for noncommercial use only. For commercial use, you need to contact the XForms authors at *xforms@world.std.com*.

XView

XView provides a different style of coding than Motif or XForms. Unlike the use of Xt functions and the very strange *XtSetArg* macro, XView applications use a small number of functions that take a variable number of parameters. This makes learning the basics of XView programming rather easy.

XView follows in interface style called *Open Look,* which differs from Motif's style in a number of respects. The main functions in the XView API appear in Table 3.1.

Table 3.1 Main XView functions.

Function	Usage
xv_create	Create widgets
xv_destroy	Destroy widgets
xv_find	Look up objects
xv_get	Get attributes of an object
xv_init	Initialize the toolkit
xv_main_loop	Main event loop
xv_set	Set attributes of an object

Of course, there's many more functions in the API, but the ones in Table 3.1 form the most-used core set.

To get a flavor for XView programming, try the following program:

```
/* Example xview program. */
#include <xview/xview.h>
#include <xview/frame.h>
#include <xview/panel.h>

static Frame    parent;

void
exitCB()

{
```

```
    xv_destroy_safe(parent);
}

int main(int argc, char** argv)

{   /* main */
    Panel   panel;

    xv_init(XV_INIT_ARGC_PTR_ARGV,
        &argc, argv,
        NULL);

    parent = (Frame) xv_create(NULL,
        FRAME,
        FRAME_LABEL,    "XView Example",
        XV_WIDTH,   500,
        XV_HEIGHT,  200,
        NULL);

    panel = (Panel) xv_create(parent,
        PANEL,
        NULL);

    (void) xv_create(panel,
        PANEL_BUTTON,
        PANEL_LABEL_STRING, "Exit",
        PANEL_NOTIFY_PROC,  exitCB,
        NULL);

    xv_main_loop(parent);
    return 0;

}   /* main */

/* end of xview.c */
```

You'll notice that most of the functions in the XView program take a variable number of parameters. Because of this, you'll often see XView code that ends each function call with a *NULL* sentinel parameter to tell the function that all the parameters are complete. In addition, most of the parameters come in pairs, with a name, such as *PANEL_LABEL_STRING* and a value, such as *Exit*.

With this model, you can pass parameters in whatever order you want, as long as you supply the required parameters at the start of the function call.

To compile XView programs, you need the xview and olgx libraries in addition to the low-level X library. You can use a command like the following:

```
$ cc -I/usr/openwin/include -o xview xview.c \
   -L/usr/openwin/lib -lxview -lolgx \
   -L/usr/X11R6/lib -lX11
```

XView libraries are located in **/usr/openwin/lib** and include files in **/usr/openwin/include**.

Fresco, a C++ Toolkit

If you've migrated from C to C++, Fresco provides one of the most interesting toolkits. Built on similar concepts to an earlier C++ toolkit called InterViews, Fresco combines four concepts into one toolkit:

- A set of run-of-the-mill widgets, as you'd expect.
- Lightweight glyphs that allow for just about any object to be transformed.
- Fresco supports structured graphics and widgets.
- The ability to distribute objects across a network.

The widgets in Fresco follow a similar vein to most other X APIs. We must add that Fresco isn't complete at this time, so not everything you'd expect is available right now.

Glyphs

One of the oddest parts of Fresco is the use of glyphs. A *glyph* is a lightweight object, and in Fresco you use glyphs for each letter of the alphabet. For example, if you display the word *Hello*, each letter is a separate glyph. Fresco then aligns the glyphs together to display the word *Hello*. This may seem like overkill, but it provides some interesting benefits.

For example, by using glyphs for letters and then containers called *Boxes*, you can create effects that other toolkits can't (at least without a lot of effort). If a Box aligns glyphs along one axis (horizontally or vertically), each line of text appears in a horizontally aligned Box. Because a Box is also a glyph, you can align the lines of text Boxes into columns, having a multicolumn display. Columns can then be aligned onto pages, and so on.

And, because quite a few Fresco objects are glyphs, you can align nearly anything. You can mix text with graphics and create all sorts of interesting layouts.

Structured Graphics

In addition to widgets, Fresco supports structured graphics, such as a CAD drawing of an automobile. Because each graphic item is a glyph, you can display and transform any graphics as well as widgets in your windows. This allows you to have a drawing program, such as **fdraw**, that can manipulate widgets as well as traditional lines, circles, and squares.

Distributed Objects

Fresco uses the CORBA object model for distributing objects across a network or between applications. Using the CORBA model, you can embed objects, such as a spreadsheet, into Fresco applications, such as a word processor. And you can embed Fresco glyphs into other applications as well. As such, this is like the facilities provided by OLE on Windows or OpenDoc on Macintosh systems.

Fresco goes a step further than OLE or OpenDoc, though; it allows graphical transformations on embedded objects, such as zooming in on the spreadsheet and word processor.

You can go beyond embedding to allow for fully distributed applications, applications of the sort envisioned by the Object Management Group (OGM), makers of the CORBA standard.

To support CORBA distribution, you need to define your objects using the CORBA Interface Definition Language (IDL). This language, very much like header files from C++, defines the API for a distributed object.

Fresco then adds C++ support to this mix, providing things like smart pointers and the glue necessary to translate what looks like a C++ object into a distributed network object. It's all incredibly interesting and complex.

Compiling Fresco Applications

On Linux, you need at least the libraries in the following command:

```
$ CC -o foo foo.cc -L/usr/X11R6/lib -lbase -ldefs -locs -ldl -lg++
```

Many of the Fresco example applications also require their own libraries.

For more information on Fresco, check out the main Web page at the following URL:

http://www.faslab.com/fresco/HomePage.html

Toolkits for Other Languages

If you're using something other than C or C++, Linux still provides a number of toolkits. Java, covered in Chapter 6, provides the AWT toolkit (short for Abstract Window Toolkit). Tcl, covered in Chapter 4, has the Tk toolkit, as does Perl, covered in Chapter 5.

Summary

There's a lot of choice in X Window programming from the APIs you choose to how you put your programs together.

The main X Window programming API is Motif, but because Motif is a commercial product, you won't find many programmers writing to the Motif API on Linux. If you're used to Motif, you can try the freeware LessTif, a clone of the Motif API.

In addition to Motif, there are a number of other X Window APIs supported on Linux. This chapter provided the smallest taste of these various APIs.

To help remember the libraries required for compiling and linking with various APIs, you can use Table 3.2 as a guide.

Table 3.2 Compiling and linking with X APIs.

Library	Requires
Athena	-lXaw -lXmu -lXt -lX11
Athena with X extensions, like Shape	-lXaw -lXmu -lXt -lXext -lX11
Fresco	-lbase -ldefs -locs -ldl
Motif	-lXm -lXt -lX11
Motif with X extensions, like Shape	-lXm -lXmu -lXt -lXext -lX11
Xlib	-lX11
Xlib with X extensions, like Shape	-lXext -lX11
XView	-lxview -lolgx -lX11
XForms	-lforms -lX11 -lm

Note that most X libraries are located in **/usr/X11R6/lib** and **/usr/openwin/lib** for XView.

Using Tcl

This chapter covers:

- The Tcl scripting language
- The Tk toolkit, which adds graphical widgets to Tcl
- Tcl's syntax
- Tcl variables
- Associative arrays
- Tcl procedures
- Mathematical functions
- Tcl wildcards
- Creating push buttons
- A Tcl script for launching editors, **make**, and programs

Linux Scripting Languages

Not all Linux programming is done under the auspices of C and C++, despite what you might think after reading through the previous two chapters. In addition to C- and C++-based programming languages, Linux offers a number of scripting languages. A scripting language is a lot like the language that comes with the Linux shell. The main difference between a programming language and a scripting language is that *scripting languages* are usually interpreted instead of compiled. In addition, scripting languages usually make it easier to launch Linux commands from within your programs (or, rather, your scripts). As you can tell, the line between programming languages and scripting languages is blurry.

This chapter introduces Tcl, a very popular cross-platform scripting language from which you can quickly and easily create graphical user interfaces and launch Linux tasks.

Tcl

Tcl (pronounced *tickle* and short for the Tool Command Language) is a very handy scripting language that runs on most UNIX platforms and Windows NT. Combined with Tcl's X Window toolkit, Tk (pronounced *teekay*), Tcl can be used to build X Window graphical programs without much coding. Some of the more famous Tcl/Tk applications include TkMan, a program that displays Linux online manual files (shown in Figure 4.1), and TkDesk, one of the best file managers for Linux, shown in Figure 4.2.

In addition, Tcl is made to be embedded in C programs, so you can use Tcl as a standard extension language for your spreadsheet, game, or other software you write. The Tcl interpreter is really just a C function that you can call from within your C programs.

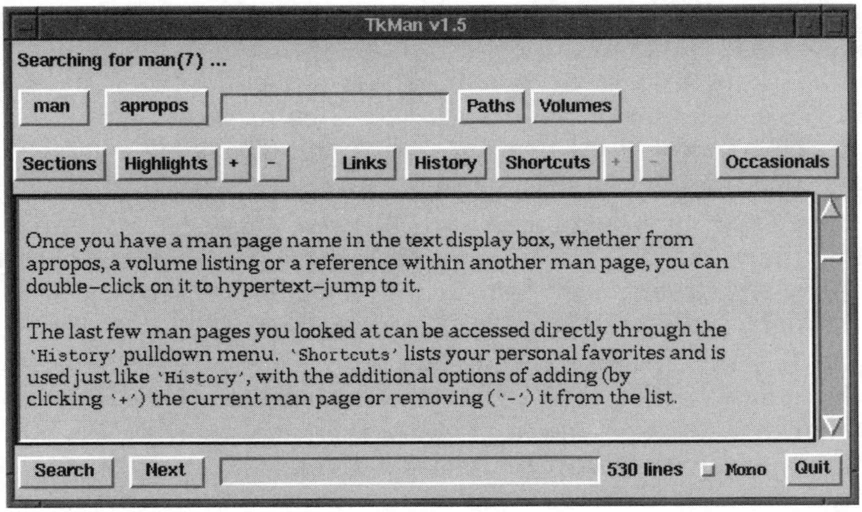

Figure 4.1 Viewing online manual files with TkMan.

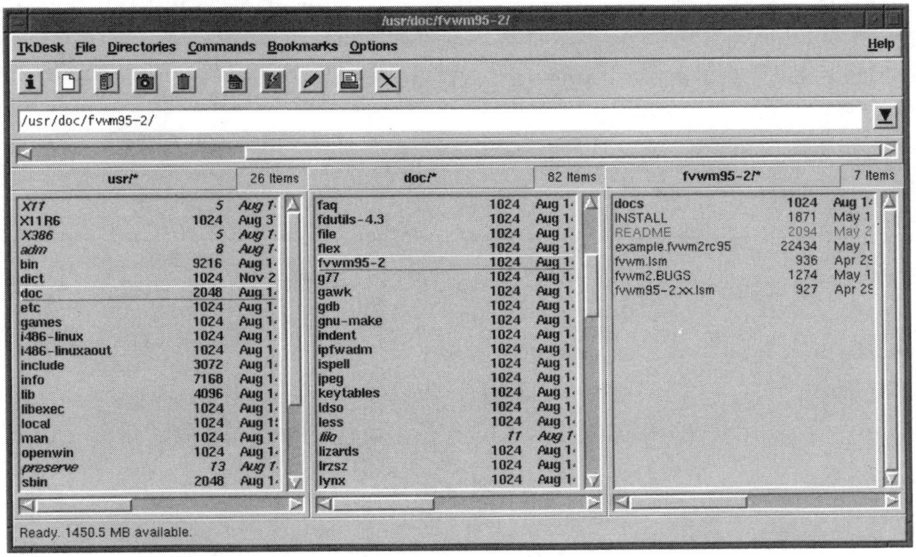

Figure 4.2 Exploring your hard disk with TkDesk.

We mostly use Tcl to create programs that have a friendly user interface, look like Motif programs, and can run on a wide number of systems. Tcl and the Tk toolkit present something akin to the Motif look and feel—not close enough for purists, but close enough for most users. This is a great benefit because the freeware LessTif libraries aren't complete yet and the true Motif libraries don't ship with Linux, while Tcl does.

Tcl is a scripting language, much like the languages built into the **bash** command shells. The language has some nice features for handling strings and lists of strings (just about everything is a string in a Tcl program).

The Tk toolkit then acts as an add-on to Tcl, allowing you to easily build widgets and create an X Window user interface. The whole concept of widgets, though, is likely to be daunting unless you've programmed with one of the many X toolkits, such as Motif. Each widget acts as a part of your user interface, for example, a list of files or a push button to exit the program. If you have worked with Motif or the Athena widgets, you'll catch on to the concepts of Tk pretty fast. Even if you haven't worked with the Motif or Athena libraries, we found the basics of Tcl very easy to grasp. (There are some frustrating parts to Tcl, though, as you'll see throughout this chapter.)

Table 4.1 lists the available widgets in Tk.

Table 4.1 Tk widgets.

Widget	Use
button	Push button, calls Tcl code when clicked on
canvas	Drawing area widget
checkbutton	On-off button
entry	Text-entry widget
frame	Frames widgets inside 3D bevel
label	Displays a text message
listbox	Scrolled list
menu	Menu
menubutton	Pulls down menu from menu bar

continued...

Widget	Use
message	Multiline label
radiobutton	On-off button; only one can be on at a time
scale	Analog value from *min* to *max*
scrollbar	Scrollbar
text	Text-entry widget
toplevel	Dialog or application window

Tcl exceeds Motif in a number of areas, too, especially with the canvas widget, which allows you to place graphic "objects" such as lines, rectangles, Bezier curves, and even other widgets inside the canvas.

Scripting with Tcl

The Tcl language itself is exceedingly simple, making for a very small interpreter. The Tcl interpreter just deals with commands and arguments. Each distinct line starts with a command. Anything else on the line is an argument that gets passed to that command. *Everything* is text.

Tcl complicates this slightly in that a single line to Tcl may span more than one line in your Tcl script files. To tell the Tcl interpreter that a command extends to the next line, end the line with a backslash, the line-continuation marker. For example:

```
button .b1 \
  -text "My first button" \
  -command { exit }
```

This command spans three lines of text but appears to Tcl as one single line—a command. In addition to the backslash, items within curly braces ({ and }) may span multiple lines, as shown here:

```
if {$i < 5} then {
    puts "$i is less than 5"
}
```

The *if* command above is one line to Tcl. This can be quite confusing.

While some parts may look like involved syntax (especially for the clever—or deranged—*if* commands just shown), a Tcl script is really made up of a set of commands and their arguments.

Commands and their arguments are separated by spaces. That's how the Tcl interpreter divides one part from another. Simple, huh? Unfortunately, it gets more complex. From these simple roots, you start to see some complexity—and quirks—of the language.

Because commands and their arguments are separated by spaces, how can you get spaces into text you want to display? Here comes the first exception to the rules: If you want to place spaces in an argument, you can enclose the full argument in double quotation marks, "".

This handy piece of syntax appeared in an example in the last chapter:

```
button .c -text "This is new text" -command { exit }
```

The text *This is new text* is treated as one single argument and passed to the button command.

The Tcl interpreter breaks up the preceding command into the following elements:

```
button
.c
-text
This is new text
-command
{ exit }
```

As you can see, the curly braces ({ and }) are like the double quotation marks, in that spaces are preserved inside the braces. These curly braces form the key to Tcl scripting, for they defer execution until later.

The curly braces are like double quotation marks (" and "), except for the following:

- You can nest sets of curly braces, for example, { { } } (not that this particular argument will do much).

- The curly braces delineate code to be executed later.
- The interpreter does not make *substitutions* within the curly braces until executed (later). You'll see more on substitutions in a bit (under the section titled "Variables and Substitutions").

Tcl Variables

One of the most useful features of the Tcl language is the use of variables. Like virtually all programming and scripting languages, Tcl lets you store a value (or a list of values) into something called a *variable*. A variable is a lot like the $c = a + b$ you learned back in algebra. Tcl lets you pick a name and then use that name to represent a value. In computer terms, you set the value into the variable.

To set in a value into a variable, you use the **set** command:

```
set var 6
```

You may want to test this command, and the others in the chapter, using **wish**, the Tcl interpreter in interactive mode. (There's also a text-only interpreter called **tclsh**.)

Type **wish** (or **tclsh**) at your shell command-line prompt. You should soon see the **wish** prompt, a percent sign, % character (or something like *tcl>*). At the **wish** prompt, you can type any Tcl command you want.

When you type the preceding command, you'll notice that **wish** prints the value set into the variable:

```
% set var 6
6
```

Most Tcl commands print their return values, unless the return value is used for some other command.

N O T E

Variables in Tcl are stored as strings, even though the preceding example could fool you into thinking it is a number. A nice part about Tcl is that the string can grow as large as necessary, so you don't have to worry about string lengths or allocating memory (like you do in C and C++ programs).

You can set any type of value into a variable:

```
set var marley
```

You can see what's stored in a variable using the **puts** (short for put string) command:

```
% puts $var
6
```

Notice the dollar sign, $, in the preceding example. This is our first experience of variable substitution, one of the trickier parts of Tcl.

Variables and Substitutions

The dollar sign signifies variable substitution. That is, if you have *$var*, this tells the Tcl interpreter to substitute the value stored in the variable in place of the string "$var". Remember, everything in Tcl is text, so the interpreter would have no way of knowing whether you wanted the value held in *var* (6, from our example) or the string "*var*" itself. Hence the $ for variable substitution.

Place the $ before the variable name, e.g., *$var*, to have the interpreter substitute the current value held in *var*. The trick to remember is that the value substituted is the value held in *var* when it is parsed. You can sometimes get into problems with this, which is why the curly braces defer execution (and parsing) until later.

If *$var* means to substitute the contents of the variable named *var*, how can you display a string in Tcl with the letters "*$var*"? You use the backslash (familiar to C programmers) with the dollar sign.

Try the following commands:

```
% set var2 $var
6
% set var3 \$var
$var
```

These examples just use the **set** command. The same concepts apply to all Tcl commands, such as the **expr** (expression) command, shown here:

```
set var4 42
expr 2 * $var4
```

You should see the result, 84.

The **expr** command takes in most kinds of math or logical operations and returns the result. This is another area where Tcl may appear strange. You need to perform all your mathematical expressions with the **expr** command.

Command Substitution

Many times you need to save the result of a command and use that value as an argument for another command. The way to do this is through the magic of command substitution.

If you see the square braces ([and]) in a command, this means that the contents between the square braces are to be parsed and executed first and then the results substituted into the overall command, as shown in the following example:

```
set var5 [expr 2 * $var4]
```

In the preceding code, the *[expr 2 * $var4]* part gets executed first, and the result, 84, is substituted to make a new command:

```
set var5 84
```

You can use any valid Tcl command within the square braces command-substitution markers; you aren't limited to the handy **expr** command. You can also nest the embedded commands. For example:

```
puts [set var6 [expr $var5 + 1] ]
```

If you type in this command, you should see the result, 85, printed out. Also, the variable *var6* gets set to the same value.

The Tcl interpreter works in what is called *two-phase execution*. In the first phase, the interpreter parses substitutions like the dollar sign and backslash. In the second phase, the commands are executed. If you nest things, such as with the command-substitution markers, this two-phase process is started again, for the data within the square bracket characters. This is really very simple, but it can trip you up if you aren't careful.

Table 4.2 shows the various types of substitution in Tcl.

Table 4.2 Variable and command substitution.

Tcl	Meaning
$*variable*	Substitute variable value
${*variable*}*text*	Prepend *variable* value onto *text* with no spaces
[expr 1+1]	Substitute results of command
"string $*variable*"	Substitute *variable* into quoted text
{string $*variable*}	Don't substitute *variable* into quoted text; defer to later

Array Variables

Tcl provides what is called *associative arrays*. You can treat an array as one identifier that represents a set of variables (keys) and values.

This is different from most programming languages, except Perl, which also offers associative arrays. In most programming languages, an array holds a set of values. In Tcl, an array holds a set of variables and values.

The syntax for accessing an element in an array is:

arrayname(variable)

where *arrayname* is the name of the array and *variable* is the name of one of the variables (keys) in the array. An example will help:

```
set employee(name) "Eric Johnson"
set employee(city) "St. Paul"
set employee(state) "Minnesota"
set employee(attitude) "Programs on Linux"
```

Controlling the Flow of the Script

A Tcl script normally executes from the start to the end, top to bottom. Each command is parsed and executed in turn, although you can defer execution using syntax elements like the curly braces.

This situation normally works fine until you want a slightly more complex scripts. To aid this, Tcl offers a number of commands that allow for branching and decision making including if-then statements, for, and while. If you've used a programming language before, all these statements will be familiar. All you need to learn is the syntax under Tcl, so you'll probably want to just skim the next sections. There's one more thing you should pay attention to, though.

Even though these statements look like real syntax, keep aware that *if*, *while*, *for*, and so on are merely Tcl commands with (usually long) arguments. A common mistake is to think that the Tcl interpreter is smarter than it is. Tcl is a very simple language. Most of the syntax, such as the *if* statement, is just for the sake of appearances. The **if** command is really just a normal Tcl command, though it is very easy to be fooled into thinking the Tcl language supports the idea of an *if* statement.

The basic format of an **if** command looks like the following:

if *{expression}* then *{body}*

For example:

```
if {$i < 5} then {
    puts "$i is less than 5"
}
```

If you're used to C programming, you may mistake the curly braces for C's parenthesis that surround the *if* expression. Unlike C, Tcl uses curly braces around the expression *and* the body.

The *then* part is optional. If the expression result is true, that is, if it generates a nonzero value (usually 1), then the body code gets executed. If the expression result is false (0), then the body code does not get executed.

The **if** command is really getting three arguments (or two, if you omit the optional *then* part), including an expression and a body. The curly braces allow you to place a lot of Tcl commands within one argument to the **if** command. Clever, huh?

Writing Your Own Procedures

There's two ways you can extend Tcl. You can write procedures strictly within the Tcl language, or you can create new Tcl procedures by writing functions in the C programming language that follow special conventions, which are most useful for application-specific behavior (such as recalculating a spreadsheet). Writing C functions is an advanced topic. But for now, there's a lot you can do by staying strictly within the Tcl language, using the **proc** command.

The **proc** command registers a procedure by name and allows you to execute it like any other command in Tcl. The syntax is:

proc *name {arguments} {body}*

For example, you can try the following simple procedure:

```
proc add_one { value } {
    return [expr $value+1]
}
```

Once you call **proc**, that procedure is ready to be used at any time in the future, as in:

```
% add_one 5
6
```

In this case, *5* is the argument passed to the procedure *add_one*. When invoked, the variable *value* will get set to the argument's value (5). Each time you invoke the *add_one* procedure, the *value* variable will get set with a new value, the value passed to *add_one* as an argument.

Inside a procedure, you can place any number of Tcl commands. You can also use variables and set values.

Working with Tcl

To try out some Tcl programs, you should run the Tcl interpreter, called **wish**, which allows you to enter Tcl commands as if you were in a Tcl-based shell, which is what **wish** is.

The most interesting use of Tcl is to create graphical programs including widgets such as push buttons. To create a push button in Tcl, use the **button** command:

```
% button .b1 \
  -text "My first button" \
  -command { exit }
```

This command creates a button widget named **.b1** (the leading period is important).

NOTE Just like Linux uses the / character to mark the root directory, Tcl uses the period (.) to mark the root widget (your application's main window). We're then creating a button widget that sits like a subdirectory beneath the root widget.

The *-command* sets the Tcl command that will run when the button gets pushed. In our case, the **exit** command exits **wish** and our Tcl script.

It's important to note that the code for the *-command* gets evaluated only when the button is pushed, usually sometime after the button is created and the Tcl program is in another procedure. Because of this, local variables no longer have their values at execution time. This can be very difficult to debug.

Widgets are created invisible. To get a widget to appear, we must pack it. The **pack** command takes a lot of parameters, including the name of the widget or widgets to pack:

```
% pack .b1
```

Tcl widgets don't appear until you pack them.

Making Script Files for Tcl

You can put together a set of Tcl commands into a script file, just like C and Bourne shell scripts. The program to execute the script is, again, **wish**. The following script assumes that **wish** is located in **/usr/bin**, the default location on Slackware Linux.

Tcl is a standard part of Slackware Linux, but other UNIX systems typically install **wish** in **/usr/local/bin**.

To turn our first example into a working script, we do the following. First type the following script into a text editor:

```
# example1.tcl
#
# Create a button.
button .b1 \
   -text "My first button" \
   -command { exit }
```

```
pack .b1

# example1.tcl
```

Save the script under the name **example1.tcl**. You can then execute this Tcl script by using the **wish** command from a Linux shell:

```
$ wish example1.tcl
```

To show you more of a flavor of Tcl scripting, we put together the following file. You can use Tcl's ability to create a graphical interface and easily launch Linux programs to create a simple little tool to aid common programming tasks, creating a simple development environment.

By launching Linux programs, you can make a small button bar with buttons to edit your files, make the program, run the program, launch a debugger on the program, call up online manuals, and launch **xterm** windows for miscellaneous usage.

Figure 4.3 shows the **progtool** window.

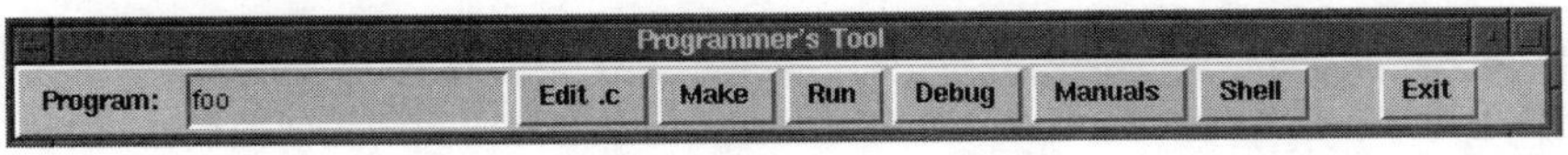

Figure 4.3 A simple programmer's tool.

The various buttons run very simple commands to:

- Call up the **elvis** text editor in an **xterm** window (using the **xterm -e** syntax that launches a program from within **xterm**). If you'd rather run another text editor, such as the graphical **textedit** or **emacs**, simply change the command launched in the *edit_file* procedure.
- Run **make** on the program name. Again, this gets launched from within an **xterm** window. You can extend this simple script to pipe the output of **make** into a scrolled Tk *text* widget to better see the results of **make**.
- Run the program itself, again from within **xterm**.

- Debug the program. For this, you have two main choices: running **gdb** in an **xterm** window or the X interface to **gdb**, **xxgdb**, if you have installed **xxgdb**.

- Call up online manuals from the **xman** command. You can also install TkMan and use the superior interface of TkMan.

- Launch a shell window (**xterm**). We get a lot of use out of lowly **xterm**, don't we?

- Change the program name by typing in a new one in the *entry* widget.

As you can tell, this simple script could use a lot of improvement, especially because it relies on **xterm** for most of the work. Even so, it demonstrates the small amount of Tcl code needed to create a graphical interface and launch Linux tasks.

The Tcl script to do all this requires just a small amount of code:

```
#!/usr/bin/wish
#
# progtool
# Simple programmer's tool written in Tcl.
# There's a LOT you can do to expand this
# and make it better.


#
# Executes a command as a Linux process.
#
proc exec_cmd { command } {

    # Execute as a Linux process in the background.
    # We use eval to handle the messy details of
    # separating the command into its elements.
    # (Try it without eval and you'll see why.)
    #
    eval exec $command &
}


proc edit_file { } {

    global progname
```

```
    # Note: we like vi; change this to emacs
    # or any other editor if you like.
    #
    # Note: .c at end of $progname.
    #
    exec_cmd "/usr/bin/X11/xterm -ls -e /usr/bin/vi $progname.c"
}

proc make_program { } {

    global progname


    #
    # You may want to capture the output of make
    # and display it in a Tk text widget.
    #
    exec_cmd "/usr/bin/X11/xterm -ls -e /usr/bin/make $progname"
}

proc run_program { } {

    global progname


    #
    # You may want to capture the output of make
    # and display it in a Tk text widget.
    #
    exec_cmd "/usr/bin/X11/xterm -ls -e $progname"
}

proc debug_program { } {

    global progname

    # If you've installed xxgdb, you can run that instead.
    #exec_cmd "/usr/X11/bin/xxgdb $progname"

    exec_cmd "/usr/bin/X11/xterm -ls -e /usr/bin/gdb $progname"
}


#
# Name of the program we're editing.
#
```

```
global progname

if { $argc > 0 } {
    set progname [lindex $argv 0]
}


#
# Main program.
#
#   Set window manager values.
wm geometry         .   +0+0
wm title . "Programmer's Tool"


#
# Frame to hold everything.
#
set back lightgray

frame .frame -relief raised -bd 2 -bg $back
.frame config -cursor top_left_arrow


#
# Widgets to enter program name
#
label .frame.label -text "Program:" \
  -relief flat -padx 8

entry .frame.progname -width 20 \
  -textvariable progname -bg $back

# Edit
# Note use of braces not quotes to
# avoid substituting now.
button .frame.edit -text "Edit .c" \
 -command { edit_file } \
 -padx 8 -bg $back

# Make program
button .frame.make -text "Make" \
 -command { make_program } \
 -padx 8 -bg $back

# Run program
```

```
button .frame.run -text "Run" \
 -command { run_program } \
 -padx 8 -bg $back

# Debug program
button .frame.debug -text "Debug" \
 -command { debug_program } \
 -padx 8 -bg $back

# Online manuals
button .frame.man -text "Manuals" \
 -command \
 { exec_cmd "/usr/bin/X11/xman -notopbox -bothshown" } \
 -padx 8 -bg $back

# Launch a shell
button .frame.term -text "Shell" \
 -command { exec_cmd "/usr/bin/X11/xterm -ls" } \
 -padx 8 -bg $back

# Exit program
button .frame.exit -text "Exit" \
 -command { exit } \
 -padx 8 -bg $back

# Pack all the buttons, in order.
pack .frame.label .frame.progname \
   .frame.edit .frame.make .frame.run \
   .frame.debug .frame.man \
   .frame.term \
   -side left -fill y

# Pack exit button with extra space to
# avoid accidental exiting.
pack .frame.exit -padx 28 -side left -fill y

pack .frame

# end of file progtool
```

Enter this script and save it under the name **progtool**.

In the **progtool** script, we create a number of procedures, called *procs* in Tcl. The *exec_cmd* procedure executes a text string as a Linux command. We use the *eval* statement to deal with text-string issues and evaluate any Tcl variables within the command. Try this Tcl script without the *eval* in the *exec_cmd* procedure and you'll see why we need it. (It has to do with evaluating the arguments as one string or as a command.)

The next step to get this script to run is to make the **progtool** file executable. For example:

```
$ chmod +x progtool
```

We use a special syntax for the first line of the **progtool** script that uses a neat Linux trick. If you place a special comment on the first line of a script, starting with #! and naming an executable program, Linux shells will pass the script file to the proper program, in this case **wish**. For example:

```
#!/usr/bin/wish
```

If you place this line at the top of your Tcl script files—in the very first line—and mark the file as executable, you can just run the script from the command line as any other program. For example:

```
$ progtool
```

When you run the **progtool** script, though, you should pass the name of the program you want to edit, for example:

```
$ progtool foo
```

Because this script is so simple, you need to be in the directory where your program exists before starting the **progtool** script. Of course, there's a lot you can do to improve this script.

You can use these two scripts as examples to get you started scripting Tcl applications.

Summary

Tcl is a handy scripting language for putting together small programs with graphical interfaces. In addition, you can embed the Tcl interpreter into your software, making for a very handy extension language you can place into your programs for free.

The Tk toolkit that comes with Tcl allows you to create a number of widgets similar to those of most other graphic toolkits like Motif.

In the next chapter, we delve into another Linux scripting language, Perl.

Using Perl

This chapter covers:

- Perl
- Installing Perl through **setup**
- A first Perl script
- Variables
- Scalar variables
- Associative arrays
- Controlling the flow of your Perl scripts
- Subroutines
- String comparisons
- Numeric comparisons

Perl

Perl is a freeware scripting language originally developed to handle a number of system administration tasks. For the programmer, Perl offers the mother of all scripting languages, which you can use for converting program files from one format to another and automating your development process. In addition, because Perl is so good with handling text strings, you can get a lot of mileage out of Perl for scanning your source code. You could scan for include files (and the files included from include files, and so on) or search for all variables and functions in a large software base, providing a database of functions and their locations.

Perl is also a major language for Web programmers, who use it to create Common Gateway Interface (CGI) scripts to handle Web-based data-entry forms.

For all these reasons, it's good to be knowledgeable about Perl. This chapter provides a brief introduction to Perl and some ideas for using this handy tool in your development environment.

Perl stands for *Practical Extraction and Report Language*. The whole point of the language is to make it easier for you to extract data from UNIX—specifically text file son UNIX—and output reports on things such as Usenet news disk usage and a list of all users on your systems, sorted in order of largest disk usage. Perl tends to excel at tasks that revolve around reporting system information or delving into text files. Because all programs start out as text files (that mantra again), you can make effective use of Perl extracting data from your source code.

If you chose Perl when you installed Linux, you should already have it loaded on your system. To make sure you've installed Perl when you install Linux, type the following:

```
$ perl -v
```

If you have Perl on your system, you should see the version number for Perl. If not, you need to run the **setup** program again. (The **setup** program installs Perl 5.003.)

A First Perl Script

Perl, like most UNIX scripting languages, uses the # as a comment marker. Any line with # is ignored from the # onward. To print data in a Perl script, use the *print* statement, as shown here:

```
#! /usr/bin/perl
print "Linux runs perl!\n";
print "Oh, joy!\n";
```

Enter this data into a file and name the file **hello.pl**.

When you run this script, you'll see the following output, as you'd expect:

```
$ perl hello.pl
Linux runs perl!
Oh, joy!
```

The \n stands for a newline, or linefeed character, and is typical UNIX parlance for the character that goes at the end of a line.

You can also prompt for data in Perl, using the following odd syntax:

```
#! /usr/bin/perl
# askname.pl
# Prompting for input in perl.

print "What is your first name: ";

# <STDIN> stands for standard input: the keyboard.
$first_name = <STDIN>;

# Remove trailing linefeed.
chomp($first_name);

printf "What is your last name: ";
$last_name = <STDIN>;

chomp($last_name);

print "Your name is $first_name $last_name.\n";
```

When you run this script, you'll see the following prompts:

```
$ perl askname.pl
What is your first name: Eric
What is your last name: Johnson
Your name is Eric Johnson.
```

Variables

Perl variables allow you to store text, numbers, or lists of either. Perl attempts to hide any sort of limit, so string variables, for example, can hold as much text as you can fit into your system's virtual memory. String variables simply grow as needed, as do all other Perl variables.

Perl's variables fall into three major types: scalars, arrays, and associative arrays.

Scalar Variables

Scalar variables hold a single value, either a text string or a number. You can set the same variable to hold either text or numeric data, and you can switch by setting a string variable to hold a number, and vice versa.

Use a dollar sign, *$*, before the name of a scalar value. This tells Perl the value is a scalar, as used in the *$last_name* variable.

Arrays

In addition to scalar variables, Perl supports lists and arrays. A *list* is simply an ordered set of scalar values, text or numbers, or both.

An *array* is a named list. When you use an array variable, you use the @ character rather than the *$*, as in the following:

```
@array = (1,2,3,4,5,6);
```

This array has the values 1 through 6. You can also intermix text and numeric values, as shown here:

```
@array = (1, 2, 3, 4, "Linux is out the door");
```

This command then sets an array variable, *@array*, to the value of the list, which is all the elements in the list.

Each element of an array is simply a scalar value, which you can access using the Perl syntax for scalars, *$*, with an index into the array. For example:

```
 # Access
print "$array[1]\n";
```

```
 # Assignment.
$array[2] = 'maroon';
```

Like C and C++, Perl starts counting array indices with 0. Thus 1 represents the *second* element of the array.

Perl treats *@array* and *$array* as completely different values that have no relation to another. This is even more confusing in that *$array[value]* refers to an element of *@array*, not to *$array*.

You can place scalar variables in lists and arrays, as in the following:

```
$element = "Ouch";
@array = ($element, 1, 2, 3, 4);
print "@array\n";
```

To determine the number of elements in an array, use the strange *$#array* syntax. Replace the word *array* with the name of your array.

The value *$#array* is the last element. Because the elements go from 0 to *$#array*, the total is *$#array* plus 1.

Associative Arrays

A great strength of Perl is its *associative arrays*, where you can use a key value for an array index and associate this with a data value. Regular arrays allow you to access elements by their index numbers, starting at zero. Associative arrays allow you to access elements by key names. That is, an associative array holds a set of key/value pairs.

A *key name* is any arbitrary scalar value, such as "HOME", "LINUX", or anything else you care to use.

Associative arrays are very useful for storing attributes of some item, especially when you don't know in advance how many attributes an item will have. For example, you can have a Perl array for a first name, last name, and street address, with each item being a separate key/value pair in an associative array.

Perl uses a percent sign, %, to indicate a variable is an associative array. Thus, *%assoc* represents a variable named *assoc* that is an associative array.

To access individual values in an associative array, though, you use a different syntax. Any value in an associative array can be accessed through its key name, using the following syntax:

```
%assoc{keyname}
```

For example, you could access street addresses as shown here:

```
#! /usr/bin/perl
# assoc.pl
# Associative arrays in perl.

# zippy is an associative array.

$zippy{"firstname"} = "Zippy";
$zippy{"address"} = "1600 Pennsylvania Ave.";

# Print the data.
print $zippy{"firstname"};
print "'s address is ";
print $zippy{"address"};
```

```
# End with a carriage return.
print "\n";
```

This example stores a first name and an address in the associative array named *zippy*. Associative arrays form a very powerful feature and can be used effectively in a lot of system administration tasks.

The output of the preceding script looks something like the following (and predicts the results of the next election):

```
$ perl assoc.pl
Zippy's address is 1600 Pennsylvania Av.
```

Working with Linux

Perl is intimately tied to UNIX and provides Linux users a number of ways to interact with your operating system.

The Environment Associative Array

One of the most useful associative arrays is *%ENV*, which holds your shell's environment variables. These variables, supported on UNIX and Windows, provide a number of values set up by the user (or for the user) that pertain to the computer's environment. On Linux, for example, the *SHELL* environment variable holds the user's desired command-entry shell program, such as **/bin/bash** for the **bash** shell.

Using the *keys* operator, you can easily access the *%ENV* associative array and see what's available on the system. Enter the following script and try it on your system:

```
# Access environment variables.

@key_names = keys(%ENV);

foreach $key (@key_names) {
```

```
    print "$key=$ENV{$key}\n";
}

# env.pl
```

On a Linux system, you'll see a lot of output, including the following (edited for space):

```
HOSTTYPE=i486-linux
LOGNAME=erc
OSTYPE=linux
WINDOWID=29360141
SHLVL=1
OPENWINHOME=/usr/openwin
MANPATH=/usr/local/man:/usr/man/preformat:/usr/man:/usr/X11/man:/usr/o
penwin/man
LESSOPEN=|lesspipe.sh %s
HOME=/home/erc
PWD=/home/erc/perl/book/scripts
DISPLAY=:0.0
LESS=-MM
SHELL=/bin/csh
TERM=xterm
MACHTYPE=i386
HOST=yonsen
ignoreeof=10
HOSTNAME=yonsen.yonsen.org
USER=erc
```

Assessing the Password File

Perl also provides a number of shortcuts for common Linux activities, like accessing the password file, **/etc/passwd**, as we show here:

```
#! /usr/bin/perl
# passwd.pl
# Accessing the password file.

# Get Eric's password entry and print it.
```

```
@erc_entry = getpwnam("erc");

($username, $realname, $homedir) = @erc_entry[0,6,7];

print "User $realname has";
print " a home directory of $homedir";
print " and a username of $username.\n";
```

When you run this script, you'll see output like the following:

```
$ perl passwd.pl
User Eric F. Johnson has a home directory of /home/erc
and a username of erc.
```

Naturally, you'll want to use a username available on your system.

Executing Programs

Perl offers a number of commands, most of which mimic C functions like *exec*, to launch Linux processes. The easiest such command is **system**. The **system** command executes a command and waits until that command completes. In most cases, this is what you want. For example:

```
$return_value = system(command);
```

The *command* is any Linux command.

When the *command* finishes, the *$return_value* will hold an integer value, the value that was returned by the *command*. You must divide this value by 256 to get the actual return value. By convention, a return value of 0 means OK.

Controlling the Flow of Your Scripts

Perl offers a number of commands for controlling the flow of your scripts, such as *if, while, for,* and *foreach.*

The basic *if* statement follows:

```
if ( $lang eq "Perl" ) {
    print "Congratulations, you chose Perl!\n";
}
```

This code compares whether the text string held in the variable *$lang* equals the string *Perl*. The *eq* part compares for string equality. Perl offers a number of string comparisons, shown in Table 5.1.

Table 5.1 String comparisons.

Perl	Usage
eq	Equal
ge	Greater than or equal to
gt	Greater than
le	Less than or equal to
lt	Less than
ne	Not equal
cmp	Returns −1 if less than, 0 if equal, and 1 if greater than

In addition to string comparisons, Perl allows for numeric comparisons, using the operators shown in Table 5.2.

Table 5.2 Numeric comparison.

Perl	Usage
==	Equal
!=	Not equal
<	Less than
<=	Less than or equal to
>	Greater than
>=	Greater than or equal to
<=>	Returns −1 if less than, 0 if equal, and 1 if greater than

You can use these comparisons in the *if* statement and other Perl conditionals, such as *while*, shown here:

```
# Example of the while statement.
$i = 0;
while ($i < 10) {
   print "Iteration $i.\n";
   $i++;
}
# while1.pl
```

The *for* loop comes straight from C. To have a loop iterate 10 times, you can follow the C language convention:

```
# Example of the for statement.
for ($i = 0; $i < 10; $i++) {
   print "Iteration $i.\n";
}
# for1.pl
```

In the parenthesis, you see three parts, called the initialization, expression, and continuation parts, respectively. The *initialization* part gets executed first, and normally initializes the loop variable, *$i*, to zero or 1. The *expression* is checked on each iteration through the loop, for example: *$i < 10*. If true, *for* iterates again. The *continuation* part gets executed at the end of the loop, just before the *expression* is evaluated again. The *continuation* part usually increments the loop-controlling variable, with *$i++* in this case.

Similar to *for*, the *foreach* statement lets you iterate for each element in a list or array. Each time through the loop, *foreach* places an element of the list into the scalar variable, repeating until all the elements in the list have been processed. For example:

```
# Example of foreach.
@languages = ("Perl","Tcl","Java","Oberon","python");

foreach $lang (@languages) {

   if ($lang eq "Perl") {
      print "The most wonderful language is $lang.\n";
```

```
    } else {
        print "$lang has some neat ideas.\n";
    }
}
# foreach.pl
```

Subroutines

A *subroutine* is a named section of Perl code that you can call to execute special commands. If your program in C or C++, a subroutine in Perl is like a function in C.

Normally, you'll use subroutines as a way to better organize your Perl scripts. You define subroutines with the *sub* statement:

```
sub my_subroutine {

    print "In a subroutine.\n";

}

# Invoke the subroutine
print "Before subroutine.\n";

&my_subroutine;

print "Before subroutine.\n";

# sub.pl
```

The *sub* statement defines a block, from { to }, that is your subroutine. Each subroutine requires a name, given by you (*my_subroutine* in the **sub.pl** example).

The Perl commands defined in the *sub* block don't execute right away. Instead, you need to use the *&subroutine_name* syntax to invoke, or execute, the subroutine at the place or places you want. You can invoke subroutines as many times as you like.

Summary

This chapter provided a whirlwind tour of Perl. The time was spent on the major actions performed by Perl including the management of variables and Linux-specific actions. The next chapter deals with Java.

This chapter covers:

- Java programming
- An overview of Java
- Obtaining the JDK
- Java development tools
- Hello, World!
- Creating an application
- Creating an applet
- Kaffe
- Guavac
- Java online resources

Insert Bad Coffee Pun Here: A Look at Java

It's hard to wander through your local bookstore without stumbling across a display of Java books. Java, as developed by Sun Microsystems, is supposed to be the greatest thing since sliced bread, a tool for single-handedly realigning world economies (as suggested with a straight face by a Sun Microsystems employee), and in general serve as a revolutionary tool in the development of personal computing.

Whether or not Java is revolutionary or merely evolutionary is something computer historians will have to debate. Our concern here is to explain Java and the Java programming tools on the accompanying CD-ROM and to point you in the general direction of other Java programming tools on the Internet.

What Is Java?

Simply put, *Java* is a programming language structurally similar to C and C++, with multiple threads and the same syntax. If you can handle C++, you can handle Java, as it is not quite as complex (or robust, for that matter) as C++. Others have made comparisons to Lisp (because of Java's garbage collection) and Smalltalk (the quip goes that Java is "Smalltalk with sane syntax"). It's also network-aware, which means it can deal quite easily with the rigors of the Internet.

You create Java applications as you do any other applications, by creating source code with an editor and then running the code through a compiler. In the case of Java, however, you're not actually creating executables with the compiler; you're creating applets in "J-Code," which is essentially byte code that is interpreted by a Java-compatible Web browser (like Netscape Navigator). These byte codes are not tied to any operating system or hardware architecture, so they can be run by any Web client that supports Java, such as the many versions of Netscape Navigator (for the Microsoft Windows, Windows 95/NT, Macintosh, UNIX, and Linux operating systems) and Microsoft Internet

Explorer (for Windows 95, Windows, and Macintosh operating systems).

However, Java differs significantly from C and C++ when it comes to the implementation of actual programs. Java applets are worked by a call from within a Web page. When a Web browser requests the applet, the applet is transferred to the client's computer and run there. The overhead on the originating Web server is therefore minimized; applications run on the client and not on the server (which is opposite from the approaches taken by CGI programming techniques with Perl and Tcl, which you learned about in previous chapters). This frees the server to serve more clients over time.

What sort of applications can be created with Java? Pretty much anything that you can code. You can use Java for mundane tasks like forms and data input. Currently, Java has been used on the Internet mainly to add multimedia flash to Web pages, such as inserting graphics into a Web page. Other applets have been incorporated into Web pages to provide real-time stock quotes and sports tickers.

Of course, you might expect there to be some drawbacks to this approach. For starters, Java's overall security is somewhat in question; it's been modified over the last couple of years to improve security on the client side by not allowing access to the client's filesystem. And its speed is somewhat in question as well, because these programs are interpreted as byte codes and not compiled (read: *optimized*) for a particular operating system. In fact, you should expect that the more extensive your Java applet, the greater the drag it will cause on your client's Web browser.

This chapter won't convince you of the superiority of Java as opposed to the other programming tools discussed here. We could spend a lot of time discussing how Java's object-oriented approach is superior to your favorite programming tools, how Java's limited functionality is actually a virtue instead of a vice, and so on. We strongly suggest you check out Java and treat it as another programming tool in your Linux arsenal.

You can get more information about the JDK for Linux at *http://www.blackdown.org/java-linux.html*.

NOTE

You'll also need a few extra tools before you dive into Linux/Java programming, even if you get a copy of the Linux JDK via the Internet. You'll probably want to use a Web browser that supports Java to test your Java applets. Netscape Navigator (version 2.0 or better) does indeed support Java, but it's commercial software, and hence not available for us to ship to you on the accompanying CD-ROM. If you're not yet using Netscape Navigator, you'll want to grab it via FTP either from *http://home.netscape.com* or *ftp://ftp.netscape.com*.

HotJava, the Java-enabled Web browser from Sun Microsystems, was not yet available in a Linux version when this book was written.

In addition, you can grab a tool that lets you edit Java code in GNU Emacs, which you'll find at *ftp://java.sun.com/pub/java/contrib/emacs*.

Creating Java Applications

Basically, there are only four tools that are part of creating Java applications:

- An *editor* to create source-code files.
- A *Java compiler* to convert Java source code into byte code.
- A *Web browser*, such as Netscape Navigator, to run the Java applets.
- A *Java interpreter* to run Java applets.

The JDK from Sun Microsystems includes these tools and more, including a profiler, header-file generator, debugger, and documentation.

The Inevitable "Hello World!" Application

We don't want to upset the delicate balance found in the programming world by not using a simple "Hello World!" file to explain how Java works. In this case, we'll use the example found in the official Sun Java documentation. You'll want to use **elvis** or **emacs** to create a file named **HelloWorldApp.java** with the following contents:

```
/**
 * The HelloWorldApp class implements an application that
 * simply displays "Hello World!" to the standard output.
 */
class HelloWorldApp {
    public static void main(String[] args) {
        System.out.println("Hello World!"); //Display the string.
    }
}
```

This is your source code.

Your next step is to compile the source code from a Linux command line using the following:

```
$ javac HelloWorldApp.java
```

A new file named **HelloWorldApp.class** should be created if everything compiled successfully. (If compilation wasn't successful, check for typos; a simple error is about all that can go wrong when creating such a simple application.)

To run the program with the Java interpreter, use the following command line:

```
$ java HelloWorldApp
```

If you have any programming experience, you should recognize some familiar elements in the amazingly simplistic "Hello World!" example. Because Java doesn't support global functions or stray variables, all functions are part of a class or an object (hence the beginning of the actual code with *class*, followed by the name of the class). Comments are strewn throughout, beginning with /** and ending with */. A comment that follows actual code on the same line begins with //. And, like C and C++ (and a host of other programming languages), comments can be bracketed with /* and */, although we didn't use any in this example.

Creating an Applet

A Java application is merely a program that can be run through an interpreter on a command line. An *applet*, on the other hand, is an application that's designed to be embedded in a Web page and run after being transferred to a client machine. This is a trickier proposition, because an applet must make the proper calls to make sure that windows and screen elements are created on the client. Witness the following code, which is used in the Sun documentation as an example of an applet:

```
import java.applet.Applet;
import java.awt.Graphics;

public class HelloWorld extends Applet {
    public void paint(Graphics g) {
        g.drawString("Hello world!", 50, 25);
    }
}
```

This is your source code. Save it with the filename **HelloWorld.java**.

Your next step is to compile the source code from a Linux command line using the following:

```
$ javac HelloWorld.java
```

A new file named **HelloWorld.class** should be created if everything compiled successfully. (If compilation wasn't successful, check for typos; a simple error is about all that can go wrong when you're creating such a simple application.)

Your next step will to be create a Web page that invokes the applet on the client through a Web browser. Your Web page should look something like this:

```
<HTML>

<HEAD>

<TITLE> A Simple Program </TITLE>
```

```
</HEAD>

<BODY>

Here is the output of my program:

<APPLET CODE="HelloWorld.class" WIDTH=150 HEIGHT=25>

</APPLET>

</BODY>
</HTML>
```

You don't need to know much about HTML code to see what this Web page will do. Basically, there are only three elements to this Web page:

- A title, *A Simple Program*.
- Some text that forms the body of the page: *Here is the output of my program:*.
- An applet called **HelloWorld.class**, which has its own formatting information (*WIDTH=150 HEIGHT=25*). This applet is called using the *<APPLET CODE></APPLET>* combination, which is an HTML tag that must be supported in a Web browser that claims to support Java.

There isn't a lot of excitement accompanying this Web page. When you do load the Web page into a Web browser, you'll see a single line of text that looks like the following:

Here is the output of my program: Hello world!

How this applet works isn't especially complicated. It beings with two *import* statements, which allow other classes to be included as part of the applet. In this case, the **java.awt.Graphics** class refers to the Abstract Windows Toolkit, which is used to create windows on a variety of operating systems. The Applet class is extended by the HelloWorld subclass; such a definition is true of every applet. In the example, only one method was called—the *paint()* method. All applets must call on one of the *init()*, *start()*, or *paint()* methods. (There's no need to invoke a *main()* method.) The *g.drawString* is used to draw the text string.

You are now a Java programmer.

There's more to learn about Java programming. In Appendix B we list some useful guides to Java programming. In addition, there are several useful online Java programming guides, including Javasoft documentation at *http://www.javasoft.com*.

Distributing Your Applications

Sun Microsystems allows you to redistribute Java applications free of charge. The only thing Sun specifically prohibits is if you make major changes to Java and pass it off as being Sun's own Java.

WARNING

This may have changed with the most recent version of the JDK. Check the license that ships with the Linux version of the JDK to determine if this is still true.

Kaffe

Despite Sun's feet-dragging about accommodating ports of the JDK to the Linux world, it hasn't stopped a set of hardy souls in the Linux world from working on their own Java projects. One such project is Kaffe, under the direction of Tim Wilkinson (*tim@sarc.city.ac.uk*).

As the Kaffe FAQ states: "Kaffe is a virtual machine design to execute Java bytecode. Unlike other virtual machines available, this machine performs 'just-in-time' code conversion from the abstract code to the host machine's native code. This will ultimately allow execution of Java code at the same speed as standard compiled code while maintaining the advantages and flexibility of code independence."

You can find out more information about Kaffe at *http://web.soi.city.ac.uk/homes/tim/kaffe/kaffe.html*. The Kaffe FAQ can be found at *http://web.soi.city.ac.uk/homes/tim/kaffe/faq.html*.

We've included the latest version of Kaffe on the accompanying CD-ROM. Keep in mind that it's still in development.

Guavac

A similar project is Guavac, a Java compiler that makes no use of Sun technology. With Guavac, programmers can compile Java applets that are compliant with the Sun standards. However, the restrictions Sun places on its development tools don't apply to Guavac, since it uses no Sun technology.

More information about Guavac can be found at *http://http.cs.berkeley.edu/~engberg/guavac*.

We've included the latest version of Guavac on the accompanying CD-ROM. Keep in mind that it's still in development.

For More Information

As you might expect for a programming tool that's primarily for use on the Internet and intranets, there are many Internet Java resources.

One valuable resource is the **comp.lang.java** newsgroup and its FAQ, which is posted regularly. You can read the FAQ with your favorite Usenet newsreader as it passes you by, or you can use the Web to read it at *http://www.city-net.com/~krom/java-faq.html*. A page of Java/Linux tips can be found at *http://www.parnasse.com/java.shtml*.

General-interest Java sites that include example applets include Gamelan at *http://www.gamelan.com/*.

Another excellent source of Linux/Java information is the Linux Java HOWTO, which is included on the accompanying CD-ROM. It's maintained by Eric S. Raymond (*esr@snark.thyrsus.com*); you can find Eric's Home Page at *http://www.ccil.org/~esr/home.html*.

Summary

This short chapter introduced the Java programming language and the tools available under Linux for creating Java applets and applications.

The next chapter covers a wide range of lesser Linux programming tools.

7

Miscellaneous Tools and Languages

This chapter covers:

- BASIC
- FORTRAN
- Objective C
- LISP
- Pascal
- Modula
- Oberon
- Eiffel

Programming Linux

Linux remains steadfastly popular in the freeware community, making a wide variety of tools and languages available to the Linux program.

We've been pleasantly surprised on more than one occasion while researching this book. Linux seems to offer the widest possible array of computer languages with scads of free tools.

This chapter covers a wide variety of programming languages and the tools that come with them. We hope you'll find your favorite language here if you haven't in the previous coverage of C, C++, Java, Perl, and Tcl.

The alternative languages available on Linux systems include BASIC, FORTRAN, Objective C, LISP, Pascal, Modula, Oberon, and Eiffel.

BASIC

BASIC forms one of the easiest-to-learn computer languages. Linux includes BASIC in the form of Bywater Basic 2.10, a minimalist ANSI BASIC interpreter.

To use Bywater BASIC, you need to install the **bwbasic.tgz** package, found on the CD-ROM in the **BASIC** directory. Use **installpkg** or **pkgtool** to add the package do your system.

Bywater BASIC comes with source code, so you can recompile the program if necessary.

To run Bywater BASIC, use the **bwbasic** command:

```
$ bwbasic
Bywater BASIC Interpreter/Shell, version 1.10
Copyright (c) 1993, Ted A. Campbell
Default English-Language Messages
bwBASIC:
```

Type **Ctrl-C Ctrl-C** to exit **bwbasic**.

As a language, BASIC is, well, basic. Bywater BASIC supports most of the ANSI BASIC commands but doesn't do much more. As such, it's more suitable as a learning environment than for serious programming. Table 7.1 lists the commands available in Bywater BASIC, from the **README** file that comes with Bywater BASIC. The **bwbasic** package installs some additional documentation and source code in **/usr/doc/bwbasic**.

Table 7.1 Bywater BASIC commands.

Command	Command
ABS(number)	ENVIRON variable-string = string
ASC(string$)	ENVIRON$(variable-string)
ATN(number)	EOF(device-number)
CHAIN [MERGE] file-name [, line-number] [,ALL]	ERASE variable[, variable]...
CHR$(number)	ERL
CINT(number)	ERR
CLEAR	ERROR number
CLOSE [[#]file-number]...	EXP(number)
COMMON variable [, variable...]	FIELD [#] device-number, number AS string-variable
COS(number)	[, number AS string-variable...]
CSNG(number)	
CVD(string$)	FOR counter = start TO finish [STEP increment]
CVI(string$)	GET [#] device-number [, record-number]
CVS(string$)	GOSUB line
DATA constant[,constant]...	GOTO line
DATE$	HEX$(number)
DEF FNname(arg...)] = expression	IF expression THEN statement [ELSE statement]
DEFDBL letter[-letter](, letter[-letter])...	INPUT [# device-number]|[;]["prompt string";]list of variables
DEFINT letter[-letter](, letter[-letter])...	
DEFSNG letter[-letter](, letter[-letter])...	INSTR([start-position,] string-searched$, string-pattern$)
DEFSTR letter[-letter](, letter[-letter])...	
DELETE line[-line]	INT(number)
DIM variable(elements...)[variable(elements...)]...	KILL file-name
END	LEFT$(string$, number-of-spaces)
	LEN(string$)

Command

LET variable = expression

LINE INPUT [[#] device-number,]

  ["prompt string";] string-variable$

LIST line[-line]

LOAD file-name

LOC(device-number)

LOF(device-number)

LOG(number)

LSET string-variable$ = expression

MERGE file-name

MID$(string$, start-position-in-string

  [, number-of-spaces])

MKD$(double-value#)

MKI$(integer-value%)

MKS$(single-value!)

NAME old-file-name AS new-file-name

NEW

NEXT counter

OCT$(number)

ON variable GOTO|GOSUB line[,line,line,...]

ON ERROR GOSUB line

OPEN O|I|R, [#]device-number, file-name [,record length]

  file-name FOR INPUT|OUTPUT|APPEND

   AS [#]device-number [LEN = record-length]

OPTION BASE number

POS

PRINT [# device-number,][USING format-string$;] expressions...

PUT [#] device-number [, record-number]

RANDOMIZE number

Command

READ variable[, variable]...

REM string

RESTORE line

RETURN

RIGHT$(string$, number-of-spaces)

RND(number)

RSET string-variable$ = expression

RUN [line][file-name]

SAVE file-name

SGN(number)

SIN(number)

SPACE$(number)

SPC(number)

SQR(number)

STOP

STR$(number)

STRING$(number, ascii-value|string$)

SWAP variable, variable

SYSTEM

TAB(number)

TAN(number)

TIME$

TIMER

TROFF

TRON

VAL(string$)

WEND

WHILE expression

WIDTH [# device-number,] number

WRITE [# device-number,] element [, element]....

Fortran

Very common for scientific and numerical software, Fortran, one of the earliest computer languages, still hangs in there. Because Linux is used in many academic sites, Fortran is a priority for many programmers and nonprogrammers who need to get some number-crunching software to run on Linux.

Well, help is on the way, in the form of **gcc**—yes, the C compiler; the ever-handy GNU C compiler, **gcc**, turns up in the oddest places. Soon after **gcc** was created, programmers started to extend **gcc** to allow front ends for languages other than C. The first efforts yielded C++, and soon after that, Objective C. These efforts also yielded a Fortran compiler, called **g77**.

If you installed FortranN from the setup program (choose the D disk set), you should have the program **g77**—the Fortran compiler—installed in **/usr/bin**. G is a small program that acts as a front end to **gcc**, calling **gcc** in the proper mode to compile Fortran programs instead of C.

When compiling a file, **gcc** looks at the filename extension and the code in the file (and command-line parameters) to determine what language to use when compiling. At the back end, all languages get converted to Linux object code, so **gcc** handles that part the same for all languages it can compile.

To get a glimpse of what **g77** does, you can use the -v (shorthand for verbose) option to have **g77** print all the commands it executes.

N O T E

Because **g77** really launches **gcc**, you can take advantage of some C-like features. For example, you can have **g77** call the C preprocessor, **cpp**, before compiling your code. This allows you to use the **cpp** constructs such as *#define*, *#ifdef*, and *#include*.

Table 7.2 lists the default file extensions **g77** looks for.

Table 7.2 g77 Fortran file extensions.

Extension	Meaning
.f	Fortran source, with no preprocessing
.for	Fortran source, with no preprocessing
.F	Fortran source, preprocessed by **cpp**
.fpp	Fortran source, preprocessed by **cpp**

If you name your Fortran files ending in a **.F** or **.fpp**, **g77** will run **cpp** first and then compile your code.

Also, because **g77** is based on GNU C, you can use a number of **gcc** command-line parameters, such as **-I** and **-g**, as for **gcc**.

Table 7.3 lists the most common command-line parameters for **g77**.

Table 7.3 G77 command-line parameters.

Parameter	Meaning
-ff90	Use the Fortran 90 dialect
-ffree-form	Allow Fortran 90 free-form source code.
-fno-fixed-form	Same as -ffree-form
-g	Compile in debugging information
-Idirectory	Look for include files in directory
-finit-local-zero	All unitialized local variables and arrays get set to 0

In addition to **g77**, there's a program called **f2c** that converts Fortran code to C. **g77** uses a lot of **f2c** features under the hood. You can also use **f2c** on its own to convert Fortran files into C code.

Objective C

The handy GNU C compiler handles more than Fortran It can also compile Objective C, an object-oriented add-on to C that is most popular on the NeXTStep system. For most Linux usage, C++, another object-oriented add-on to C, has proven far more popular.

All you need to do to compile an Objective C program is to use **gcc** the same way we described in Chapter 2.

You will need one extra command-line option, though, **-lobjc**, to tell **gcc** to use the Objective C libraries.

Pascal, Modula, and Oberon

All designed by Niklaus Wirth, Pascal, Modula, and Oberon haven't been very popular on UNIX systems. For one thing, UNIX and C are intimately tied together and the UNIX philosophy goes against the grain of Pascal, which tried to prevent programmers from doing potentially harmful things. Even so, you can run all these languages on Linux.

Pascal

Linux takes a somewhat unusual approach with Pascal. Most Linux programmers who use Pascal make use of the **p2c** translator, a tool which converts Pascal source code into C source code. The C code can then be compiled using the GNU **gcc** compiler. If you've installed the **p2c.tgz** package from the D series on the CD-ROM, then you're all set to use **p2c**.

The **p2c** translator is remarkably flexible with its input requirements, accepting several dialects of Pascal. The default dialect is H-P Standard Pascal, but **p2c** will work with Turbo Pascal input files, or will even attempt to translate Modula-2 source code if you provide the appropriate switch on the command line.

To see how **p2c** does its job, lets take a look at **hello.p**, a simple "Hello, World" program written in Pascal:

```
program Hello (input, output);
```

```
begin
  writtenln("Hello, world.");
end.
```

To translate the program run p2c on the file **hello.p**:

```
p2c hello.p
```

This produces an output file named hello.c which contains the following:

```
/* Output from p2c, the Pascal-to-C translator */
/* From input file "hello.p" */

#include <p2c/p2c.h>

main(argc, argv)
int argc;
Char *argv[];
{
  PASCAL_MAIN(argc, argv);
  printf("Hello, world.\n");
  exit(EXIT_SUCCESS);
}

/* End. */
```

To compile this file, you use the GNU **gcc** compiler. Like all **p2c** output, the program must be linked with a special p2c library:

```
gcc -o hello hello.c -1p2c
```

More sample programs for use with **p2c** can be found in the **/usr/doc/p2c** directory.

NOTE There is a GNU Pascal compiler project working on a Pascal front end for the GNU C compiler, but at the time of this writing the version for GNU's latest C compiler was not yet ready. If you're interested in this compiler, you can check out its Internet FTP archive on **kampi.hut.fi** in directory **/jtv/gnu-pascal**.

Modula

The follow-on language to Pascal was Modula-2 and its more object-oriented successor, Modula-3. You can clearly see the Pascal roots for these languages, and they continue the Pascal family tradition. Linux supports both of these languages.

Modula-2

Modula-2 adds the very important concept of *modules* to Pascal. (Very few people ever saw Modula-1.) In addition, with the standardized system module, Modula-2 programmers can write real programs that interface with their operating system, as opposed to standard Pascal, which really can't do much.

Linux comes with the MOCKA Modula-2 compiler, found in the Modula-2 directory on the CD-ROM. **Mc** is the main program for compiling Modula-2 programs.

The **README** file in the **mocka** package contains the instructions for building and installing Modula-2.

The MOCKA Modula-2 sources are actually written in Modula-2, so don't get rid of your binary programs!

WARNING

Modula-3

Modula-3, developed originally by Digital Equipment, continues Modula-2 and adds more object-oriented features, including objects, threads, exceptions, and generic types.

The Modula-3 package, found in the Modula-3 directory of the CD-ROM, comes with a host of goodies. There's an X Window toolkit, a user interface builder and the ability to create networked objects.

The main program for building Modula-3 executables is **m3build**. (Modula-3 uses the term *build* in place of compile.) You can debug your programs with **m3gdb**.

Mm3totex and **m3tohtml** format Modula-3 programs for output to TeX and HTML Web pages, respectively.

Oberon

Just when the world was getting ready for Modula (2 and 3), Niklaus Wirth came up with Oberon, a new language in the Pascal family. Oberon provides even more object-oriented features, but in a minimalist fashion.

Oberon comes out of a project of Wirth's to build a whole new type of workstation (called *Ceres*) that runs the Oberon system, an operating system written in Oberon, instead of UNIX or Windows. This Oberon system has a windowing system different from X (and a lot more primitive), and all programming is done in Oberon—the language.

Oberon the language adds inheritance and some limited object-oriented capabilities to a Modula base but does not go as far as C++ or other truly object-oriented languages. The goal was to keep the language as simple as possible and add only those features that were absolutely necessary.

For Linux, the CD-ROM with the book comes with the **Jacob** Oberon-2 compiler. (*Jacob* is short for Just a Compiler for Oberon-2.)

The **Jacob** compiler supports a number of options that mimic GNU C, such as -*c* to compile a module but not link, and -*I* to specify include directories. The -*h* option provides short online help, which is very useful, as **Jacob** doesn't come with much documentation.

The binary version for Linux and Oberon sources for a number of modules (named with **.ob2** filename extensions) come with **Jacob**, as does a shell script front end, **oc**, that can drive the **Jacob** compiler.

LISP

LISP, short for List Processing (or lots of irritating single parenthesis to its detractors), is another very old computer language commonly used in artificial-intelligence applications.

Linux supports Common LISP, the most important LISP dialect, and the subset of Common LISP included in the **emacs** text editor (see the section on **emacs** in Chapter 2).

Emacs and LISP

If you just want to play around with LISP, the version inside **emacs** may be good enough. If your needs are a little more demanding, you can load the Common LISP package into **emacs** for more features that the standard versions of LISP.

In **emacs**, if you want to use the Common LISP package, simply place the following line at the beginning of your LISP code:

```
(require 'cl)
```

This should force **emacs** to automatically load the Common LISP, or **cl.el** module. If this fails, chances are you didn't install this package when you installed **emacs**.

For most programming tasks, you'll need more than the version of LISP in **emacs**.

Common LISP

Real LISP programmers, of course, require the full-blown Common LISP package. Originally started as Kyoto Common LISP (which you may have heard of), this package is now called GNU Common LISP, or GCL.

To start GCL, simply type **gcl** at the UNIX command line:

```
$ gcl
GCL (GNU Common Lisp)  Version(2.2) Sat May 18
00:03:47 CDT 1996
Licensed under GNU Public Library License
Contains Enhancements by W. Schelter
>
```

If you don't see output like this, then **gcl** was not installed or was installed in the wrong place (a common practice on Linux). By default, **gcl** wants to be installed in **/usr/local/bin** with support files in **/usr/local/lib**.

On some versions of Linux, you'll see an error such as the following:

```
/usr/bin/gcl: /usr/local/lib/gcl-2.2/unixport/saved_gcl:
No such file or directory
exec: /usr/local/lib/gcl-2.2/unixport/saved_gcl:
cannot execute: No such file or directory
```

To get around this on Linux, create the directory **/usr/local/lib/gcl-2.2** and copy the contents of **/usr/lib/gcl-2.2** to **/usr/local/lib/gcl-2.2**. At this point, **gcl** should work fine, and you can type Lisp commands like the following at the > *LISP* prompt:

```
> (+ 4 5)
9
```

Use **Ctrl-D**, the Linux end-of-file marker, to exit **gcl**.

N O T E

Eiffel

Eiffel is an object-oriented programming language developed by Bertrand Meyer and popular among those who worry about the ease at which programmers can shoot themselves in the foot in C++. Because of this, Eiffel differs from C++ in a number of ways, mostly in making the Eiffel language safer than C++.

The major emphasis of Eiffel is on creating working, re-usable components. One of the basic tenets of the language is the idea of design by contract. Using this method, each function—called a *feature* in Eiffel—promises to perform a certain task. The caller, though, must maintain its side of the bargain, forming a type of contract. Eiffel enforces contracts using built-in language constructs for beginning and ending conditions. Before a feature is executed, the beginning condition must be met or Eiffel generates a form of protest over a contract violation called an *exception*. This enforces the caller's requirement that certain conditions be met before calling the feature.

Eiffel also enforces the contract that the feature must perform a certain task by using ending conditions. If these conditions aren't met, the writer of the feature failed, and again Eiffel issues a contract violation exception.

While you could emulate much of this behavior in C or C++ using assertions, Eiffel provides this capability built into the language and makes it much easier to enforce.

Like Java, Eiffel manages memory for you, making the programmer's life a lot easier and removing a major source of errors in C and C++ programs. Because of this, there are no destructors in Eiffel.

Ironically, though, for all of Eiffel's anti-C attitude, Eiffel compilers typically compile Eiffel code to C. The C compiler then executes to compile the resulting C code and ending up with a Linux executable. This is unlike many other languages, such as Fortran, that extend the GNU C compiler to compile new languages. Instead, Eiffel calls your system's C compiler—GNU C for Linux—to compile C code that the Eiffel compiler generates. Thus, Eiffel doesn't need to modify your C compiler.

Small Eiffel

For many years, the development of Eiffel stalled because the language was kept proprietary. This couldn't have come at a worse time, because C++ was rapidly gaining steam when while Eiffel only ran on a few platforms and Eiffel tools were only available from one company. It's not hard to tell which language won the battle for the hearts, minds, and pocketbooks of programmers worldwide.

Luckily, all that has changed. The Eiffel definition is open to the world, and many Eiffel compilers have sprung into existence. By compiling Eiffel programs to C, the Eiffel compiler itself becomes relatively easy to port to multiple platforms, because C seems to run on just about every computer ever invented.

This book comes with an Eiffel package called Small Eiffel, where the *small* comes from trying to make Eiffel as easy to use as SmallTalk, another object-oriented language.

Small Eiffel is located in the **Small Eiffel** directory on the CD-ROM.

Programming in Eiffel

Eiffel looks much more like Ada or Modula than C or C++. This starts in the very beginning with comments, as Eiffel uses two dashes, – –, for comments.

Eiffel also diverges from the UNIX and C concept of using a backslash for special characters, such as \n for a newline; Eiffel uses %N to represent a newline character.

To get a flavor of Eiffel, you can look at the ubiquitous "Hello World" program, shown in **hello.e**:

```
--
-- Hello world in Eiffel.
--
-- Note: Eiffel comments start with --
--

class HELLO

creation main

feature

main is
do
   io.put_string("Hello from Eiffel.%N");
end;

end -- HELLO
```

Most Eiffel programs use a **.e** filename extension.

Compiling Eiffel Programs with Small Eiffel

To compile the **hello.e** Eiffel program, use the **compile** command. To compile and link our Eiffel example, you can use the following command:

```
$ compile HELLO main -o hello
```

The **compile** command converts **hello.e** to the executable named **hello**. In the process, the command results in eight **.c** files (**hello1.c** to **hello8.c**), all of which are compiled by the GNU C compiler. When the files are all compiled and linked, you have a new executable program, **hello**.

You can run **hello**, and you'll see the following highly original output:

```
$ hello
Hello from Eiffel.
```

All that work to make one simple line of output!

The **compile** command requires a few parameters and allows for many options. Each time you compile an Eiffel program, you're required to list the root class, *HELLO* in our example, and the starting, or root, procedure. This is the procedure that gets called when the Eiffel program starts up, sort of like C's *main* function.

In the **hello.e** example, this procedure is named *main*.

Other options to compile get passed directly to the C compiler. For example, the **-o hello** command-line parameter gets passed directly to the C compiler, telling the C compiler the name of the executable program to produce.

Thus, it helps if you've programmed with C before starting Eiffel. If you omit the **-o** command-line parameter, the C compiler outputs an executable program named **a.out**, a name virtually no one uses.

Small Eiffel comes with a number of tools, including the ones listed in Table 7.4.

Table 7.4 Eiffel tools.

Tool	Usage
clean	Cleans up intermediate files produced by **compile**
compile	Compiles Eiffel code to C
compile_to_c	The actual compiler called by **compile**
finder	Helps determine which file contains which Eiffel class
pretty	Reformats your code to make it pretty

For More Information on Eiffel

An overview of Eiffel appears on the Internet at the following URL:

http://www.eiffel.com/doc/manuals/language/intro/

Small Eiffel is located at an Internet site (and on the CD-ROM that comes with this book):

ftp://ftp.loria.fr/pub/loria/genielog/SmallEiffel

At that location, you can get Small Eiffel versions for Linux, UNIX (BSD, HP-UX, Irix, Xenix), NeXT, DOS, OS/2, Windows 95, and Macintosh systems.

Summary

Linux offers a host of programming languages. In fact, Linux offers more languages than most people have ever heard of. Some of the best tools for Linux include Fortran, part of the GNU C compiler, Common LISP, and Eiffel.

Programmer Information Sources

This chapter covers:

- Additional sources of information
- Online-manual pages
- The **man** command
- Documentation
- Frequently asked questions
- How-Tos
- Mini-How-Tos
- The **info** command
- Additional Perl information
- Additional Tcl/Tk information

Looking for the Elusive Needle

Linux comes with a surprisingly large amount of programmer information. The problem is finding it. This chapter covers the main locations for Linux information, which differ from other versions of UNIX.

As you read through this chapter, you'll note many divergent sources of information. One of the main strengths of UNIX and Linux is the huge developer base creating all sorts of neat programs. One of the main drawbacks, especially of Linux, is the wildly divergent set of organizations promoted by various groups and individuals that make up the huge developer base for Linux.

Manual Pages

Linux comes with extensive online manuals that are accessible from the **man** command. Most online manuals are stored in subdirectories under the **/usr/man** directory. A few manuals are stored in **/usr/local/man** (mostly for software that isn't part of the standard Linux distribution that you've loaded onto your Linux system), **/usr/openwin/man** (for Open Look X Window programming information), and **/usr/X11/man** (for X Window programming information).

All these directories should be listed in the *MANPATH* environment variable, which is used by the **man** command to determine where to look for online manuals. The default *MANPATH* on Linux follows:

```
MANPATH=/usr/local/man:/usr/man/preformat:/usr/man:/usr/X11/man:/usr/o
penwin/man
```

Documentation

In addition to the online manuals, Linux comes with an extensive set of documentation in the **/usr/doc** directory. The documents stored in **/usr/doc** tend to provide a lot more expository information than the infamously terse online manuals.

Under **/usr/doc**, you'll find about 80 subdirectories, each for a major Linux program, programming library, or set of programs. Inside these subdirectories, you'll find everything from short **README** files to much longer documents that explain things in much greater depth than the online manuals.

Of particular interest to programmers are the subdirectories listed in Table 8.1.

Table 8.1 Subdirectories in /usr/doc of particular interest to programmers.

Directory	Contains Information on
SlingShot	Using C++ with XView
bash	The Bourne Again shell, **bash**
emacs-19.31	The **emacs** text editor
faq	Frequently asked questions
flex	The flex lexical analyzer
g77	GNU FORTRAN
gawk	GNU **AWK** scripting language
gdb	GNU debugger
gnu-make	GNU **make**
indent	A program for automatically indenting code
jpeg	A library to manipulate JPEG image files
less	A paging program like **more**
m4	A preprocessor like the C preprocessor
p2c	A Pascal-to-C converter
perl5.003	Perl
rcs	Revision Control System
strace	A means to trace execution of system calls
tar	UNIX tape archiver, used for packing files
tcl7.5	Tcl
tclX7.5.0	Tcl with TclX extensions
tcsh	**tcsh** and C shells

continued...

Directory	Contains Information on
texinfo	GNU documentation system
tk4.1	Tcl/Tk
vim	**Vi** editor clone
xpaint	For creating program icons
xpm-3.4c	Library of color bitmap routines

Frequently Asked Questions

The UNIX community contains many frequently asked questions documents, some of more value than others. Basically, each document is tied to a particular subject, such as LISP, and answers the most commonly asked questions posted on the Internet.

You can often find the answers to your questions in such documents. The Slackware Linux distribution includes the frequently asked questions (FAQ) directories listed in Table 8.2.

Table 8.2 Frequently asked questions directories.

Directory	Contains Frequently Asked Questions on
/usr/doc/faq/lang/	C, Objective C, Fortran, Tcl
/usr/doc/faq/lisp/	LISP
/usr/doc/faq/perl/	Perl
/usr/doc/faq/xfaq/	X Window System, Open Look, PEX

How-Tos

In addition to lists of frequently asked questions, Linux popularized a set of documents called How-Tos. Each How-To document describes—as the name implies—how to do something.

While most of these How-To documents describe particular hardware or networking configurations, you'll also find information that is useful in programming in the **/usr/doc/faq/howto/** directory, the main repository of How-To documents. The ELF-HOWTO, on the extended linking format used by Linux, is probably the most useful How-To.

Some How-Tos haven't graduated to prime time yet and are called mini-How-Tos. Stored in the **/usr/doc/faq/howto/mini/** directory, these documents tend to be shorter than the main How-Tos. The most useful document in **/usr/doc/faq/howto/mini/** is the GUI-Development document on the multiple libraries available for creating X Window applications.

Info Tools and Documents

Long before there were How-To documents, and even long before Linux existed, the GNU project developers created what they thought would be the future of publishing and hypertext: a format called **info**. They used the **info** format to document all GNU tools, including the **emacs** text editor, the GNU C and C++ compilers, and **gdb**, the GNU debugger.

The info format supports hypertext links. If you use **emacs** as your text editor, you won't have any problem viewing **info** documents because **emacs** automatically supports the **info** format.

For the rest of us, though, there's a program called **info**. This program purports to display the **info** documentation stored in the **/usr/info** directory, but we've found **info** to be one of the most frustrating programs in existence.

To start **info**, simply type **info** at the shell command prompt:

```
$ info
```

You'll see a top-level display of information and not much more. Typing **?** will call up **info**'s help in a split-screen mode, but nothing on the first page will be of much use at all (hence our initial frustration with **info**).

Items marked with an asterisk (*) are topics you can call up via the **m** key. Type **m** and then the name of the topic you want. For example, in the following **info** text, there are four topics: **gcc**, **cpp**, **make**, and **gdb**:

```
Developing in C and C++:
==========================
* GCC: (gcc).          Information about the gcc Compiler
* CPP: (cpp).          The C Preprozessor
* Make: (make).        The GNU make Utility
* GDB: (gdb).          The GNU Debugger
```

To get around in **info**, try the commands listed in Table 8.3.

Table 8.3 Some useful info commands.

Command	Action
f	Follows, jumps to topic name underneath cursor
m *topicname*	Jumps to *topicname*
n	Jumps to next topic in list, if you've visited topics
p	Jumps to previous topic in list—if you've visited topics
q	Quits **info**.
Alt-f	Jumps forward one word
Alt-b	Jumps backward one word
Ctrl-l	Jumps to next topic
Space	Presents next page of information

WARNING

While you can navigate around in the **info** file, the **info** utility is quirky. It often refuses to bring up a topic depending on how you navigated to the location.

In general, **info** is a very frustrating program. Luckily, all the **info** files in **/usr/info** are text files that can be viewed with any text editor.

N O T E

The files in **/usr/info** may be compressed with GNU **zip**. If the files have names ending in **.gz** or **.Z**, you can uncompress the files with the **gunzip** command.

The **/usr/info** directory contains a lot of information on the topics listed in Table 8.4.

Table 8.4 Information in /usr/info.

Tool	Files
GNU assembler	as.info*
GNU binary utilities	binutils.info*
Common LISP	cl*
GNU **configure**	configure.info*
diff	diff.info*
dired **emacs** mode	dired*
ediff	ediff*
emacs	emacs*
GNU file utilities	fileutils*
find	find.info*
flex	flex.info*
Fortran	g77.info*
gawk	gawk.info*
GNU C compiler	gcc.info*
GNU debugger	gdb.info*
DBM database library	gdbm.info*
Performance profiling	gprof.info*
The **info** program	info*
ld linker	ld.info*
Standard C library	libc.info*
C++ library	libg++.info*
m4 preprocessor	m4.info*
make	make.info*
tar archiver	tar.info*

You may have installed some other GNU programs, libraries, or tools that use **info** files. If so, look in **/usr/local/info** for more **info** files.

Programming Language Information

Most of the information on the GNU C and C++ compilers resides in **/usr/info** with the rest of the GNU documentation.

Other languages provide more information in separate directories. For example, GNU Common LISP provides some information in the **/usr/lib/gcl-2.2/doc** directory.

Perl

Like the GNU tools, Perl comes with its own documentation format, called *POD* for Plain Old Documentation. POD files are ASCII text files with some basic formatting. Handy Perl scripts convert the POD files into UNIX manual files—accessible by the **man** command—or HTML Web documents, which you can view from any Web browser.

The main Perl directories are **/usr/lib/perl5/man** for online manuals (discussed earlier in the section on manuals) and **/usr/lib/perl5/pod** where the Plain Old Documentation source files reside.

Even though the Perl manuals are available to the **man** command (try **man perl**, for example), take a look in **/usr/lib/perl5/man**. There are many Perl modules that you can use to dramatically speed development of Perl scripts.

Tcl

Linux includes extensive information on Tcl as well as a set of Posix extensions called *TclX*. In addition to the online manuals, you probably want to check in a number of directories in **/usr/doc**.

Table 8.5 lists the relevant directories.

Table 8.5 Extra Tcl information.

Directory	Contains Information on
/usr/tcl**X**/7.5.0/help/tcl/	TclX extensions
/usr/doc/tcl7.5	Tcl (very small amount of information here)
/usr/doc/tk4.1	Tk toolkit
/usr/tk**X**/4.1.0/help/tk	TclX Tk extesions

Finally, also check **/cdrom**, the default mount point for any CD-ROMs you've mounted. Often, you'll find even more sources of information on your Slackware CD-ROMs.

Summary

This short chapter covered the additional sources of information that can be of use to the Linux programmer. There's really no single depository of information with Slackware Linux, but by looking at several different sources—FAQs, HOWTOs, and online-manual pages—you can learn more about the programming tools discussed throughout this book.

Debugging on Linux

This chapter covers:

- The Linux debugger, **gdb**
- Compiling for debugging
- **Gdb** commands
- Using debuggers to find errors in your programs
- Debugging a buggy example program
- Mapping **dbx** commands to **gdb**
- **Emacs** and **gdb**
- The **xxgdb** graphical front end to **gdb**
- Debugging Java applications with **jdb**
- Useful **jdb** commands

Debugging

Linux provides most of the GNU set of freeware programming tools, including the GNU debugger, **gdb**, which can help a lot at tracking bugs in your code. This chapter covers debugging and testing C, C++, and Java applications with Linux tools.

Debuggers

The **gdb** debugger provides a fairly mature tool for tracking down bugs in your code. You'll find **gdb** of most use when for some reason your program crashes and you cannot figure out why. A debugger like **gdb** allows you to set breakpoints, which stop the program's execution at a particular point of interest. Once stopped, you can examine variables and verify if your program is working correctly or—hopefully—find out why the program misbehaves. You can also examine variables and data structures.

In order to work with **gdb**, though, you first need to recompile your programs with the proper debugging options.

Compiling with Debugging Options

Most C and C++ compilers aim at creating compact, fast executables. This means any extraneous data, like symbol table information, gets removed. In order for a debugger to work, though, your program must contain this extra information.

The main purpose of this debugging information is to provide a connection between the code that gets executed and the actual location—usually a line number—in a source-code file. Remember, programs get compiled to machine code, so all relations to the original lines of code gets lost in the compilation process.

To place debugging information in your code, you need to use the *-g* command-line parameter to **cc** or **gcc**. For example:

```
$ cc -g -c prog.c
$ cc -g -o prog prog.o
```

The above commands compile the file **prog.c** and places debugging information into the resulting executable, **prog**.

You need to compile each source code file with the *-g* command-line parameter, and you need to link together the whole program also using the *-g* command-line parameter. The *-g* command-line parameter is required for both steps.

The Linux GNU C compiler allows you to mix the *-O* optimize option with the *-g* debugging information option. Virtually all other UNIX C compilers prohibit this combination, so you may be under the false impression that you can't do this on Linux as well. With the GNU compiler, though, you can track down errors coming from the optimizer as well as in your code.

Don't use the *-s* command-line parameter when compiling for debugging. This option strips out all the symbol table information you just added with the *-g* option.

Using Gdb

Once you've compiled your program with debugging information, you can then use **gdb** to debug your program. You can use **gdb** in two ways. You can run the debugger on your program, execute the program from within the debugger, and then watch what happens. Or, you can use a debugger in post-mortem mode. In this mode, after your program has crashed and core dumped—leaving a file named **core**—the debugger can examine both your program's executable file and the **core** file to try to figure out what went wrong.

In post-mortem debugging, you often won't be able to find out exactly what happened, but you can usually get a stack trace. A *stack trace* shows the chain of function calls where the program exited so ungracefully. Such information can usually pinpoint where the program went down. You can see a stack trace in **gdb** with the **bt**, **backtrace**, or **where** commands (all perform the same operation).

In most cases, the stack trace shows you the offending routine. It's up to you then, to examine the parameters to the routine that crashed the program and the variables inside the routine to see if you can determine what went wrong.

To use **gdb** with a program, the basic syntax follows:

```
gdb program
```

Program is the name of your program. **Gdb** runs in text mode and presents you with a prompt (*gdb*), at which you enter **gdb** commands.

Trying Out Gdb

To help get a better feel for how **gdb** works, we'll start with a small C program sporting a clear bug and show how you can help track down the source of the problem with **gdb**. In addition, this bug appears in a LessTif graphical program, so you can get an idea of how to debug X Window applications as well.

The following C program, **bugmotif.c**, contains a nasty bug: it writes to a *NULL* pointer, using the string copying function *strcpy*. The code for **bugmotif.c** follows:

```
/*
 * bugmotif.c
 * A first Motif program.
 */

#include <Xm/Xm.h>
#include <Xm/Label.h>      /* XmLabel */
#include <Xm/PushB.h>      /* XmPushButton */
#include <Xm/PanedW.h>     /* XmPanedWindow */

/*
 * This function has a bug.
 */
void bugCB(Widget widget,
    XtPointer client_data,
    XtPointer call_data)
```

```
{   /* bugCB */

    /* Copy data into NULL pointer. */
    strcpy(client_data, "This is a string.");

}   /* bugCB */

/*
 * exitCB() is a callback for the
 * pushbutton widget we create below.
 */

void exitCB(Widget widget,
    XtPointer client_data,
    XtPointer call_data)

{   /* exitCB */

    exit(0);

}   /* exitCB */

int main(int argc, char** argv)

{   /* main */
    Widget          parent;
    XtAppContext    app_context;
    Widget          pane, push, bug;
    Arg             args[20];
    int             n;

    /*
     * Initialize the X Toolkit
     * Intrinsics.
     */
    n = 0;
    parent = XtAppInitialize(&app_context,
            "LinuxProgramming",         /* app class */
            (XrmOptionDescList) NULL,    /* options */
            0,                           /* num options */
            &argc,                       /* num cmd-line */
            argv,                        /* cmd-line opts */
            (String*) NULL,              /* fallback rsc */
```

```
                args, 0);

    /*
     * Create a paned window
     * widget to contain all
     * the child widgets. Note that
     * the paned window is a child
     * of the top-level parent.
     */
    n = 0;
    pane = XmCreatePanedWindow(parent,
        "pane", args, n);

    /* We manage the pane later, below. */

    /*
     * Create a pushbutton widget,
     * as a child of the paned window.
     */
    n = 0;
    push = XmCreatePushButton(pane,
            "quit", args, n);

    /*
     * Set up a callback for the
     * pushbutton widget.
     */
    XtAddCallback(push,              /* widget */
        XmNactivateCallback,        /* which callback */
        (XtCallbackProc) exitCB,    /* callback function */
        (XtPointer) NULL);          /* extra data to pass */

    /*
     * Manage the pushbutton widget.
     */
    XtManageChild(push);

    /*
     * Create push button to exercise a bug.
     */
    n = 0;
    bug = XmCreatePushButton(pane,
            "bug", args, n);
```

```
    XtAddCallback(bug,            /* widget */
        XmNactivateCallback,      /* which callback */
        (XtCallbackProc) bugCB,   /* callback function */
        (XtPointer) NULL);        /* extra data to pass */

    XtManageChild(bug);

    /*
     * Note that we manage the paned window
     * container *after* we fill in the
     * child widgets of the pane.
     */
    XtManageChild(pane);

    /*
     * Realize widget hierarchy, which
     * brings the top-level widget
     * (and all its children) to
     * reality. That is, create windows
     * for the widgets and then map
     * the windows.
     */
    XtRealizeWidget(parent);

    /*
     * Process events forever.
     */
    XtAppMainLoop(app_context);

    return 0;

}   /* main */

/* end of file bugmotif.c */
```

This program also uses a resource file. Save this file as **LinuxProgramming** and place the file in your home directory:

```
! Resource file for bugmotif.c
!
! Global Resources
!
! Set font.
```

```
*fontList:  lucidasans-12

! Set program background color.
*background:  lightgrey

! Set up window title.
*title:     Bug

! Widget-Specific Resources
!
! Set up quit message.
*quit.labelString:   Push here to exit

*bug.labelString:  Generate Bug

! end of resource file
```

The program **bugmotif.c** is very similar to the **exmotif.c** program in Chapter 3. You can save yourself some typing if you already input that program by just adding the new push-button widget—named *bug*, and the new callback—*bugCB*.

The **bugmotif.c** program should compile fine, using a command like the following:

```
$ cc -g bugmotif.c -o bugmotif -I/usr/X11R6/include \
    -L/usr/X11R6/lib -lXm -lXt -lX11
```

In order to compile and link this program, you must have installed the LessTif libraries and include files, described in Chapter 3 in the section on "Installing LessTif." You also need the X Window System libraries and include files, which you can install with the **setup** program if you have not yet done so. See Chapter 1 for more on using the **setup** program.

Remember to compile your code with the -g command-line parameter. If you don't **gdb** will not be able to provide you with much information about what went wrong.

When you run the program, you'll see a window like that shown in Figure 9.1

Figure 9.1 The simple buggy LessTif program.

When you click on the **Generate Bug** button, the program crashes with the following error message:

```
Bus error (core dumped)
```

Our program, of course, has a problem. You need to run the program from **gdb** to find out more information about what went wrong. Use a command like the following:

```
$ gdb bugmotif
```

You can then run this LessTif program from within **gdb** using the **run** command:

```
(gdb) run
```

When you click on the **Generate Bug** button, the program will crash, and **gdb** will print a message like the one below:

```
Program received signal SIGBUS, Bus error.
0x7afd12e4 in strcpy ()
```

Since you're running the program from within **gdb**, though, the debugger keeps running and you can try to find out what happened, even though the program itself crashed. To figure out where the program crashed, you can use the **back trace** command, as shown below:

```
(gdb) backtrace
#0   0x7afd12e4 in strcpy ()
#1   0x217c in bugCB (widget=0x4001d660, client_data=0x0,
```

```
      call_data=0x7b03b25c "") at bugmotif.c:23
#2   0x7ae11f10 in XtCallCallbackList ()
#3   0x7ad1e028 in ActivateCommon ()
#4   0x7ad1dd8c in Activate ()
#5   0x7ae3d60c in HandleActions ()
#6   0x7ae3df90 in HandleComplexState ()
#7   0x7ae3e080 in _XtTranslateEvent ()
#8   0x7ae1cc90 in DispatchEvent ()
#9   0x7ae1d7d0 in DecideToDispatch ()
#10  0x7ae1d8a8 in XtDispatchEvent ()
#11  0x7ae1dd08 in XtAppMainLoop ()
#12  0x2410 in main (argc=1, argv=0x7b03aacc) at bugmotif.c:152
```

The top function is the deepest in the stack trace, *strcpy*, and is the likely cause of the error. At the very least, you should check out the top function for bad data. You must be careful, though, as the function where the error manifests itself is not always the function where the error occurred.

Sometimes the top function comes from a library for which you don't have the source code, such as *strcpy* in this case. (While you may have the full source code for Linux, few users load the whole thing.) In that case, you need to go down the stack trace until you find a function for which you have the source code—*bugCB* in our case. Start looking for errors at this point. Note that **gdb** provides the file name and line number.

Viewing Code Files

In **gdb**, you can call up the file in which the error occurred—if you have the source code—and then set break points in the code.

A break point is a place you want **gdb** to break—or stop. Usually you set a break point at a line number in a file, or at the beginning or end of a particular function.

In the example above, we probably want to break at line 23 in the file **bugmotif.c**, where the error occurs. We show the **gdb** commands to do this below:

```
(gdb) break 23
Breakpoint 1 at 0x2164: file bugmotif.c, line 23.
(gdb) run
```

```
The program being debugged has been started already.
Start it from the beginning? (y or n) y
```

This time, when you click on the Generate Bug button, **gdb** stops the program at line 23, the current break point, as shown below:

```
Breakpoint 1, bugCB (widget=0x4001d660, client_data=0x0,
    call_data=0x7b03b25c "") at bugmotif.c:23
23          strcpy(client_data, "This is a string.");
```

The **list** command shows the source code around the break point:

```
(gdb) list
18
19      {   /* bugCB */
20
21
22          /* Copy data into NULL pointer. */
23          strcpy(client_data, "This is a string.");
24
25      }   /* bugCB */
26
27
```

At this point, you can print out the value of variables, as shown below:

```
(gdb) p client_data
$1 = (String) 0x0
```

The **c** command continues execution:

```
(gdb) c
Continuing.

Program received signal SIGBUS, Bus error.
0x7afd12e4 in strcpy ()
```

The program crashes, of course, after the break point.

Gdb Commands

Gdb supports a huge number of commands, with many ways to accomplish the same goal. The main **gdb** commands appear in Table 9.1.

Table 9.1 The most important gdb commands.

Command	Meaning
bt	Display stack trace.
Backtrace	Display stack trace.
info stack	Display stack trace.
quit	Quits debugger.
run	Runs program.
run *args*	Runs program with *args* as command-line parameters.
break *func*	Sets breakpoint at start of function *func*.
break *line_num*	Sets breakpoint at line number in current file.
list *filename.c:func*	View *filename.c*.
c	Continue from breakpoint.
step	Execute next program line.
print *var*	Print value of variable *var*.
help	Get help.

Gdb provide extensive online help with the **help** command. This is very useful because few programmers are more than casual users of any debugger program.

Dbx Emulation

Most commercial versions of UNIX don't ship with **gdb** (nor any of the GNU tools). Instead, the most common debugger is called **dbx**. However, Linux doesn't ship with **dbx**. If you're used to working with **dbx** on another UNIX box, however, you'll find that **gdb** can be an acceptable substitute. Because **dbx** is so popular on other versions of UNIX, **gdb** supports the most common **dbx** commands in addition to the **gdb** set. Table 9.2. helps you map between **dbx** and **gdb** commands.

Table 9.2 Mapping dbx commands to gdb.

dbx	gdb	Meaning
where	where	Display stack trace.
quit	quit	Quits debugger.
run	run	Runs program.
run *args*	run *args*	Runs program with *args* as command-line parameters.
stop in *func*	break *func*	Sets breakpoint at start of function *func*.
stop at *line_num*	break *line_num*	Sets breakpoint at *line number*.
file *filename.c*	list *filename.c:func*	View *filename.c*.
c	c	Continue from breakpoint.
step	step	Execute next program line.
print *var*	print *var*	Print value of variable *var*.
help	help	Get help.

In many cases, such as with the **where** command, **gdb** and **dbx** both support the same command. Of course, **gdb** also supports other commands for the same task, such as **backtrace**.

WARNING

For some bizarre reason, **gdb** will accept without complaint the **dbx** break point commands **stop in** and **stop at**. But, while **gdb** accepts the commands, these commands do *not* set break points in **gdb**. So, even though **gdb** supports many **dbx** commands, don't get lulled into believing that **gdb** supports all **dbx** commands.

In both **dbx** and **gdb**, you can just type in the first letter of a command, or a short abbreviation, instead of the full text. For example, **q** for quit or **bt** for **backtrace**. Be careful, though, for commands that start with the same letter.

Graphical Front Ends To Debuggers

You may find the **gdb** syntax tedious and long for a nice integrated environment with a graphical debugger, such as ships with Microsoft's

C++ compiler. Linux comes with **xxgdb**, a graphical front end to **gdb**. **Xxgdb** launches **gdb** from a UNIX pipe and then presents the **gdb** output to you in a friendlier format, as shown in Figure 9.2.

Figure 9.2 The xxgdb front end to gdb.

You may find **xxgdb** a lot friendlier than **gdb**. In addition, even with the graphical environment, you can still execute **gdb's** text-mode commands from the main **xxgdb** window.

Emacs and Gdb

The **M-x gdb** command in **emacs** starts the **gdb** debugger from within an **emacs** window.

> **NOTE**
>
> Remember that the **Meta** key in **emacs** is the **Alt** key on your keyboard, so that **M-x gdb** is really **Alt-x gdb** on your keyboard. All the **emacs** documentation will state **M-x gdb**, though.

When you run this **emacs** module, you'll see a new menu on the menu bar, if you're running the graphical X Window version of **emacs**. This new menu, *Gud* (no, we don't know what the name means either), contains a number of choices for commonly used debugging commands, like **Set Breakpoint** and **Remove Breakpoint**.

Using the **bugmotif.c** program from previously in this chapter, **emacs** automatically places the cursor at the place the program crashes, as shown in Figure 9.3.

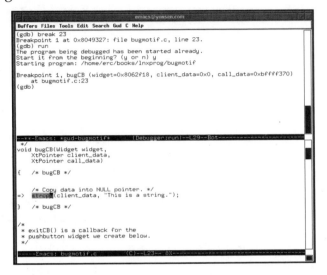

Figure 9.3 Emacs in gdb mode.

This tight integration provides a nice front end to **gdb**.

Other Debugging Techniques

The age-old debugging technique is to place *printf* calls into your code at a strategic location. We use this technique only if the debugger can't tell us what's going on. For example, if your code tries to execute a bad function pointer, **gdb** can't always keep track of where the program failed. If you face errors like this, you may also need to use this low-tech method.

When using *printf* calls for debugging, we usually combine *printf* with the ANSI C __FILE__ and __LINE__ macros, which resolve to the current file (as a string) and the current line (as an integer). This tells you that the program got to a certain line before crashing. The *printf* call usually looks something like the following:

```
printf("%s %d\n", __FILE__, __LINE__);
```

When you run your program, then, you'll see output like that below:

```
bugmotif.c 70
bugmotif.c 87
bugmotif.c 107
bugmotif.c 130
bugmotif.c 141
bugmotif.c 153
bugmotif.c 21
```

Debugging Java Applications

In addition to **gdb**, which debugs C and C++ programs, Java also provides a debugger, built on many of the same assumptions as **dbx**. And, since **dbx** is similar to **gdb**, the Linux debugger, you should be able to move from **gdb** to **jdb** fairly easily.

Jdb, the Java debugger that comes with the Java development kit, is a text-mode application much like **gdb**. Also like **gdb**, you must first recompile your Java code with the **-g** command-line parameter in order to work with a debugger.

To test out **jdb**, we'll revisit the small Java application shown in Chapter 6, which originally came from the Sun Java documentation. The **HelloWorldApp.java** file appears below:

```
/**
 * The HelloWorldApp class implements an application that
 * simply displays "Hello World!" to the standard output.
 */
class HelloWorldApp {
    public static void main(String[] args) {
        System.out.println("Hello World!"); //Display the string.
    }
}
```

To compile this file with debugging information, you can use the following command:

```
$ javac -g HelloWorldApp.java
```

Remember, you must compile your Java code with the -g command-line parameter in order to work with a debugger.

N O T E

You can run this application in the **jdb** debugger:

```
$ jdb HelloWorldApp
Initializing jdb...
0x404c4628:class(HelloWorldApp)
```

The **jdb** debugger acts as both a Java interpreter and debugger, so it can run your Java programs as well as help you find out what's wrong.

At the **jdb** prompt, you can enter any of **jdb's** commands, listed in Table 9.3.

Table 9.3 Jdb commands.

Command	Usage
!!	Repeat last command.
catch *class*	Break on exception for class.
classes	List all classes—a large list.
clear *class:line_num*	Clear break point.
cont	Continue execution from break point.
down *num_frames*	Move down a thread's stack.
dump *object*	Print all object information.
exit	Quits **jdb**.
gc	(Garbage collect) free unused objects.
help	Get information on available commands.
ignore *class*	Ignore exception for class.

continued...

Command	Usage
list *line_num*	Print source code—did not work.
load *class*	Loads class into debugger.
locals	Print all local variables.
memory	List memory usage.
methods *class*	List a class's methods.
print *object*	Print data.
print *object.field*	Print data.
quit	Quits **jdb**.
resume *id*	Resume thread.
run *class args*	Runs program.
step	Execute current line.
stop at *class:line_num*	Set break point at line number in class.
stop in *class.method*	Set break point at method.
suspend *id*	Suspend thread.
threads	List threads.
thread *id*	Set default thread.
threadgroup *name*	Name current thread group.
threadgroups	List thread groups.
up *num_frames*	Move up a thread's stack.
use *source_file_path*	Change source file path.
use	List source file path.
where *id*	List a thread's stack.
where *all*	List all thread stacks.

Because Java is a multithreaded language, this makes the debugger quite complex. Most of the commands in **jdb** relate to threads. It's likely that most of the problems you have with Java will also deal with threads, since concurrent programming is a tough task. The use of threads also makes the stack trace tougher, since each thread has its own stack.

To try out **jdb**, you can enter some of the available commands listed in Table 9.3.

For example, the **methods** command lists out all the methods for a class. When you try this with the example Java application, above, you'll see the following output:

```
$ jdb HelloWorldApp
Initializing jdb...
0x404c4628:class(HelloWorldApp)
> methods HelloWorldApp
void main(String[])
void <init>()
```

You can also run the **methods** command on the built-in Java classes, as shown below:

```
> methods java.io.DataOutput
void write(int)
void write(byte[])
void write(byte[], int, int)
void writeBoolean(boolean)
void writeByte(int)
void writeShort(int)
void writeChar(int)
void writeInt(int)
void writeLong(long)
void writeFloat(float)
void writeDouble(double)
void writeBytes(String)
void writeChars(String)
void writeUTF(String)
```

The command above prints out the methods for the built-in Java class of *java.io.DataOutput*.

You can use the **methods** command to find out a lot about various Java classes, although for the built-in classes, the Java documentation is probably a better bet.

The **dump** command prints out information on a class:

```
> dump HelloWorldApp
HelloWorldApp = 0x404c4628:class(HelloWorldApp) {
```

```
    superclass = 0x404b8018:class(java.lang.Object)
    loader = null
}
```

For objects, the **print** command is less useful than **dump**:

```
> print HelloWorldApp
HelloWorldApp = 0x404c4628:class(HelloWorldApp)
```

Print works much better at printing data members of an object.

You can view the current source-code file path with the **use** command:

```
> use
.:/usr/local/java/bin/../classes:/usr/local/java/bin/../lib/classes.zi
p:/usr/local/java/bin/../bin/../classes:/usr/local/java/bin/../bin/../
lib/classes.zip
```

You can also change the source file path with **use**.

The **memory** command lists the amount of memory used:

```
> memory
Free: 608384, total: 1048568
```

And, most importantly, the **run** command runs the application:

```
> run
run HelloWorldApp
running ...
main[1] Hello World!

The application has exited
$
```

Note that when the application quits, the debugger also quits, which is not always the behavior you want.

Break points in **jdb** work much like those in **gdb**, except that since all functions are members of a class, all break points must be in a class. To set a break point in **jdb**, you can use the following example as a guide:

```
> stop in HelloWorldApp.main
Breakpoint set in HelloWorldApp.main
> run
run HelloWorldApp
running ...
main[1]
Breakpoint hit: HelloWorldApp.main (HelloWorldApp:6)
main[1]
```

In a break point, the **cont** command continues execution:

```
main[1] cont
Hello World!
```

And, the **exit** or **quit** command exits the debugger:

```
> exit
pid 650 status 0
Received sigchild for 650 exit=0
```

This should give you a head start for when you need to debug your Java applications.

Summary

This chapter covers debugging, never a fun task. Linux ships with the GNU debugger, **gdb**. Debuggers help you find out why your program crashed and hopefully tell you where the crash occurred. You can use the text-mode **gdb** interface or the graphical **xxgdb** interface for debugging.

The Java debugger, **jdb**, debugs Java programs.

More Linux Commands
for Programmers

This chapter covers:

- Merging file differences with **sdiff**
- Searching for data within files with **grep**
- Finding files with **fin**d
- Examining binary files with **objdump**
- Checking executables for shared library usage with **ldd**
- Managing software versions with RCS
- Making screen shots of your Linux programs
- Converting image files
- Editing bitmap icons
- Logging on to remote machines
- Copying files to and from remote machines

Handy Linux Commands

This chapter covers miscellaneous Linux commands that help programmers in their day-to-day tasks. These commands include utilities for comparing files, merging changes from the differences between files, finding files, searching for data within files, creating online manual files, capturing screen images, creating icon bitmaps, and connecting to remote machines.

Comparing Files

As you modify program source code and use source code modified by others, you'll often need to figure out what changed between one version and another. To help with this, you can use the Linux **diff** command.

Diff compares two files and prints out a terse listing of the differences. The basic syntax follows:

```
diff options file1 file2
```

Diff is most useful when used on two modified versions of the same original file. With two completely different files, **diff** will then detect every line as being different and that won't be of much use. **Diff** works best at finding the small areas where files differ. (It also works well at comparing large chunks of data. For instance, you can specify directories instead of files and have **diff** compare the two.)

For example, suppose you have the following text in a file:

```
Online manual entries are
specially-formatted ASCII text
files, using commands from the
nroff/troff family of text
formatters. nroff and troff
are both Linux text formatters
that come from the dark ages of
UNIX history. Documents in
this format contain dot commands,
```

```
commands that start with a
period.
```

And, let's say you compare that file against a similar, but slightly changed file, as shown below:

```
Online manual entries are
specially-formatted ASCII text
files, using commands from the
nroff/troff family of text
formatters. nroff and troff
are both completely evil text formatters
that come from the dark ages of
UNIX history. Documents in
this format contain cryptic dot commands,
commands that start with a
period.
```

With short files like these, you can point out the differences with a quick glance. For long program source files, though, this is a much harder task. Using **diff** automates the process.

If you run **diff** on the two files above, you'll see the following output identifying the differences:

```
$ diff file1 file2
6c6
< are both Linux text formatters
---
> are both completely evil text formatters
8,10c8,10
< UNIX history. Documents in
< this format contain dot commands,
< commands that start with a
---
> UNIX history. Documents in
> this format contain cryptic dot commands,
> commands that start with a
```

Lines that start with < represent something different in the first file passed to diff. Lines starting with > represent something different in the second file passed to diff. The --- lines separate the different sections.

Diff is the most-used file comparison program. Other Linux utilities that act similarly to **diff** include **cmp**, **comm**, **diff3**, and **sdiff**.

Other File-Comparison Programs

Cmp does nothing if the files are the same. If the files differ, **cmp** prints out the first byte position where the files differ. Because **cmp** isn't a text-only utility, you can use **cmp** to detect differences in binary files. For example, if you want to compare executable files, you can use **cmp**.

For example, if you have two programs that should be the same, but you're unsure if they differ, you can use **cmp** to compare the files. If we compare two bitmap editing programs, the command would be as follows:

```
$ cmp bitmap /usr/X11/bin/bitmap
bitmap /usr/X11/bin/bitmap differ: char 25, line 1
```

The -*l* command-line parameter tells **cmp** to print out every different byte, instead of just the first difference. If there were no difference between the two files, there would be nothing returned at all.

With the -*s* (short for silent) command-line parameter, **cmp** will just return a status code telling whether the files are the same or different. You can then use this as a simple test in shell scripts for **Makefiles** to determine if two files are the same.

Table 10.1 lists the status codes returned by **cmp**.

Table 10.1 Status codes returned by **cmp**.

Code	Meaning
0	The files are identical
I	The files differ
> I	An error occurred

Comm is not very useful for programmers, because **comm** only compares sorted files (and source code files are rarely sorted). With two sorted files, **comm** prints out the lines that are the same, the lines that exist only in the first file and the lines that exist only in the second file.

Diff3, on the other hand, is quite useful for programmers. **Diff3** compares three files, not two. The main purpose for **diff3** is to compare two changed files with a common baseline. For example, if two programmers need to modify the same file—to fix different bugs, perhaps—when both sets of changes are complete, you need to integrate both files back into the mainline version of your code. This is where **diff3** comes in. **Diff3** compares your changes against the older baseline to another programmer's changes.

The basic syntax for **diff3** follows:

```
diff3 mine baseline yours
```

You compare your changes—*mine*—with the older *baseline* against someone else's changes—*yours*.

When comparing files, **sdiff** brackets its output with the markers shown in Table 10.2.

Table 10.2 How sdiff brackets output.

Marker	Meaning
====1	File 1 differs
====2	File 2 differs
====3	File 3 differs
====	All three files differ

To show **diff3** in action, we can make another modification to the above example baseline file used above, as follows:

```
Boring manual entries are
specially-formatted ASCII text
files, using commands from the
nroff/troff family of text
formatters. nroff and troff
are both Linux text formatters
that come from the dark ages of
```

```
UNIX history. Documents in
this format contain dot commands,
commands that start with a
period.
```

We now have three versions of the same file. Two files were modified from the same base version. Now, you can use **diff3** to try to find where each of the modified files differs from the baseline.

When you run **diff3** on these three files, you'll see the following output:

```
====3
1:1c
2:1c
  Online manual entries are
3:1c
  Boring manual entries are
====1
1:6c
  are both completely evil text formatters
2:6c
3:6c
  are both Linux text formatters
====1
1:8,10c
  UNIX history. Documents in
  this format contain cryptic dot commands,
  commands that start with a
2:8,10c
3:8,10c
  UNIX history. Documents in
  this format contain dot commands,
  commands that start with a
```

Sdiff compares two files and tries to merge the changes. This is also most useful when trying to combine two changed versions of a source code file. The basic syntax follows:

```
sdiff -o output_file from_file to_file
```

Sdiff acts interactively, writing the merged output to the *output_file*. So, for each difference **sdiff** prints out the differences and then you need to choose which version to use to place into the output file. The left version comes from the first file passed to **sdiff**, the *from_file*. The right version comes from the second file passed to **sdiff**, the *to_file*. For example:

```
$ sdiff -o changes from_file to_file
Online manual entries are  | Boring manual entries are
%
```

At the **sdiff** % prompt, you need to enter one of **sdiff** commands, as listed in Table 10.3.

Table 10.3 Sdiff commands.

Command	Usage
l	Uses the left version
r	Uses the right version
e l	Edits then use the left version
e r	Edits then use the right version
e b	Edits then use the left and right versions concatenated
e	Edits a new version
s	Silently includes common lines
v	Verbosely includes common lines
q	Quits

In the example above, we can specify to use the left side, with the **l** command:

```
% l
```

The data chosen gets written to the output file, identified with the *-o* command-line parameter.

Sdiff presents a prompt for each difference. You can accept either side as is, or edit the changes, using the commands listed in Table 10.3.

Searching For Files in All the Wrong Places

The two main Linux searching tools are **grep** and **find**. **Grep** searches for data inside a file while **find** looks for files by name (although you can literally do anything with **find** if you wish).

Searching For Data In Files

Grep, short for generalized regular expression parser, searches Linux text files for patterns and prints out the lines that match. We find **grep** useful for tracking down files that use a particular function or data type.

The basic syntax for **grep** follows:

```
grep pattern files
```

The most simple pattern is a literal string. For example, to search through all the *.c* files in the current directory that have the text string *XtAppInitialize*, you could use the following command:

```
$ grep XtAppInitialize *.c
exaw.c:     parent = XtAppInitialize(&app_context,
exmotif.c:     parent = XtAppInitialize(&app_context,
```

The *-i* command-line parameter tells **grep** to ignore case when searching. Uppercase and lowercase strings will match, as will mixed case strings. Since C function names are case sensitive, the *-i* command-line parameter isn't of great use unless the data structures and functions use similar prefixes but different case. For example, with the X Window toolkits discussed in Chapter 3, many toolkits use variations on *arg* for arguments, such as *XV_INIT_ARGC_PTR_ARGV*, a constant from the XView toolkit; *Arg*, a data structure used in the Xt Intrinsics, and *XtSetArg*, a macro also used in the Xt intrinsics.

To track down all uses of *arg*, *ARG*, *Arg*, and every combination thereof in the *.c* files in the current directory, you can use the following command:

```
$ grep -i ARG *.c
exaw.c:int main(int argc, char** argv)
exaw.c:    Arg            args[20];
exaw.c:        parent, args, n);
exaw.c:        XtSetArg(args[n], XtNx, 10); n++;
xview.c:int main(int argc, char** argv)
xview.c:        xv_init(XV_INIT_ARGC_PTR_ARGV,
xview.c:            &argc, argv,
```

GNU **grep** on Linux supports regular expressions and extended regular expressions, two different syntaxes to describe just about every combination of text imaginable.

The -G command-line parameter tells **grep** to treat the expression as a regular expression. The -E command-line parameter tells **grep** to treat the expression as an extended regular expression. Unlike other versions of **grep**, with GNU **grep** there is no loss of functionality when using the plain regular expressions. The online-manual entry for **grep** describes regular expressions in detail.

Finding Files

Linux systems present a huge, complicated directory structure, making it hard to find files tucked away somewhere on disk. For example, when looking for a file or directory, it's hard to tell whether the file should be in **/var** or in **/usr**. There are simply a lot of files that make up a complete Linux system. And, to be fair, Linux provides a huge number of tools, including more programming tools than most other UNIX systems provide, that justify the large number of files.

To help track down files, you can use the **find** command.

The **find** command searches from a top-level directory and applies a test to each file it looks at. If the file passes the test, **find** performs an action on the file. This action can be to backup the file to tape, or simply print out the file name and full path if there's no other option defined.

The simplest case is to use **find** to track down files with a given name. For example, if your hard disk starts filling up, you need to remove some files. If you've been programming a lot, chances are a number of **core** files—created when Linux programs crash—remain strewn around your hard disk. **Core** files tend to be large, so getting rid of them could potentially free a lot of space. In addition, you normally don't need to keep **core** files, so removing these kinds of files can be considered eliminating the low-hanging fruit. There's no need to decide whether or not you really need some feature. You don't need the **core** files.

We can use **find** to track down **core** files. You could also use **find** to remove these files, but watch out. There may be legitimate files named **core**. (Strangely enough this is true. The one that first comes to mind is **/dev/core**.) So, instead of having **find** remove the files, we'll just ask **find** to print out the names, so we can go back and examine which ones should be deleted. Any **core** file in a system directory should be treated with care. In many cases, it will mean a system program crashed and left behind a **core** file (and can therefore be safely eliminated). In other cases, you won't be sure whether the system needs the file or not. When in doubt, don't delete.

To find all files named **core**, starting in the root directory, and print out the paths for the file names, you can use the following command:

```
$ find / -name core
```

The above command starts searching in the root directory, /. The test **find** applies is the **-name core** test, which passes if the file checked has a name of core.

When you run this command, you'll see output like the following:

```
/dev/core
find: /var/spool/cron: Permission denied
find: /var/spool/atjobs: Permission denied
find: /var/spool/atspool: Permission denied
find: /var/lib/uucp/taylor_config: Permission denied
find: /var/lib/uucp/hdb_config: Permission denied
find: /var/games/sasteroids: Permission denied
find: /usr/doc/emacs-19.31: Permission denied
/usr/src/linux-2.0.0/net/core
find: /root: Permission denied
find: /cdrom/programming/xforms/xforms/contrib: Permission denied
find: /cdrom/programming/xforms/xforms/DEMOS: Permission denied
/proc/sys/net/core
/home/erc/programs/wunderword/core
```

```
/home/erc/programs/wunderweb/core
/home/erc/programs/wundercalc/core
```

Any **core** file under your home directory or a subdirectory should be safe to delete. **Find** also complains about every directory that it didn't have permission to enter. If **find** can't look in the directory, you most likely won't be able to delete files there either.

Find's Test

Find tests each file to see whether or not to perform something—the action—on the file. The most common test used by **find** include the following.

```
-name pattern
```

The *-name* test checks for files with a given name. You can use the name directly, such as the **-name core** test used above, or you can use wildcards like ***** and **?**. If you use wildcards, you should enclose the argument in quotation marks, ", because the **bash**, **tcsh**, or other Linux shells will expand the wildcards before the test gets passed to find. For example, to print out all find ending in *.c* starting in your home directory, you can use the following command:

```
$ find ~ -name "*.c"
/home/erc/src/untab/detab.c
/home/erc/src/untab/untab.c
/home/erc/src/undos/undos.c
```

Note the double quotation marks around the *"*.c"* pattern to prevent the shell from expanding the pattern to include just the files that match in the current directory.

Find includes other useful tests as well. The *-newer* test tells **find** to look for files that are newer than the file given on the command line. The syntax appears as follows:

```
-newer filename
```

For example:

```
$ find ~ -newer file1
/home/erc/.tkdesk/_history
/home/erc/.tkdesk/_layout
/home/erc/.tkdesk/_bookmarks
/home/erc/books/lnxprog/file3
/home/erc/books/lnxprog/file2
/home/erc/books/lnxprog/file4
```

The above command looks for files starting in your home directory that have been changed more recently that the file **file1**.

The **-user** test looks for files owned by a particular user. The syntax follows:

```
-user username
```

For example, to look for files in **/usr/local** that are owned by a particular user, say user *erc*, you can use a command like the following:

```
$ find /usr/local -user erc
```

The *-fprint* action prints the names of the files found into the given filename. This is useful if you run **find** in the background and want to save **find**'s output. The syntax follows:

```
-fprint filename
```

The *-exec* action executes a Linux command for each file found. Due to the syntax of **find**, you need to place a {} in the command to execute to signify the current file name. The syntax follows:

```
-exec command ;
```

The command continues until the semicolon (;).

N O T E
Your shell likely interprets a semicolon to be a command separator and won't pass the ; on to **find** unless you escape the semicolon with a backslash, making it \;.

If **find** responds with the following error, then you need to use the \; to end the command:

```
find: missing argument to '-exec'
```

For example:

```
$ find ~ -newer file1 -exec /usr/bin/wc -l {} \;
```

The above command lists the number of lines in each file found.

Find needs the full path to commands it executes, **/usr/bin/wc** in this case. Just using **wc** fails.

N O T E

The online manual entry for **find** describes a large number of options should you want to get into greater depth on **find**.

Tools To Work With Object Modules and Binary Files

A lot of programming work results in the creation of object modules, whether left as .o files or combined in a library archive (.*a* file).

The **objdump** command prints out information about Linux object modules and libraries. The basic syntax follows:

```
objdump option object_files
```

Each time you call **objdump** you need to pass an option, which determines what information gets printed out. The simplest option is the --*file-headers* command-line parameter. (Note the two dashes, **--**, at the start of the --*file-headers* command-line parameter.)

When you call **objdump** with --*file-headers* command-line parameter, **objdump** prints out basic information about the type of object module (ELF versus a.out, and so on). You can use a command like the following:

```
$ objdump —file-headers cmdlne.o

cmdlne.o:     file format elf32-i386
```

```
architecture: i386, flags 0x00000011:
HAS_RELOC, HAS_SYMS
start address 0x00000000
```

 NOTE While most Linux commands use a single dash, -, for command-line parameters, **objdump**, like many GNU tools, supports both short parameters marked with a single dash and longer command-line parameters marked with a double dash, --, such as *--file-headers*.

The _d (or *--disassemble*) command-line parameter disassembles the object code and prints out the Linux assembly code for all the functions in the file.

The *--source* command-line parameter goes further and tries to combine disassembly with the actual source code from the C or C++ program. For example, using just the disassembly of one C++ function (a class destructor), you have the following output:

```
$ objdump —source cmdlne.o

        virtual ~CommandLine() { }     // Does nothing.
000000f4 <_._13CommandLine> pushl   %ebp
000000f5 <_._13CommandLine+1> movl    %esp,%ebp
000000f7 <_._13CommandLine+3> movl    0x8(%ebp),%eax
000000fa <_._13CommandLine+6> movl    $0x0,0x8(%eax)
00000101 <_._13CommandLine+d> testb   $0x1,0xc(%ebp)
00000105 <_._13CommandLine+11> je      0000010d <_._13CommandLine+19>
00000107 <_._13CommandLine+13> pushl   %eax
00000108 <_._13CommandLine+14> call    00000109 <_._13CommandLine+15>
0000010d <_._13CommandLine+19> movl    %ebp,%esp
0000010f <_._13CommandLine+1b> popl    %ebp
00000110 <_._13CommandLine+1c> ret
```

The example above shows how much code gets executed for a NULL inline virtual destructor on a C++ class, which is a surprisingly large amount of code for a function that does nothing.

The *--debugging* command-line parameter prints out the debugging information compiled into an object file with the *-g* command-line parameter to **gcc**:

```
$ objdump —debugging cmdlne.o
```

```
static struct __vtbl_ptr_type /* id 1 */ _vt.13CommandLine[2] /* 0x0
*/;
void _._13CommandLine (CommandLine *this /* 0x8 */, int __in_chrg /*
0xc */)
{ /* 0xf4 */
  /* file ../kh/util.h line 211 addr 0xf4 */
  { /* 0x101 */
    register CommandLine *this /* 0x0 */;
  } /* 0x101 */
} /* 0x111 */
```

The --*syms* command-line parameter prints out symbol table from the object file, as follows:

```
$ objdump —syms cmdlne.o

cmdlne.o:      file format elf32-i386

SYMBOL TABLE:
00000000 l     df *ABS*  00000000 cmdlne.cxx
00000000 l      O .rodata        00000010 _vt.13CommandLine
00000000 l      d .rodata        00000000
00000000 l      d .text  00000000
00000000 l      d .data  00000000
00000000 l      d .bss   00000000
00000000 l      d .note  00000000
00000000 l      d .stab  00000000
00000000 l      d .stabstr       00000000
00000000 l      d .comment       00000000
00000000 g      F .text  00000022 Argv__C13CommandLinei
00000024 g      F .text  0000006b FindOption__C13CommandLinePci
00000000        *UND*  00000000 strcmp
00000000        *UND*  00000000 strncmp
00000090 g      F .text  00000029 Option__C13CommandLinePci
000000bc g      F .text  00000035 OptionAndData__C13CommandLinePci
000000f4  w     F .text  0000001d _._13CommandLine
00000000        *UND*  00000000 __builtin_delete
```

The -*a* command-line parameter prints out information on each file added to a library archive, as shown below:

```
$ objdump -a libkh.a
In archive libkh.a:
```

```
cmdlne.o:      file format elf32-i386
rw-r--r-- 501/100    7316 Oct 12 15:03 1996 cmdlne.o

compos.o:      file format elf32-i386
rw-r--r-- 501/100   47620 Oct 12 15:03 1996 compos.o
```

Checking for Shared Libraries

While **objdump** concentrates on object files, **ldd** works with executables. **Ldd** prints out the dynamic libraries that an executable program depends on. This is very useful in trying to determine why a Linux executable won't work. You'll often find a shared library mismatch.

For example, the **netscape** application depends on the following Linux shared libraries:

```
$ ldd /home/erc/bin/netscape
    libXt.so.6 => /usr/X11R6/lib/libXt.so.6.0
    libSM.so.6 => /usr/X11R6/lib/libSM.so.6.0
    libICE.so.6 => /usr/X11R6/lib/libICE.so.6.0
    libXmu.so.6 => /usr/X11R6/lib/libXmu.so.6.0
    libXpm.so.4 => /usr/X11R6/lib/libXpm.so.4.3
    libXext.so.6 => /usr/X11R6/lib/libXext.so.6.0
    libX11.so.6 => /usr/X11R6/lib/libX11.so.6.0
    libdl.so.1 => /lib/libdl.so.1.7.14
    libc.so.5 => /lib/libc.so.5.3.12
```

Ldd is very useful for Motif programs. since most Linux systems don't come with the Motif libraries, you need to get binary versions of Motif applications that have been statically, rather than dynamically linked to the Motif library, **libXm.a**. The **netscape** application mentioned above is indeed a Motif application, but the version used here was linked statically to the Motif library. All the other X libraries used are dynamically linked, except for Motif.

Examining Binary Files

The **hexdump** program prints out binary files in a variety of forms that are a lot easier to read that raw binary data. Despite the name, hexdump supports octal, hexadecimal, and ASCII output.

The major options are whether to display the file using octal, decimal or hexadecimal characters. You can control this with the options given in Table 10.4.

Table 10.4 Hexdump's formatting options.

Option	Format
-b	Octal
-c	Character
-d	Two-byte decimal
-o	Two-byte octal display
-x	Two-byte hexadecimal

For example, the single-byte octal format results in a print-out like the following:

```
$ hexdump -b cmdlne.o | more

0000000 177 105 114 106 001 001 001 000 000 000 000 000 000 000 000
000
0000010 001 000 003 000 001 000 000 000 000 000 000 000 000 000 000
000
0000020 230 027 000 000 000 000 000 000 064 000 000 000 000 000 050
000
0000030 017 000 014 000 125 211 345 213 105 010 213 125 014 205 322
174
0000040 017 071 020 176 013 213 100 004 213 004 220 211 354 135 303
220
0000050 061 300 211 354 135 303 215 066 125 211 345 127 126 123 213
165
```

The numbers on the far left of each line are the byte addresses in the file, in hexadecimal.

In two-byte hexadecimal output format, you'll see output like the following:

```
$ hexdump -x cmdlne.o | more
```

```
0000000    457f    464c    0101    0001    0000    0000    0000
0000
0000010    0001    0003    0001    0000    0000    0000    0000
0000
0000020    1798    0000    0000    0000    0034    0000    0000
0028
0000030    000f    000c    8955    8be5    0845    558b    850c
7cd2
```

In ASCII character mode, you'll see output like the following:

```
$ hexdump -c cmdlne.o | more

0000000 177   E   L   F 001 001 001  \0  \0  \0  \0  \0  \0  \0  \0
\0
0000010 001  \0 003  \0 001  \0  \0  \0  \0  \0  \0  \0  \0  \0  \0
\0
0000020 230 027  \0  \0  \0  \0  \0  \0   4  \0  \0  \0  \0  \0   (
\0
```

Note the leading ELF in the file above, starting with the second byte. This stands for the ELF object-file format.

Managing Versions with RCS

Version control is the task of managing revisions to software. You can make this task as hard or as easy as you'd like, but sooner or later every software project needs some way to manage revisions to files. You need to be able to back out of changes and recover a previous version in the case that something new doesn't work out. You need to be able to ensure that you don't lose changes like bug fixes. And, you need to be able to manage the case where more than one person needs to edit the same file, somehow merging the changes together when complete. If you've released software, you need the ability to fix bugs reported on one release while working on the next release. In fact, you may release interim maintenance versions of your software—based on minor changes to the most recent release, all the while adding bells and whistles for the next release. With any significant software project, you need to do all this and more.

RCS is the main method for managing versions on Linux. With RCS, you're able to:

- Store and retrieve different versions of the same file.
- Maintain a history of all versions of each file in the RCS system.
- Recreate an earlier version of your software, say release 1.0, restoring all files to their state as of that version.
- Use a check-in and check-out system to prevent two users from editing the same file at the same time.
- Help merge separate revisions of the same file.
- Help identify revisions.

How Version Control Systems Work

All version control systems maintain a form of database for each file you want to control. Virtually all of these files are source code files—that is, text. If you use third-party libraries, you may sometimes need to archive binary files, most usage of version control tools sticks to text files.

At certain times, normally then you're at a good stopping place and things work, you may want to make a snapshot or checkpoint for your files, placing the files into the version control system's database. Whenever you make a checkpoint, you're saving a version of your files that you can recover at some later time.

If you're using a manual form of version control, checkpointing your code requires you to make a copy of the current directory hierarchy and archive that copy somewhere. While this may work for small projects, it soon becomes unworkable for large projects. You normally need something more.

RCS: The Revision Control System

RCS provides the main version-control suite for Linux. It includes a number of utilities for working with files under version control, and an established convention for numbering versions and creating branches. When you installed Slackware Linux, you were prompted to install RCS. If you did not, you'll need to go back to the **setup** program and do so.

RCS scales quite well, going from simple check in and check out control to allowing you to add version labels and manipulate the versions of your code in complicated ways. That's a great feature of RCS. You can get started with very little effort and just a few simple commands.

The Only RCS Commands You Really Need

For most usage, you really only need to create the **RCS** directory and use two RCS commands. To get started with RCS, you need to create a directory named **RCS** in each directory where you have files you want to manage versions. Usually, this is every source code directory. Create a directory named **RCS**:

```
$ mkdir RCS
```

The next step is to check in all your source code files for the first time, placing each file under version control by RCS. To do this, you can use the following command:

```
$ ci -u filename.c
RCS/filename.c,v  <--  filename.c
enter description, terminated with single '.' or end of file:
NOTE: This is NOT the log message!
>> Initial version
>> .
```

When you first check in a file, **ci**, short for check in, prompts you for a descriptive message. Your message may span a number of lines and continues until you enter a period all alone on the line to end the message.

When you check in the same file again, **ci** prompts you for a log message, which you enter the same way and end with a period all alone on the line.

The **ci** command copies the file into the RCS directory, with a ,*v* extension. When you first check in a file, the ,*v* file contains the full text of the original file, plus any RCS log messages. When you check in later versions, the ,*v* file changes. RCS stores all the revision history for the file in the ,*v* file. RCS keeps the full text of the latest version, and the differences necessary to recreate any earlier version.

By keeping the full text of the latest version, RCS assumes you'll most likely want to check out the latest version. Checking out earlier versions involves more work, as RCS must recreate the earlier versions from the difference information stored in the ,*v* file.

By keeping only the differences for the earlier versions, RCS saves you a lot of disk space, at a price in slower access times for earlier versions.

The **ci** command also removes the file from the current directory, which can be disconcerting. The -*u* command-line parameter takes care of this and checks out the file again, in unreserved mode. An unreserved file has read-only permissions.

Any number of users can check out files unreserved (read-only). Only one user at a time can check out a file for editing (read-write). Such a file is said to be reserved or locked in RCS terminology.

To check out a file for editing, use the **co** command with the -*l* (for lock) command-line parameter, as shown below:

```
$  co -l filename.c
RCS/filename.c,v  -->  filename.c
revision 1.1 (locked)
done
```

The **co** command, short for check out, checks out the file from RCS. **Co** generates an error if someone already has the file checked out in reserved mode. The -l command-line parameter creates a lock on the file. This ensures that no one else can check out the file while you have the file locked, and it gives you a read-write version of the file in the current directory.

When you're done editing the file, and want to store the current version of the file in RCS, check the file back in with the **ci** command, as shown below:

```
$ ci -u filename.c
RCS/filename.c,v  <--  filename.c
new revision: 1.2; previous revision: 1.1
enter log message, terminated with single '.' or end of file:
>> Latest version.
>> .
done
```

Again, you're prompted for a log message, ending with a period in a line of its own. (Normally, you'll want a more descriptive message than the one shown above.) The *-u* command-line parameter keeps a read-only copy of the file in the current directory. This is the same as using **co -u** to check out a file unreserved.

More RCS Commands

RCS offers more than the simple check in and check out commands. RCS extends the ci and co commands with a number of command-line parameters. In addition, RCS offers a number of other useful commands for controlling your source code. Table 10.5 lists the most important RCS commands and their command-line parameters.

Table 10.5 RCS commands.

Command	Meaning
ci -l *filename*	Check in *filename*, then check out again and lock
ci -u *filename*	Check in *filename*, then check out again unlocked (read-only)
ci -i *filename*	Initial check in for *filename*, won't work if already checked in
ci -m*Message filename*	Check in *filename*, uses Message as the log message
co -r *filename*	Check out a file for read-only use
co -l *filename*	Check out a file for modification

continued...

Command	Meaning
rcs -u *filename.c*	Abandon changes and uncheck out *filename.c*
rcs -l *filename.c*	Check out without overwriting *filename.c*
$ co -r3.5 -l *filename.c*	Check out a particular version, 3.5 in this case
rlog *filename.c*	View RCS log for *filename.c*
$ rlog -R -L -l*username* **RCS/***	Lists all files locked by user *username*

For beginners, the only commands to worry about are **ci -u**, which checks a file in and then retrieves a read-only copy of the file, and **co -l** which checks out a file, locking the file from modification by other users.

The RCS Directory

Each directory you keep source code in needs an **RCS** subdirectory. Inside the RCS subdirectory, RCS keeps all of its version information. This makes it extremely important for you to back up the contents of all the **RCS** directories. Remember, these directories contain the crown jewels of your source code.

Inside each **RCS** directory, you'll see a, *v* file for each file in the source code control system, for example:

```
$ ls RCS
Makefile,v        khdata.h,v       khevent.h,v      khstring.h,v
kh.h,v            khdebug.cxx,v    khiter.cxx,v     khtest.cxx,v
khcompos.cxx,v    khdebug.h,v      khrect.cxx,v     khtypes.h,v
khdata.cxx,v      khdraw.h,v       khstring.cxx,v   khwidget.cxx,v
```

Working in Groups With RCS

If you work alone, you normally create an **RCS** subdirectory in each source code directory. If you work in a group, you need to share the **RCS** directories, because that's where RCS stores all the version and locking information.

The usual procedure is to create source code directories on a shared disk, usually a network-mounted disk. Inside each of these source code directories, you place the crucial **RCS** subdirectories.

When working, though, you do not work in the shared directories. Instead, you make your own directory hierarchy—without the RCS directories—somewhere within your own account. This is called creating a *local work area*. Despite the fancy name, all you're doing is mirroring the main set of directories. When you do this, you need to use slightly more complicate RCS commands to check out files and check them back in.

What you need to do is refer to the exact filename in the **RCS** directory, in the shared location. For example, to check out a file from a shared **RCS** location and place the checked-out file into the current directory—called your local work area, you can use a command like the following:

```
$ co -l /shared_source/RCS/khiter.cxx,v
/shared_source/RCS/khiter.cxx,v  -->  khiter.cxx
revision 1.2 (locked)
done
```

Note the ,v at the end of the filename in the command above. You need to refer to the exact name in the shared **RCS** directory, called **/shared_source/RCS** for the purposes of this example. You're free to place your source code anywhere you want.

When you check the current directory, you should see the file you checked out, as shown below:

```
$ ls
khiter.cxx
```

In order to work in this mode, you normally need to check out all files unreserved, using the **co -u** command. This is how you get a starting set of files into your local work area.

To check the file back in, you need to use a command like the following:

```
$ ci -u /shared_source/RCS/khiter.cxx,v
new revision: 1.3; previous revision: 1.2
enter log message, terminated with single '.' or end of file:
>> Fix bug # 7089
```

```
>> .
done
```

All your RCS commands need to refer to the source files in the proper shared directories. Because this makes for more complicated RCS commands for all users, what most people do is create utility shell scripts for working with RCS. These shell scripts hide the location of the shared source code RCS repositories and make for much easier commands. For example, here's a shell script, called **mycheckin**, to check in files into the shared source code base:

```
#!/bin/sh
ci -u /shared_source/RCS/$1,v
```

The *$1* gets replaced with the filename you pass on the command line. To mark this file as executable, you need to run the **chmod** command. For example:

```
$ chmod +x mycheckin
```

Then, to check in a file, all you need to do is pass the name of the file to the **mycheckin** shell script, as shown below:

```
$ mycheckin khiter.cxx
new revision: 1.3; previous revision: 1.2
enter log message, terminated with single '.' or end of file:
>> Fix bug # 7089
>> .
done
```

The shell script to check out files is also quite simple. The mycheckout script follows:

```
#!/bin/sh
co -l /shared_source/RCS/$1,v
```

You can use these scripts by changing the **/shared_source** directory to the name of the directory where you keep the **RCS** subdirectory. If you use multiple **RCS** directories, perhaps one for each source code library, you'll need to change the shell scripts shown above to reflect your directory organization. This makes for more complicated shell scripts, but is relatively easy to accomplish.

Checking the RCS Log

Whenever you check a file into RCS, the **ci** command prompts you for a log message. You can then view these messages with the **rlog** command, as shown below:

```
$ rlog khwidget.cxx
RCS file: RCS/khwidget.cxx,v
Working file: khwidget.cxx
head: 1.2
branch:
locks: strict
access list:
symbolic names:
keyword substitution: kv
total revisions: 2;      selected revisions: 2
description:
Initial RCS version
----------------------------
revision 1.2
date: 1996/10/05 09:48:02;  author: erc;  state: Exp;  lines: +2 -1
Call khData constructor.
----------------------------
revision 1.1
date: 1996/09/22 13:59:31;  author: erc;  state: Exp;
Initial revision
```

The **rlog** command supports some command-line parameters to get different information about the files managed by RCS. The *-L* command-line parameter forces **rlog** to only look at files that are checked out. The *-l* command-line parameter allows you to specify only files locked by a particular user. The *-R* command-line parameter tells **rlog** to merely list the RCS file name.

You can combine these command-line parameters as follows:

```
$ rlog -R -L -lerc RCS/*
RCS/khstring.cxx,v
RCS/khstring.h,v
RCS/khtest.cxx,v
```

The above command lists out all files locked by user erc.

Abandoning Changes

If you've made changes to a file and things haven't worked out, you can abandon changes made to a checked out file with the **rcs -u** command:

```
$ rcs -u filename.c
```

The **-u** command-line parameter to **rcs** unchecks out a file.

Locking Without Overwriting

When you check out a file with the co command, RCS generates a version of the file from the data stored in the RCS directory and writes this new file into the current directory. This can be a problem if you have modified the file without checking it out. You shouldn't do this, but may get into a situation where you need to apply changes already made to a file that hasn't been properly checked out.

To get around this problem, you can use the **rcs -l** command:

```
$ rcs -l filename.c
```

The *-l* command-line parameter to **rcs** locks the file, but does not overwrite the file with the latest version from the **RCS** directory.

Breaking Locks

If someone else has a file reserved, then RCS prevents you from checking out that file in reserved (read-write) mode. You can always check out a file unreserved to get a read-only copy.

Sometimes, though, you need to edit a file checked out by someone else. For example, if you discover a critical bug and need to fix it now. In this case, you need to break the lock on the file held by the other user. To do this you use the same **rcs -u** command to uncheck out a file, but you uncheck out a file checked out by someone else. For example:

```
$ rcs -u khtest.cxx
RCS file: RCS/khtest.cxx,v
Revision 1.3 is already locked by erc.
Do you want to break the lock? [ny](n): y
State the reason for breaking the lock:
(terminate with single '.' or end of file)
>> Sorry, I need to fix Bug # 7076 NOW
>> .
1.3 unlocked
done
```

When you break the lock on a file held by someone else, that person gets an email message containing the reason you gave for breaking the lock. For example:

```
From: Eric Foster-Johnson <efj@yonsen.com>
Subject: Broken lock on khtest.cxx,v
Your lock on revision 1.3 of file
/home/erc/src/toolkit/kh/RCS/khtest.cxx,v
has been broken by efj for the following reason:

Sorry, I need to fix Bug # 7076 NOW
```

Version Numbers

RCS applies a version number to each revision of a file you check in, starting with version 1.1. After version 1.1, the next revision is 1.2, then

1.3 and so on. If these version numbers are fine, you need to nothing, as RCS automatically updates version numbers when you check files out.

To start the next major revision, such as 2.1, you can use the following command-line parameters when checking a file in:

```
$ ci -r2.1 filename.c
```

You can also use the following shortcut:

```
$ ci -r2 filename.c
```

When you later check in the file, it will have a version number of 2.1.

Extracting Particular Versions

To check out a particular version, such as 3.5, you can use the following command:

```
$ co -r3.5 -l filename.c
```

If you want to check out the latest 3.n version, you can use the following command:

```
$ co -r3 -l filename.c
```

By default, **co** always checks out the highest regular version, i.e., 3.6. If you want to check out a different version, you need to use the -r command-line parameter.

Branching

You can use RCS to create a branch in the source-code tree. Much like on a tree, a branch diverges from the main source-code trunk. For example, if you're still finishing version 1.0 of your software but another team has already started long-term projects on version 2.0, chances are you need to branch the source code tree. You still need to be able to fix bugs on the version 1.0 branch and the other team needs to be able to check in files on their version 2.0 branch.

To create a branch in RCS, you add an extra digit to the revision number when checking a file out. For example, to create a branch off of revision 1.6, you'd use a command like the following:

```
$ co -l -r1.6.1 filename.c
```

The above command actually creates revision number 1.6.1.1. Revision numbers nested this deep tell you you're working on a branch.

In general, branching is an advanced topic and you should become familiar with RCS before attempting to create one. Look at the online manual entries for **co**, **rcs**, **rcsdiff**, **rcsfile**, **rcsmerge**, and **rcsintro** for more information on branching.

Placing RCS IDs in Your Code

You can use RCS to automatically update your source code files with information from the RCS log. By convention, RCS looks for specially-formatting text strings in your code using the format of *$string$*. The most common such string is *Id*. If you place *Id* in your source code files, RCS expands the *Id* part to include the RCS filename, revision number, date, time, username of the person making the changes and the RCS state (usually *Exp*) of the file.

In most cases, place the *Id* into a comment. For example:

```
/* $Id$ */
```

When you check in a file with a *$string$* message that RCS understands, RCS expands the message. For example:

```
/* $Id: khwidget.h,v 1.3 1996/10/05 13:22:20 erc Exp $ */
```

This allows you to keep RCS information up to date inside your files.

If you place the *Id* string inside a comment, this won't get compiled into the executable program (unless you use Tcl or another interpreted language). Sometimes, you want to place RCS versioning information into your binary executable files. To do this, you can add code like the following to your source files:

```
static char rcsid[] = "$Id$";
```

The name of the variable, *rcsid*, is just a convention.

The static character array will get compiled into your C and C++ programs.

To see the RCS *Id* strings in files, you can use the **ident** program. **ident** searches for *$string$* constructs in files and prints them out. For example:

```
$ ident khwidget.h
khwidget.h:
     $Id: khwidget.h,v 1.3 1996/10/05 13:22:20 erc Exp $
```

Ident also works on binary files as well, for example:

```
$ ident khtest

khtest:
     $Id: khtest.cxx,v 1.4 1996/10/05 13:31:51 erc Exp $
```

The Id string first gets expanded when you next check in the file.

N O T E

Other *$string$* keywords include *$Author$*, *$Date$*, *$Header$*, *$Locker$*, *Log*, *$Author$*, *$Name$*, *$RCSfile$*, *$Revision$*, *$Source$*, and *$State$*.

Checking the Differences Between Versions

To compare the differences between versions of the same file, you can use **rcsdiff**. In its simplest form, **rcsdiff** displays the differences between the current file and the last version checked in. The syntax follows:

```
$ rcsdiff filename.c
```

For example:

```
$ rcsdiff khstring.h
===================
RCS file: RCS/khstring.h,v
retrieving revision 1.1
diff -r1.1 khstring.h
48c48
<         khString(const char* cstring);
---
>         khString(char* cstring);
67a68
>                 // Returns 0 if there are problems.
70,71c71,73
<                 // Convert string value to double
<         operator double() const;
---
>                 // Convert string value to float
>                 // Returns NAN (not a number) if there are problems.
>         operator float() const;
```

You can also explicitly name the revisions you want to compare, as shown below:

```
$ rcsdiff -r1.4 -r1.2 khtest.cxx
```

The example above compares revision 1.4 with revision 1.2 of the file **khtest.cxx**. The ability to specify a revision number is very handy when you need to merge changes created on two RCS branches.

Merging Versions

Rcsdiff helps show you differences between versions. **Rcsmerge** tries to combine the differences of three versions together. The basic syntax follows:

```
rcsmerge -rAncestor -rDescendent -p filename.c > combined_file
```

The **-r** command-line parameters tell **rcsmerge** which versions to use when merging. The basic task of **rcsmerge** is to merge the current checked-out file with another version of the file on a different branch. The *Ancestor* version names the revision number for an ancestor version. This ancestor must be common to both the current version of the file—the one you've checked out—and the *Descendent* version.

For example, if your current **filename.c** is at version 1.8, and you need to merge the changes made on the 1.7.1 branch into this file, you can use a command like the following:

```
$ rcsmerge -r1.7 -r1.7.1.5 -p filename.c > combined_file
```

The above command tries to merge all the changes made on the 1.7.1 branch—through revision 1.7.1.5 with the changes in the current file.

The *-p* command-line parameter tells **rcsmerge** to send the combined changes to standard output (the screen) instead of overwriting the **filename.c**. In most cases, you redirect the output to a new file.

Rcsmerge is rather tricky. We suggest you use the *-p* command-line parameter to output all changes to another file instead of overwriting your working file.

WARNING

Rcsmerge does as good as it can at merging the changes between the files. There's no perfect way to combine files like this, though, so you need to carefully examine the **combined_file** output by the above command. Sometimes, the merger goes perfectly. Other times you'll see amusing results.

WARNING

Rcsmerge is the trickiest part of the whole RCS system. Be very careful with it.

Using RCS From Emacs

Emacs provides a special RCS mode, allowing you to check out files, check them back in, and perform other RCS commands from within **emacs**.

In most cases, **C-x v v** will do the next right thing. If a given file is read-only, then **C-x v v** will check it out. If you have the file already checked out, then **C-x v v** will check the file in. Table 10.6 lists the major VC commands in emacs.

Table 10.6 RCS commands in emacs.

Command	Action
C-x v v	Do next logical thing: check out, check in, etc.
C-x v l	Show version log
C-x v u	Uncheck out; revert the previous version
C-x v h	Insert RCS *Id* header at cursor
C-x v d	Run the **dired** directory mode, with RCS extensions

Working with Image Files

Most every modern program these days sports a GUI windowed interface. Many applications present toolbars with bitmap images. In addition, program documentation often includes screen shots of the application in use.

Making Screen Shots on Linux

The very useful **xv** program provides the best Linux tool for viewing, manipulating, and converting images. About the only thing **xv** can't do is bitmap editing. You can crop images, manipulate the colormap, shrink and expand images, as well as convert any image into a variety of formats: BMP (Windows), FITS, GIF, Iris RGB, JPEG, PostScript, PM, PPM, PGM, PBM (raw and ascii), Sun rasterfile, Targa, TIFF, XBM, and XPM.

N O T E The **xv** program is shareware, even though it's part of the Slackware distribution. You should register your copy.

Xv also supports making screen shots on Linux. To make a screen shot from **xv**, first launch the program:

```
$ xv &
```

Then, press the rightmost mouse button inside the main **xv** window. You should see the Xv Controls window appear, as shown in Figure 10.1.

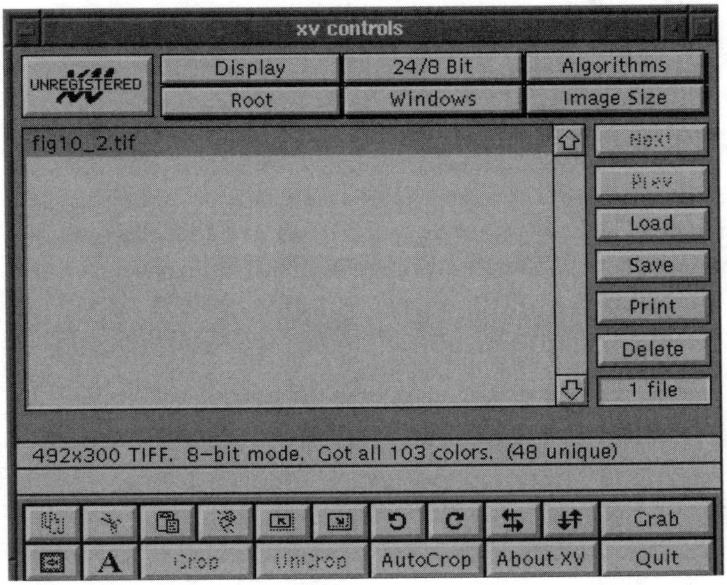

Figure 10.1 The xv controls window.

Now, select the button marked **Grab**. You'll see the Xv Grab window, shown in Figure 10.2.

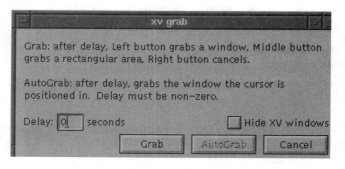

Figure 10.2 The xv grab window.

To take the screen shot, click on the Grab button in the Xv Grab window. Now, click on the window to capture with the leftmost mouse button. The window's border should flash. After the second beep, **xv** has captured the image.

If you need to capture more than one top-level window at the same time, you can click on the root window to capture the whole screen. After that, you will want to crop the image to just show the windows of our program.

N O T E

The **xv** main window should display your captured image. You can now manipulate the image and save it to disk in one of the formats listed previously.

From the Xv Controls window, the Image Size menu allows you to enlarge or shrink the image. You can also crop the image. Select the area of the image you want to retain, using the leftmost mouse button. Then, click on the Crop button. The handy AutoCrop button crops the window to the nearest border, very useful for touching up after you crop an image.

Xv also helps manage your images with the neat visual schnauzer window, shown in Figure 10.3. Call up the visual schnauzer window from the Windows menu.

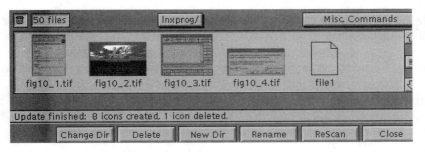

Figure 10.3 xv's visual schnauzer.

The visual schnauzer shows small thumbnail images for each image file in the given directory. This window is also useful for managing files. You can move, delete, rename and examine files, all with simple mouse commands.

Converting Images

In addition to **xv**, which converts many image formats, Linux includes JPEG image tools for converting images. The **cjpeg** program compresses an image file into the JPEG image format. **Cjpeg** supports conversion to JPEG from BMP, GIF, PPM (PBMPLUS color format), PGM (PBMPLUS gray-scale format), and Targa.

Because JPEG images are compressed, converting to JPEG can save you a lot of disk space over other formats, such as GIF (which is also compressed, but generally not as much as JPEG images).

JPEG compression reduces image quality, though, so if this is an issue, you may not want to convert to JPEG.

You can control the quality in a JPEG file, using the *-quality* command-line parameter to **cjpeg**. The *-quality* value goes from 0, the worst, to 100, the best. The default is 75, which works for most image files. Any value about 95 does not really add much the image quality.

For example, to convert a GIF image file to JPEG, you can use the following command:

```
$ cjpeg -quality 75 mryuk.gif > mryuk.jpg
```

In the example above, a 86286 byte GIF image becomes a 33326 byte JPEG image. Using a quality value of 25, the image shrinks to 14718 bytes, but at a very noticeable loss of quality.

The **djpeg** program works the opposite of **cjpeg**. **Djpeg** decompresses a JPEG image and converts the image into another format. **Djpeg** supports fewer options than **cjpeg** and only supports the BMP, GIF, PGM, PPM, GIF, and Targa output formats.

Creating Program Icons

Technically, all X Window icons must be monochrome image files. The most common format for these bitmap images are the X Bitmap format, supported by the X Library functions *XCreateBitmapFromData*, *XReadBitmapFile*, and *XWriteBitmapFile*, which create a bitmap from bitmap data, read in a bitmap file and write out a bitmap file.

The X bitmap file format cleverly looks like a snippet of valid C code:

```
#define icon_width 16
#define icon_height 16
static unsigned char icon_bits[] = {
   0xff, 0xff, 0x01, 0x80, 0xfd, 0xbf,
   0x05, 0xa0, 0xf5, 0xaf, 0x15, 0xa8,
   0xd5, 0xab, 0x55, 0xaa, 0x55, 0xaa,
   0xd5, 0xab, 0x15, 0xa8, 0xf5, 0xaf,
   0x05, 0xa0, 0xfd, 0xbf, 0x01, 0x80,
   0xff, 0xff};
```

Because of this, you can include X bitmap image data into your C and C++ programs.

You can create X bitmap images with the **bitmap** program, as shown in Figure 10.4.

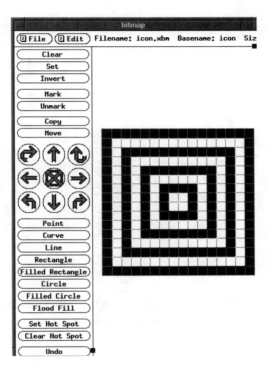

Figure 10.4 Creating an icon with the bitmap program.

When you save a file from the bitmap program, it will contain all ASCII printable characters and look like the example code snippet above.

You can also edit images with the **xpaint** program, shown in Figure 10.5.

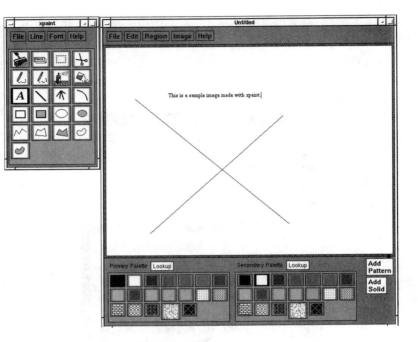

Figure 10.5 Editing images with xpaint.

Xpaint supports GIF, PPM, TIFF, XBM, XPM, XWD, and PostScript output. The main problem is that the **xpaint** program, as many freeware programs, unfortunately, isn't very robust. **Xpaint** tends to crash a lot, so save your work often.

Remote Connections

Since Linux supports networking right out of the box (or CD-ROM as the case may be), you'll often want to connect to other systems, perhaps to test programs on more than one installation.

The **rlogin** command, short for remote login, allows you to log in to a remote machine. The basic syntax requires the host name of the machine you want to log in to, as shown below:

```
rlogin hostname
```

If you want to log in to the remote machine under a different user name than your current user name, use the following syntax:

```
rlogin -l username hostname
```

In the X Window environment, you can combine **rlogin** with the **xterm** command to create a window that logs you on to the remote machine. To do this, you take advantage of **xterm**'s *-e* command-line parameter, which launches a named program instead of the default shell. To combine **xterm** with **rlogin**, then, you need a command like the following:

```
xterm -e rlogin hostname &
```

The above command creates an **xterm** window that will remain for your remote session and disappear when you log off the remote machine. **Xterm** automatically runs the **rlogin** command, which should log you in to the remote machine.

In addition to **rlogin**, Linux also supplies **telnet**, which accomplishes much the same goal, using a different protocol. The syntax of **telnet** is very similar to **rlogin**:

```
telnet hostnme
```

or

```
telnet -l username hostnme
```

Copying Files From Remote Machines

To copy files to and from remote machines, you can use **rcp**—remote copy—or **ftp**—file transfer program.

The **rcp** command works like an extended version of the traditional **cp** command. The syntax is very similar, as shown below:

```
rcp source destination
```

With **rcp**, though, you need to extend the **cp** syntax to include the names of remote machines. This syntax uses the *hostname:filename* format to identify the remote machines. For example, to copy a file named **/tmp/foo** from a machine named *yonsen* into the current directory on the local machine, you can use the following command:

```
$ rcp yonsen:/tmp/foo .
```

To copy the **foo** file from the current machine back to **/tmp** on machine *yonsen*, you can use the following command:

```
$ rcp foo yonsen:/tmp/foo
```

You can also copy files from one remote machine to another, using the *hostname:filename* format to identify both the source and destination files.

NOTE   As with all remote activity, network security may prevent your access. You must have a user account on the remote machine and permission to copy files out of the directory on that machine.

In addition to **rcp**, you can also copy files with the **ftp** program.

The **ftp** program requires you to login to the remote machine and enter commands to copy files. Because **ftp** requires you to login and **rcp** assumes you have a valid user account on the remote machine, you'll often find more security restrictions with **rcp** than with **ftp**. Such security restrictions may dictate which program you use to transfer files.

With **ftp**, the first step is to connect to the remote machine. The syntax follows:

```
ftp hostname
```

Once **ftp** connects, you'll be prompted for a user name and password on the remote machine. (Many systems allow the general public to acquire files by **ftp**. In these cases, you can use a user name of anonymous and your email address as a password.)

After logging in, you'll see the **ftp** prompt:

```
ftp>
```

At this prompt, you need to enter **ftp** commands. You can change directories with the **cd** command, copy files to the remote machine with the put command and copy files from the remote machine to your local machine with the get command. The basic syntax follows:

```
ftp> cd directory
ftp> put filename
ftp> get filename
```

To quit **ftp**, use the **quit** command:

```
ftp> quit
```

Summary

This chapter covered a number of handy Linux commands useful for programmers.

The **diff** command compares two files and prints out the differences. The **sdiff** program extends this to allow you to merge the differences, creating a merged output file with both source file's changes.

You can search for text string matches in files with the **grep** command. While **grep** looks for data within files, **find** searches for the files themselves. You can use **find** to track down files or even to select the files for backup.

The **objdump** program prints out scads of information about object files and libraries. You can use **objdump** to disassemble object files, list the debugging information and print general object file headers, including information on whether or not the file uses the ELF or a.out formats.

The **ldd** command prints out the list of shared libraries required by a Linux executable program.

The very handy **xv** program works great for capturing screen shots and converting image file formats.

You can **login** to remote machines with **rlogin** and **telnet**. You can copy files to and from remote machines with **ftp** and **rcp**.

Linux Hardware Compatibility

This appendix lists the hardware components that have proven to be friendly toward the version of Linux on the accompanying CD-ROM. This appendix is partially based on the information found at *http://sunsite.unc.edu/mdw/HOWTO/Hardware-HOWTO.html*.

Bus

Linux runs on all the major bus architectures—ISA, VLB, PCI, EISA— except for the nonstandard Micro Channel Architecture, found on most IBM PS/2 models. (Not every IBM PC features an MCA bus; the ValuePoint and PS/1 models feature an industry-standard ISA bus.)

Processor

Linux needs at least an Intel 80386-based processor to run efficiently. Don't bother with a 80286- or 80386SX-based PC. If you've got an older PC sitting in the closet and you think it might be neat to recycle using Linux, leave it there, donate it to your local charity, or give it to the kids to bang on. It won't be useful in your Linux adventure.

Basically, any PC built around the Intel 80386 or better (including the i486 and Pentium, as well as chips from AMD and Cyrix) can run Linux. If there is no math coprocessor (which may be an issue in older 80386-based PCs), Linux has built-in FPU emulation.

Graphics Card

Dealing with a graphics card has been one of the most problematic areas of Linux—or rather, XFree86, which serves as the X Window System graphical interface to Linux. XFree86 deals directly with the graphics card and must know everything about the card in a configuration file (such as the amount of RAM it has, the chipset it features, and what modes it supports), putting more stress on you than the average software. Chapter 1 details how to configure XFree86, and in almost every respect this will be the most daunting task you face as a budding Linux user.

We list the graphics cards supported by XFree86 in Tables A.1 and A.2. Table A.1 lists the accelerated chipsets.

Table A.1 Accelerated chipsets supported under XFree86.

Type	Chips and Cards
8514/A	8514/A and true clones
ATI	Mach8, Mach32, Mach64
Cirrus	CLGD5420, CLGD5422, CLGD5424, CLGD5426, CLGD5428, CLGD5429, CLGD5430, CLGD5434
IBM	XGA-2
IIT	AGX-014, AGX-015, AGX-016
Oak Tech	OTI087
S3	86C911, 86C924, 86C801, 86C805, 86C805i, 86C928, 86C864, 86C964, 86C732, 86C764, 86C868, 86C968
Tseng	ET4000/W32, ET4000/W32i, ET4000/W32p
Weitek	P9000
Western Digital	WD90C31, WD90C33

The Cirrus, Oak, and Western Digital cards are supported in the Super VGA server, **XF86_SVGA**. Each of the other types has its own X server.

The Super VGA server, **XF86_SVGA**, supports a whole range of graphics cards and chipsets, which are listed in Table A.2.

Table A.2 Super VGA chipsets supported by the XF86_SVGA server.

Vendor	Chipsets
ARK Logic	ARK1000PV, ARK2000PV
ATI	18800, 18800-1, 28800-2, 28800-4, 28800-5, 28800-6, 68800-3, 68800-6, 68800AX, 68800LX, 88800CX, 88800
Advance Logic Technology	ALG2101, ALG2228, ALG2301, ALG2302, ALG2308, ALG2401 Chips & 65520, 65530, 65540, 65545
Cirrus Logic	CLGD5420, CLGD5422, CLGD5424, CLGD5426, CLGD5428, CLGD5429, CLGD5430, CLGD5434, CLGD6205, CLGD6215, CLGD6225, CLGD6235, CLGD6410, CLGD6412, CLGD6420, CLGD6440
Compaq	AVGA

continued…

Vendor	Chipsets
Genoa	GVGA
MX	MX68000, MX680010
NCR	77C22, 77C22E, 77C22E+
Oak	OTI067, OTI077, OTI087
RealTek	RTG3106
Tseng	ET3000, ET4000AX, ET4000/W32
Western Digital/Paradise	PVGAI
Western Digital	WD90C00, WD90C10, WD90C11, WD90C24, WD90C24A, WD90C30, WD90C31, WD90C33
Trident	TVGA8800CS, TVGA8900B, TVGA8900C, TVGA8900CL, TVGA9000, TVGA9000i, TVGA9100B, TVGA9200CX, TVGA9320, TVGA9400CX, TVGA9420
Video 7/Headland Technologies	HT216-32

Hard-Drive Controllers

Unlike most PC-based Unices, Linux isn't too fussy about the hard disk or hard disks it supports; basically, if a hard disk is supported by a PC's BIOS, it will work fine under Linux. This goes for IDE, EIDE, MFM, RLL, ESDI (with controllers that emulate the ST-506 interface, that is), and most SCSI interfaces. In fact, the following Enhanced IDE (EIDE) interfaces are explicitly supported, even on systems with up to two IDE interfaces and up to four hard drives and/or CD-ROM drives:

- CMD-640
- DTC 2278D
- Intel Triton (82371FB) IDE (with busmaster DMA)
- FGI/Holtek HT-6560B
- RZ1000

However, there's still the chance you could experience some problems. For example, the Hardware Compatibility How-To reports that some

Conner CFP1060S drives may have problems with Linux when using the ext2fs filesystem. The symptoms are inode errors during e2fsck and corrupt filesystems. Conner has released a firmware upgrade to fix this problem (call 1-800-4CONNER), but you'll need the microcode version (found on the drive label, 9WA1.6x) before Conner can help you.

In addition, certain Micropolis drives have problems with Adaptec and BusLogic cards. In these situations, contact the drive manufacturers for firmware upgrades.

SCSI Controllers

The following SCSI controllers are explicitly supported under Linux: AMI Fast Disk VLB/EISA (BusLogic compatible), Adaptec AVA-1505/1515 (ISA) (Adaptec 152x compatible); Adaptec AHA-1510/152x (ISA) (AIC-6260/6360); Adaptec AHA-154x (ISA) (all models); Adaptec AHA-174x (EISA) (in enhanced mode); Adaptec AHA-274x (EISA) / 284x (VLB) (AIC-7770); Adaptec AHA-2940/3940 (PCI) (AIC-7870); Always IN2000; BusLogic (ISA/EISA/VLB/PCI) (all models); DPT PM2001, PM2012A (EATA-PIO); DPT Smartcache (EATA-DMA) (ISA/EISA/PCI) (all models); DTC 329x (EISA) (Adaptec 154x compatible); Future Domain TMC-16x0, TMC-3260 (PCI); Future Domain TMC-8xx, TMC-950; Media Vision Pro Audio Spectrum 16 SCSI (ISA); NCR 5380 generic cards; NCR 53c400 (Trantor T130B) (use generic NCR 5380 SCSI support); NCR 53c406a (Acculogic ISApport / Media Vision Premium 3D SCSI); NCR 53c7x0, 53c8x0 (PCI); Qlogic / Control Concepts SCSI/IDE (FAS408) (ISA/VLB); Seagate ST-01/ST-02 (ISA); SoundBlaster 16 SCSI-2 (Adaptec 152x compatible) (ISA); Trantor T128/T128F/T228 (ISA); UltraStor 14F (ISA), 24F (EISA), 34F (VLB); and Western Digital WD7000 SCSI.

In addition, there are other SCSI controllers that can be used under Linux only after patches have been added to an installed system. These controllers and the Internet locations of the patches are listed in Table A.3.

Table A.3 SCSI controllers needing patches and the Internet locations.

Controller	Internet Address
AMD AM53C974, AM79C974 (PCI) (Compaq, HP, Zeos onboard SCSI)	*ftp://sunsite.unc.edu/pub/Linux/kernel/patches/scsi/AM53C974-0.3.tgz*
Adaptec ACB-40xx SCSI-MFM/RLL bridgeboard	*ftp://sunsite.unc.edu/pub/Linux/kernel/patches/scsi/adaptec-40XX.tar.gz*
Always Technologies AL-500	*ftp://sunsite.unc.edu/pub/Linux/kernel/patches/scsi/al500-0.2.tar.gz*
BusLogic (ISA/EISA/VLB/PCI)	*ftp://ftp.dandelion.com/BusLogic-1.0-beta.tar.gz*
Iomega PC2/2B	*ftp://sunsite.unc.edu/pub/Linux/kernel/patches/scsi/iomega_pc2-1.1.x.tar.gz*
QLogic (ISP1020) (PCI)	*ftp://sunsite.unc.edu/pub/Linux/kernel/patches/scsi/isp1020-0.5.gz*
Ricoh GSI-8	*ftp://tsx-11.mit.edu/pub/linux/ALPHA/scsi/gsi8.tar.gz*

NOTE Parallel-port SCSI adapters (popular among laptop users) and DTC boards (327x, 328x) that are not Adaptec-compatible are not supported by Linux.

The SCSI device must support block sizes of 256, 512, or 1024 bytes. Other block sizes will not work. (Use the **MODE SELECT SCSI** command to change the block size.)

Floppy Drive

The Linux installation process assumes that you'll be creating a bootdisk and a rootdisk for use on a high-density drive. Because larger 1.2MB drives have all but disappeared from daily usage, the accompanying CD-ROM contains drivers only for the 1.44MB 3.5-inch floppies that most computers use for drive **A:**.

Tape Drives

Any tape drive that works from the SCSI connector should be fine under Linux (in other words, if your SCSI card works, so should the tape drive), such as the QIC-20. In these cases, you'll need to make sure that drives using both fixed and variable length have blocks smaller than the driver buffer length (set to 32K in the distribution sources). In addition, Linux works pretty well with other tape drives that are connected via floppy controller, like QIC-117, QIC-40/80, and QIC-3010/3020 (QIC-WIDE) drives.

Other tape drives using the floppy controller Colorado FC-10/FC-20, Mountain Mach-2, and Iomega Tape Controller II should work, but you may have to grab a patch from *ftp://sunsite.unc.edu/pub/Linux/kernel/tapes*.

There are several unsupported tape drives, including Emerald and Tecmar QIC-02 tape controller cards, drives that connect to the parallel port (like the Colorado Trakker), some high-speed tape controllers (Colorado TC-15), the Irwin AX250L/Accutrak 250 (which are not QIC-80 compatible), the IBM Internal Tape Backup Unit (which is not QIC-80 compatible), and the COREtape Light.

CD-ROM

You can use a SCSI-based CD-ROM for Linux, or you can use one of the many CD-ROM/sound board combinations from the likes of Creative Labs. If you use a SCSI CD-ROM with a block size of 512 or 2048 bytes, you'll be fine as long as Linux recognizes the SCSI card; Linux works directly with the SCSI card and not necessarily directly with the CD-ROM. Also, pretty much any EIDE (ATAPI) CD-ROM drive should work In addition, there's explicit support for the following drives: Aztech CDA268, Orchid CDS-3110, Okano/Wearnes CDD-110, Conrad TXC, GoldStar R420, LMS Philips CM 206, Mitsumi, Optics Storage Dolphin 8000AT, Sanyo H94A, Sony CDU31A/CDU33A, Sony CDU-535/CDU-531, Teac CD-55A SuperQuad, and the drives that fall under the Creative Labs label that are used in SoundBlaster Pro bundles—Matsushita/Panasonic, Creative Labs, Longshine, and Kotobuki.

You'll need patches to use the following CD-ROM drives: LMS/Philips CM 205/225/202 (*ftp://sunsite.unc.edu/pub/Linux/kernel/patches/cdrom/lmscd0.3d.tar.gz*), Mitsumi FX001D/F (alternate drivers can be found at *ftp://ftp.gwdg.de//pub/linux/cdrom/drivers/mitsumi/mcdx-1.0a.tar.gz*), NEC CDR-35D (*ftp://sunsite.unc.edu/pub/Linux/kernel/patches/cdrom/linux-neccdr35d.patch*), and Sony SCSI multisession CD-XA (*ftp://tsx-11.mit.edu/pub/linux/patches/sony-multi-0.00.tar.gz*).

Not every SoundBlaster features a proprietary interface, as some versions are based on a SCSI architecture. You'll need to know what specific SoundBlaster board you're using before you sit down for your Linux installation.

N O T E

Removable Drives

As is the case with all SCSI controllers, any removable drive connected to a working SCSI controller should work, including optical (MO), WORM, floptical, Bernoulli, Zip, SyQuest, PD, and others.

If you're using a parallel-port Zip drive, you can grab a patch from *ftp://gear.torque.net/pub/* and see if it works.

Linux supports both 512- and 1024-bytes/sector disks.

I/O Controllers

Any standard serial/parallel/joystick/combo card can be used with Linux, including those sporting 8250, 16450, 16550, and 16550A UARTs. Cards that support nonstandard IRQs (such as an IRQ of 9) can be used.

Network Cards

If you're planning on using Linux on a network, you'll need a networking card. (If you're not planning on using Linux on the network, you won't need a card.) Other PC Unices require the presence of a network card to run at all (even on a single-user installation), but Linux doesn't.

The following Ethernet cards have been tested and are supported under Linux: 3Com 3C501, 3C503, 3C505, 3C507, 3C509/3C509B (ISA) / 3C579 (EISA); AMD LANCE (79C960) / PCnet-ISA/PCI (AT1500, HP J2405A, NE1500/NE2100); AT&T GIS WaveLAN; Allied Telesis AT1700; Ansel Communications AC3200 EISA; Apricot Xen-II; Cabletron E21xx; DEC DE425 (EISA) / DE434/DE435 (PCI); DEC DEPCA and EtherWORKS; HP PCLAN (27245 and 27xxx series); HP PCLAN PLUS (27247B and 27252A); HP 10/100VG PCLAN (ISA/EISA/PCI); Intel EtherExpress; Intel EtherExpress Pro; NE2000/NE1000 (not all clones work, however); New Media Ethernet; Racal-Interlan NI5210 (i82586 Ethernet chip); Racal-Interlan NI6510 (am7990 lance chip) (this board doesn't work if your computer has more than 16 megabytes of RAM); PureData PDUC8028, PDI8023; SEEQ 8005; SMC Ultra; Schneider & Koch G16; Western Digital WD80x3; and Zenith Z-Note/IBM ThinkPad 300 built-in adapter. The following pocket and portable adapters have been tested and will work with Linux: AT-Lan-Tec/RealTek parallel port adapter; D-Link DE600/DE620 parallel port adapter. The following methods can be used to connect to a network: SLIP/CSLIP/PPP (serial port); EQL (serial IP load balancing); and PLIP (parallel port) using a bidirectional cable.

In addition, Linux works with all ARCnet cards and the IBM Tropic chipset Token Ring cards. Finally, Linux will work with the following amateur radio (AX.25) cards: Ottawa PI/PI2 and most generic 8530-based HDLC boards.

In addition, Linux will work with the following Ethernet cards once you go out and grab patches from the Internet. 3Com Demon Ethercards (3C592, 3C597 (100 mbps)) (EISA), with the patch at *http://cesdis.gsfc.nasa.gov/linux/drivers/vortex.html*; 3Com Vortex Ethercards (3C590, 3C595 (100 mbps)) (PCI), with the patch at *http://cesdis.gsfc.nasa.gov/linux/drivers/vortex.html*; DEC 21040/21140 Tulip, with a patch at *http://cesdis.gsfc.nasa.gov/linux/drivers/tulip.html*; SMC PCI EtherPower 10/100, with a patch at *http://cesdis.gsfc.nasa.gov/linux/drivers/tulip.html*; and the HP J2585 (PCI) and HP J2573 (ISA) (ATT2MDx1 / 100VG), with a patch at *http://cesdis1.gsfc.nasa.gov:80/linux/drivers/100vg.html*.

Xircom adapters (PCMCIA and parallel port) are not supported.

WARNING

Multiport Controllers

Linux supports many multiport controllers. They fall into two groups: intelligent controllers and nonintelligent controllers. Supported nonintelligent controllers are: AST FourPort and clones (4 port); Accent Async-4 (4 port); Arnet Multiport-8 (8 port); Bell Technologies HUB6 (6 port); Boca BB-1004, 1008 (4, 8 port), with no DTR, DSR, and CD; Boca BB-2016 (16 port); Boca IO/AT66 (6 port); Boca IO 2by4 (4 serial / 2 parallel, uses 5 IRQs); Computone ValuePort (4, 6, 8 port) (AST FourPort compatible); DigiBoard PC/X (4, 8, 16 port); Comtrol Hostess 550 (4, 8 port); PC-COMM 4-port (4 port); SIIG I/O Expander 4S (4 port, uses 4 IRQs); STB 4-COM (4 port); Twincom ACI/550; and Usenet Serial Board II (4 port). These nonintelligent controllers usually come in two varieties:

- The first uses standard port addresses and 4 IRQs.
- The second is AST FourPort-compatible and uses a selectable block of addresses and a single IRQ. (Addresses and IRQs are set using the setserial utility.)

Linux supports the following intelligent multiport controllers: Cyclades Cyclom-8Y/16Y (8, 16 port) (ISA/PCI); Stallion EasyIO (ISA)/EasyConnection 8/32 (ISA/MCA); and Stallion EasyConnection 8/64 and ONboard (ISA/EISA/MCA)/Brumby/Stallion (ISA).

Table A.4 lists multiport controllers that Linux will recognize after patches have been downloaded from the Internet and installed.

Table A.4 Multiport controllers and the patch locations.

Controller	Internet Address
Comtrol RocketPort (8/16/32 port)	ftp://tsx-11.mit.edu/pub/linux/packages/comtrol/
DigiBoard PC/Xe (ISA) and PC/Xi (EISA)	ftp://ftp.digibd.com/drivers/linux/
Moxa C218 (8 port)/C320 (8/16/32 expandable)	ftp://ftp.moxa.com.tw/drivers/c-218-320/linux/
Specialix SIO/XIO (modular, 4 to 32 ports)	ftp://sunsite.unc.edu/pub/Linux/kernel/patches/serial/sidrv0_5.taz

Modems

Again, if a modem works under DOS, it should work under Linux—whether the modem is internal or external. When you install Linux, you'll need to specify the location of the modem (serial port 1, 2, 3, or 4). This also goes for PCMCIA modems.

You'll need fax software to take advantage of a fax modem. Some fax modems require special programs: the Digicom Connection 96+/14.4+ needs a DSP code downloading program (which can be found at *ftp://sunsite.unc.edu/pub/Linux/system/Serial/smdl-linux.1.02.tar.gz*), and the ZyXEL U-1496 series needs ZyXEL 1.4, a modem/fax/voice control program (which can be *ftp://sunsite.unc.edu/pub/Linux/system/Serial/ZyXEL-1.4.tar.gz*).

ISDN Cards

ISDN cards fall under the category of either direct-link devices to the Internet or replacements for standard modems or network cards. If you're using an ISDN card to emulate a modem or network card, you should have no problems. However, if you're using ISDN to connect to the Internet, you'll need to install some drivers. Table A.5 lists the ISDN device that Linux will recognize, followed by an Internet location for the appropriate patch.

Table A.5 ISDN devices and the patches that love them.

ISDN Device	Internet Patch Location
3Com Sonix Arpeggio	*ftp://sunsite.unc.edu/pub/Linux/kernel/patches/network/sonix.tgz*
Combinet EVERYWARE 000 ISDN	*ftp://sunsite.unc.edu/pub/Linux/patches/network/combinet1000isdn-1.02.tar.gz*
Diehl SCOM card	*ftp://sunsite.unc.edu/pub/Linux/kernel/patches/network/isdndrv-0.1.1.tar.gz*
ICN ISDN/Teles ISDN Creatix AVM ISDN cards	*ftp://ftp.franken.de/pub/isdn4linux/*
German ISDN (1TR6) and Euro-ISDN	*ftp://ftp.uni-stuttgart.de/pub/unix/systems/linux/isdn/*

If you want more information on using Linux and ISDN devices, point your Web browser to *http://www.ix.de/ix/linux/linux-isdn.html*.

ATM Network Adapters

Work has been done on the Efficient Networks ENI155P-MF 155 Mbps ATM adapter. You can grab a driver and some description of the process from *http://lrcwww.epfl.ch/linux-atm/*.

Frame Relay Cards

Work has been done on a driver for the Sangoma S502 56K Frame Relay card. You can grab a copy from *ftp://ftp.sovereign.org/pub/wan/fr/*.

Sound Boards

Linux supports a wide range of sound cards, including: 6850 UART MIDI; Adlib (OPL2); Audio Excell DSP16; Aztech Sound Galaxy NX Pro; cards based on the Crystal CS4232 (Plug and Play)–based cards; ECHO-PSS cards (Orchid SoundWave32, Cardinal DSP16); Ensoniq

SoundScape; Gravis Ultrasound; Gravis Ultrasound 16-bit sampling daughterboard; Gravis Ultrasound MAX; Logitech SoundMan Games (SBPro, 44kHz stereo support); Logitech SoundMan Wave (Jazz16/OPL4); Logitech SoundMan 16 (PAS-16 compatible); MPU-401 MIDI; MediaTriX AudioTriX Pro; Media Vision Premium 3D (Jazz16); Media Vision Pro Sonic 16 (Jazz); Media Vision Pro Audio Spectrum 16; Microsoft Sound System (AD1848); OAK OTI-601D cards (Mozart); OPTi 82C928/82C929 cards (MAD16/MAD16 Pro); SoundBlaster; SoundBlaster Pro; SoundBlaster 16; Turtle Beach Wavefront cards (Maui, Tropez); and Wave Blaster (and other daughterboards).

In addition, the following sound boards can be coaxed into working under Linux, provided you install the proper patches and drivers (which can be found at the accompanying Internet addresses): MPU-401 MIDI (*ftp://sunsite.unc.edu/pub/Linux/kernel/sound/mpu401-0.2.tar.gz*); PC speaker/parallel-port DAC *ftp://ftp.informatik.hu-berlin.de/pub/os/ linux/hu-sound/*); and Turtle Beach MultiSound/Tahiti/Monterey (*ftp://ftp.cs.colorado.edu/users/mccreary/archive/tbeach/multisound/*).

Not every feature on every sound board is supported, however. The ASP chip on SoundBlaster 16 series and AWE32 is not supported, and neither is the AWE32's onboard E-mu MIDI synthesizer.

Also, the SoundBlaster 16 with DSP 4.11 and 4.12 have a hardware bug that causes hung/stuck notes when playing MIDI and digital audio at the same time.

Mouse and Joystick

We've used various mice with Linux, mostly under the auspices of the X Window System. Basically, if you use a serial mouse with Linux, you'll just be telling the system to look to a specific serial port for the mouse. The same goes for trackballs and joysticks that run off a serial port. The following mouse models are explicitly supported under Linux: Microsoft serial mouse, Mouse Systems serial mouse, Logitech Mouseman serial mouse, Logitech serial mouse, ATI XL Inport busmouse, C&T 82C710 (QuickPort; used on Toshiba, TI Travelmate laptops), Microsoft busmouse, Logitech busmouse, and the PS/2 (auxiliary device) mouse.

To use other mouse models, you'll need to grab a patch. These would include the Sejin J-mouse (the patch is at *ftp://sunsite.unc.edu/pub/Linux/ kernel/patches/console/jmouse.1.1.70-jmouse.tar.gz*) and MultiMouse, which uses multiple mouse devices as single mouse (the patch is at *ftp://sunsite.unc.edu/pub/Linux/system/Misc/MultiMouse-1.0.tgz*).

If your joystick doesn't work, you may want to check out one of the joystick drivers ftp://sunsite.unc.edu/pub/Linux/kernel/ patches/console/joystick-0.7.3.tgz or ftp://sunsite.unc.edu/pub/ Linux/kernel/patches/console/joyfixed.tgz.

In addition, touchpads that emulate a mouse (like the Alps Glidepoint) should work if they precisely emulate a supported mouse.

Printers

Essentially, any printer connected to a parallel or serial port that works under DOS should work under Linux. During the installation, you'll be asked to specify which port contains the printer. There are special programs that enhance the basic printing capabilities: HP LaserJet 4 users can grab free-lj4, a printing modes control program, at *ftp://sunsite.unc.edu/pub/Linux/system/Printing/free-lj4-1.1p1.tar.gz*, while those using the BiTronics parallel port interface can grab a program at *ftp://sunsite.unc.edu/pub/Linux/kernel/misc/bt-ALPHA-0.0.1.tar.gz*.

The issue becomes a little dicier when dealing with XFree86 and Ghostscript, the utility used to create and print PostScript documents. Ghostscript allows you to print PostScript-formatted documents on non-PostScript printers; much of the UNIX documentation that flows down the pike is formatted with PostScript, and this capability is very handy. Ghostscript supports the following printers: Apple Imagewriter; C. Itoh M8510; Canon BubbleJet BJ10e, BJ200, LBP-8II, and LIPS III; DEC LA50/70/75/75plus, LN03, and LJ250; Epson 9 pin, 24 pin, LQ series, Stylus, and AP3250; HP 2563B, DesignJet 650C, DeskJet/Plus/500, DeskJet 500C/520C/550C/1200C color, LaserJet/Plus/II/III/4, and PaintJet/XL/XL300 color; IBM Jetprinter color and Proprinter; Imagen ImPress; Mitsubishi CP50 color; NEC P6/P6+/P60; Okidata MicroLine 182; Ricoh 4081; SPARCprinter; StarJet

48 inkjet printer; Tektronix 4693d color 2/4/8 bit and 4695/4696 inkjet plotter; and Xerox XES printers (2700, 3700, 4045, etc.). Those using the Canon BJC600 and Epson ESC/P color printers can grab a printer program at *ftp://petole.imag.fr/pub/postscript/*.

Scanners

Slackware Linux right out of the box doesn't support any scanners. However, several folks have contributed scanner drivers and programs to the Linux community, and there may be a program available on the Internet for your particular scanner. (Be warned that some of the products listed here are commercial products, however.) Scanners with support software available include: A4 Tech AC 4096 (*ftp://ftp.informatik.hu-berlin.de/pub/local/linux/ac4096.tgz*), Epson GT6000 (*ftp://sunsite.unc.edu/pub/Linux/apps/graphics/scanners/ppic0.5.tar.gz*), Genius GS-B105G (*ftp://tsx-11.mit.edu/pub/linux/ALPHA/scanner/gs105-0.0.1.tar.gz*), Genius GeniScan GS4500 handheld scanner (*ftp://tsx-11.mit.edu/pub/linux/ALPHA/scanner/gs4500-1.3.tar.gz*), HP ScanJet and ScanJet Plus (*ftp://ftp.ctrl-c.liu.se/unix/linux/wingel/*), HP ScanJet II series SCSI (*ftp://sunsite.unc.edu/pub/Linux/apps/graphics/scanners/hpscanpbm-0.3a.tar.gz*), HP ScanJet family, including ScanJet 3c (*http://www.tummy.com/xvscan/*), Logitech Scanman 32/256 (*ftp://tsx-11.mit.edu/pub/linux/ALPHA/scanner/logiscan-0.0.2.tar.gz*), Mustek M105 handheld scanner with GI1904 interface (*ftp://tsx-11.mit.edu/pub/linux/ALPHA/scanner/scan-driver-0.1.8.tar.gz*), Mustek Paragon 6000CX (*ftp://sunsite.unc.edu/pub/Linux/apps/graphics/ scanners/muscan-1.1.5.taz*), and Nikon Coolscan SCSI 35mm film scanner (*ftp://sunsite.unc.edu/pub/Linux/apps/graphics/scanners/*).

Video-Capture Boards

Slackware Linux doesn't support any video-capture boards right out of the box. To use such a board, you'll need to first make sure that the board has a driver and then grab that driver from the Internet. Boards with Linux drivers available are: FAST Screen Machine II (*ftp://sunsite.unc.edu/pub/Linux/apps/video/ScreenMachineII.1.2.tgz*), ImageNation Cortex I (*ftp://sunsite.unc.edu/pub/Linux/apps/video/cortex.drv.0.1.tgz*), ImageNation CX100 (*ftp://sunsite.unc.edu/pub/Linux/apps/video/cxdrv-0.1beta.tar.gz*), Pro Movie Studio (*ftp://sunsite.unc.edu/pub/Linux/apps/video/PMS-grabber.2.0.tgz*), Quanta WinVision video-capture card (*ftp://sunsite.unc.edu/pub/Linux/apps/video/fgrabber-1.0.tgz*), Video Blaster/Rombo Media Pro+ (*ftp://sunsite.unc.edu/pub/Linux/apps/video/vid_src.gz*), and VT1500 TV cards (*ftp://sunsite.unc.edu/pub/Linux/apps/video/vt1500-1.0.5.tar.gz*).

Uninterruptible Power Systems

Slackware Linux doesn't support UPS systems right out of the box, but there are drivers available for APC SmartUPS (*ftp://sunsite.unc.edu/pub/Linux/system/UPS/apcd-0.1.tar.gz*) and general UPS systems with RS-232 monitoring port (known as the "unipower" package) (*ftp://sunsite.unc.edu/pub/Linux/system/UPS/unipower-1.0.0.tgz*). Others have managed to interface Linux with other UPS systems; for more details, check out the UPS-HOWTO on the accompanying CD-ROM.

Data-Acquisition Equipment

Hardware used for data acquisition is not explicitly supported in Slackware Linux, but you can grab software from the Linux Lab Project (*ftp://koala.chemie.fu-berlin.de/pub/linux/LINUX-LAB/*) to learn about supporting the following devices: Analog Devices RTI-800/815 ADC/DAC board, CED 1401, DBCC CAMAC, IEEE-488 (GPIB, HPIB) boards, Keithley DAS-1200, and National Instruments AT-MIO-16F / Lab-PC+.

Linux on Laptops

Generally speaking, Linux should run fine on most laptops with enough horsepower—that is, the newer breed of 486- and Pentium-based laptops on the market, decked out with at least 8 megabytes of RAM. Users have reported that the following laptops have posed no problems in dealing with Linux: AMS PN325, SoundPro, TravelPro 5300, and TravelPro 5366; ARM TS30A; AST Advantage! Explorer and PowerExec; Austin Active Color and Arima; BIT DU33 and FR-800; Canon Innova Subnotebook; Caravene AV-B5NT; Chicony NB5 and NoteBook 9800; Compaq Aero 4/33C, Concerto 4/33, Contura 4/25, Contura 4/25cx, 4/25 Lite, and LTE Elite 4/75 CX; Compat TS37 (Wang); Compudyne SubNote 4SL/25; DECpc 425 SL/e and 433SLC Premium (AST); Dell 320N+, Latitude 433C, and Latitude XP 4100cx; DUAL SKD-4000; Epson 700, Direct Endeavor NT-500, NB-SL/25, and Paradigma SX33; Gateway 2000 ColorBook, HandBook, and Liberty; GRID 1450SX, 1550SX, and 1660; Highscreen 486 SLC 33 and Blue Note; Hyperdata Expor CD100; IBM L40SX, PS/Note 425, ThinkPad 340CSE, ThinkPad 350, ThinkPad 500, ThinkPad 750 (Mono), ThinkPad 750CS, and ThinkPad 755C; INSI EchoBook; IPC P5 and IPC Porta-PC P5E-486/DSTN; Jetta Jetbook; Lion NB 8500; MacPerson Scriba; Magnavox Metalis SX/16; Midwest Micro Elite, Ultra, Soundbook, and Soundbook P-90; NEC Ultralite Versa E, Versa 33C, and Versa S/33D; NoteBook 3500; Notestar NP-743D; Olivetti Philos 33; Prostar 9200; Sager NP943, NP3600, NP7500, NP7600, and NP9200; SDK 4000 III Extended version; SEH Design Note; Siemens Nixdorf PCD 4 ND; Sharp PC-8650; SNI PCD-4NE; Tadpole P1000; Targa; TI Travelmate 4000E, Travelmate Win4000, Travelmate 4000M, and Travelmate 5000; Toshiba T1800, T1900C, T1910, Toshiba T1950 (mono), T1950CT/200, Satellite T2100, T2200SX, T3100SX/40, T3200SXC, T3400, T4400SX, T4400SX, T4600 (mono), T4600, T4600C, T4700, and T5200/100; Total Peripherals NBD486, TravelPro 5300, Twinhead Slim 484, Tulip NB, Vobis ModuleNote, WinBook and WinBook XP; Zenith SuperSport SX, Z-Note 425-Inc., and Z-Star 433VL; and Zeos Contenda 386 Subnotebook.

NOTE The Linux Laptop Home Page (*http://www.cs.utexas.edu/users/kharker/linux-laptop/*) contains additional information on laptops and Linux, including many sites that contain information about specific laptop models not covered here. Some of the information here is gleaned from that Web site, courtesy of Kenneth E. Harker (*kharker@cs.utexas.edu*) and some from our personal experience. If you own a laptop and want to know more about using Linux on it, the Linux Laptop Home Page is the place to start.

Another source of information is the Linux on Portables Web site, found at *http://queequeg.ifa.hawaii.edu/linux/portables.html.*

PCMCIA and Laptops

A separate package, Card Services, is used for PCMCIA support on laptops; this package is included on the accompanying CD-ROM. Common PCMCIA controllers (including those built around chips from Databook, Intel, Cirrus, Ricoh, Vadem, and VLSI) and custom controllers found in IBM and Toshiba laptops are supported. In addition, the PCMCIA How-To reports that the package is used on desktop computer systems with PCMCIA card adapters.

Be warned that the Motorola 6AHC05GA controller used in some Hyundai laptops and the proprietary controller used in Hewlett-Packard OmniBook 600 subnotebooks are not supported.

For More Information

In all likelihood, this book is only the beginning of your Linux programming voyage. You'll find that there's a sea of Linux information available, both on the Internet and in the print world. Our emphasis here is on Internet resources (specifically Linux programming resources), because they are the ones you'll find most useful. In addition, the authors maintain two Web sites with programming information: *http://www.kreichard.com* and *http://ourworld.compuserve.com/homepages/efjohnson/*.

Internet Resources

Linux is a big topic on the Internet; a recent search on the Alta Vista search engine yielded 300,000 Web pages that mention Linux. Even when discarding the Web pages created by undergraduates who tinker a little with Linux, you're left with an amazing number of Web pages that cover Linux in some depth.

We've done a little editing for you and compiled this assortment of interesting Linux-related Web pages. Naturally—this being the World Wide Web and all—most of these pages spend a lot of time pointing you to other Web pages, which point you to even more Web pages. Still, by beginning with these pages, you can significantly expand your Linux expertise.

The Linux Documentation Project

http://sunsite.unc.edu/mdw/linux.html

The home page of the Linux Documentation Project is an important source of Linux information and archived software; virtually any aspect of Linux usage and configuration can be found here. This is a page to be placed prominently in your Web browser's bookmarks list. You can search through the Linux Documentation Archives by connecting to *http://sunsite.unc.edu/architext/AT-Linuxquery.html* or *http://amelia.db. erau.edu/Harvest/brokers/LDP/query.html*.

Linux.org

http://www.Linux.org/

Linux.org is a user-driven group dedicated to—surprise!—Linux.

Walnut Creek CD-ROM

http://www.cdrom.com

This is the online repository of Slackware; you can grab updated versions of Slackware from here.

The Linux Applications and Utilities Page

http://www.xnet.com/~blatura/linapps.shtml

Bill Latura maintains this excellent list of Linux applications and utilities. Unlike the Linux Software Map (see later), the applications are listed by category, making it much easier for browsing.

The Linux Software Map

http://www.boutell.com/lsm/

This site attempts to match your software needs with what's available in the Linux world.

The Linux FAQ

http://www.cl.cam.ac.uk/users/iwj10/linux-faq/

This site contains the most up-to-date version of the Linux Frequently Asked Questions (FAQ).

LessTif

http://www.hungry.com/products/lesstif/

The Hungry Programmers' implementation of LessTif—a freely available replacement for Motif libraries, as explained in Chapter 3—has its home here.

The XFree86 Project

http://www.XFree86.org/

When you installed X Window on your Linux installation, you were really using XFree86, a version of X Window optimized specifically for the Intel architecture. This is the home page of the effort.

The Java-Linux Page

http://www.blackdown.org/java-linux.html

When this book was written, the future of Java on Linux was somewhat in doubt. To see how the porting process has gone, check out this Web site.

The Linux Configuration Page

http://www.hal-pc.org/~davidl/linux/linux.config.html

This page combines installation and configuration tips from a wide variety of users. These are the folks who have successfully installed and configured Linux on a vast assortment of PCs, and if you're having trouble with Linux on your no-name clone, you may want to check to see if someone else hasn't already invented that wheel.

The Linux Laptop Page

http://www.cs.utexas.edu/users/kharker/linux-laptop/

This page is similar to the Linux Configuration Page; it takes the experiences of many users and condenses them into a useful guide to installing Linux on a wide variety of machines. Because it's a little harder to get hardware information about a laptop (i.e., what chipset is used for graphics) and some of the laptop components can be, well, a little fussy (check out the following Web listing), this page is an essential for anyone wanting to run Linux on a laptop. Of similar interest is the **Linux and X Window on Notebook Computers** home page (*http://www.castle.net/X-notebook/index_linux.html*).

Linux PCMCIA Information

http://hyper.stanford.edu/~dhinds/pcmcia/pcmcia.html

Dave Hinds is a virtual god in the Linux community. Why? Because he's taken on the topic of making Linux work with PCMCIA ports, found mostly on laptops. PCMCIA ports are for those credit-card-type adapters (Ethernet, modem, et al.); even in the mainstream community PCMCIA support isn't all it should be. Still, thanks to Hinds' Card Services for Linux, you can generally make a PCMCIA port work. We've included Card Services for Linux on the accompanying CD-ROM; here's where you can go for more information.

If there's one thing about the Web, it's always changing. If you want to generate a more current list of Linux-related home pages, check out the Alta Vista Home Page (*http://alta.vista.com*). Alta Vista is a searchable database of Web pages across the world.

Slackware Mirrors

The Slackware distribution of Linux is maintained at the *ftp.cdrom.com* site in **/pub/linux/slackware**. At this site, you can grab the latest version of Slackware (although you shouldn't do this too often; you should upgrade in response to specific needs, not as a general practice).

This is a busy site, however, so you may want to check out a mirror site. A *mirror site* contains the same Linux files as the *ftp.cdrom.com* site, and they're updated regularly. In addition, as a good Internet citizen you should use the FTP site closest to you, keeping in mind that most of these sites are maintained for the use of local users, not global Internet users. (By the way, *ftp.cdrom.com* is in California.)

Table B.1 lists the sites known to mirror the Slackware Linux release.

Table B.1 Slackware Linux mirrors.

Country	Site	Directory
United States	*ftp.cdrom.com*	**/pub/linux/slackware**
	uiarchive.cso.uiuc.edu	**/pub/systems/linux/distributions/slackware**
	tsx-11.mit.edu	**/pub/linux/distributions/slackware**
	ftp.cps.cmich.edu	**/pub/linux/packages/slackware**
	sunsite.unc.edu	**/pub/Linux/distributions/slackware**
	ftp.rge.com	**/pub/systems/linux/slackware/**
	ftp.cs.columbia.edu	**/archives/linux/Slackware**
	ftp.ccs.neu.edu	**/pub/os/linux/slackware**
Australia	*ftp.monash.edu.au*	**/pub/linux/distributions/slackware**
Brazil	*farofa.ime.usp.br*	**/pub/linux/slackware**
Canada	*ftp.ECE.Concordia.CA*	**/pub/os/linux/dist/slackware**
	pcdepot.uwaterloo.ca	**/linux/slackware**
Chile	*ftp.ing.puc.cl*	**/pub/linux/slackware**
	ftp.dcc.uchile.cl	**/linux/slackware**
	ftp.inf.utfsm.cl	**/pub/Linux/Slackware**
Czech Republic	*vcdec.cvut.cz*	**/pub/linux/local**
Denmark	*ftp.dd.dk*	**/pub/linux/dist/slackware**
Finland	*ftp.funet.fi*	**/pub/OS/Linux/images/Slackware**
France	*ftp.ibp.fr*	**/pub/linux/distributions/slackware**

continued...

Country	Site	Directory
	ftp.irisa.fr	**/pub/mirrors/linux**
Germany	*ftp.uni-trier.de*	**/pub/unix/systems/linux/slackware**
Hong Kong	*ftp.cs.cuhk.hk*	**/pub/linux/slackware**
Hungary	*ftp.kfki.hu*	**/pub/linux/distributions/slackware**
Japan	*ftp.cs.titech.ac.jp*	**/pub/os/linux/slackware**
Mexico	*ftp.nuclecu.unam.mx*	**/linux/slackware**
The Netherlands	*ftp.leidenuniv.nl*	**/pub/linux/slackware**
	ftp.twi.tudelft.nl	**/pub/Linux/slackware**
Norway	*ftp.nvg.unit.no*	**/pub/linux/slackware**
Portugal	*ftp.di.fc.ul.pt*	**/pub/Linux/Slackware**
	ftp.ncc.up.pt	**/pub/Linux/slackware**
South Africa	*ftp.sun.ac.za*	**/pub/linux/distributions/Slackware**
Spain	*luna.gui.uva.es*	**/pub/linux.new/slackware**
	ftp.uniovi.es	**/pub/slackware**
Switzerland	*nic.switch.ch*	**/mirror/linux/sunsite/distributions/slackware**
Taiwan	*NCTUCCCA.edu.tw*	**/Operating-Systems/Linux/Slackware**
United Kingdom	*src.doc.ic.ac.uk*	**/packages/linux/slackware-mirror**

Usenet Newsgroups

The Usenet newsgroups listed in Table B.2 are devoted to the Linux operating system. These are newsgroups from around the world.

Table B.2 Usenet newsgroups related to Linux.

lt.os.linux	*comp.os.linux.answers*
alt.uu.comp.os.linux.questions	*comp.os.linux.development.apps*
at.fido.linux	*comp.os.linux.development.system*
aus.computers.linux	*comp.os.linux.hardware*
comp.os.linux.advocacy	*comp.os.linux.networking*

comp.os.linux.setup	*linux.wine.users*
comp.os.linux.x	*linux.appletalk*
comp.os.linux.announce	*linux.apps.seyon*
comp.os.linux.misc	*linux.apps.seyon.development*
de.alt.sources.linux.patches	*linux.bbs.rocat*
dc.org.linux-users	*linux.dev.680x0*
de.comp.os.linux	*linux.dev.admin*
ed.linux	*linux.dev.apps*
fido.ger.linux	*linux.dev.atm*
fj.os.linux	*linux.dev.bbs*
fr.comp.os.linux	*linux.dev.c-programming*
han.sys.linux	*linux.dev.config*
hannover.uni.comp.linux	*linux.dev.debian*
it.comp.linux	*linux.dev.diald*
linux.apps.bbsdev	*linux.dev.doc*
linux.apps.flexfax	*linux.dev.fido*
linux.apps.linux-bbs	*linux.dev.fsf*
linux.debian	*linux.dev.fsstnd*
linux.debian.announce	*linux.dev.ftp*
linux.debian.user	*linux.dev.gcc*
linux.fido.ifmail	*linux.dev.hams*
linux.free-widgets.announce	*linux.dev.ibcs2*
linux.free-widgets.bugs	*linux.dev.interviews*
linux.free-widgets.development	*linux.dev.ipx*
linux.motif.clone	*linux.dev.japanese*
linux.new-tty	*linux.dev.kernel*
linux.news.groups	*linux.dev.laptop*
linux.samba	*linux.dev.linuxbsd*
linux.samba.announce	*linux.dev.linuxnews*
linux.sdk	*linux.dev.linuxss*
linux.test	*linux.dev.localbus*

linux.dev.lugnuts

linux.dev.mca

linux.dev.mgr

linux.dev.msdos

linux.dev.net

linux.dev.new-lists

linux.dev.newbie

linux.dev.normal

linux.dev.nys

linux.dev.oasg

linux.dev.oi

linux.dev.pkg

linux.dev.ppp

linux.dev.qag

linux.dev.raid

linux.dev.scsi

linux.dev.serial

linux.dev.seyon

linux.dev.sound

linux.dev.standards

linux.dev.svgalib

linux.dev.tape

linux.dev.term

linux.dev.uucp

linux.dev.wabi

linux.dev.word

linux.dev.x11

linux.i18n

linux.jobs

linux.largesites

linux.local.chicago

linux.local.nova-scotia

linux.local.silicon-valley

linux.ports.alpha

linux.ports.hp-pa

linux.ports.powerpc

linux.pvt.png

linux.pvt.png.announce

linux.pvt.png.implement

linux.sources.kernel

linux.test.moderated

list.linux-activists.announce

list.linux-activists.gcc

list.linux-activists.ibsc2

list.linux-activists.kernel

list.linux-activists.msdos

list.linux-activists.net

list.linux-activists.normal

list.linux-activists.ppp

list.linux-activists.questions

list.linux-activists.scsi

list.linux-activists.tape

list.linux-fsstnd

list.linux-activists.680x0

list.linux-activists.admin

list.linux-activists.doc

list.linux-activists.fsstnd

list.linux-activists.laptops

list.linux-activists.newbie

list.linux-activists.postgres

list.linux-activists.serial

list.linux-activists.sound

list.linux-activists.term	*muc.lists.linux.international*
list.linux-activists.wabi	*no.linux*
list.linux-activists.x11	*sbay.linux*
maus.os.linux	*sfnet.atk.linux*
maus.os.linux68k	*tw.bbs.comp.linux*
muc.lists.isdn4linux	*zer.t-netz.linux*

Other Linux Implementations

Most Linux users work on a PC—after all, that's one of the big appeals of Linux. However, Linux has been ported to several other computer architectures, and more efforts are underway. In Table B.3 we list the port and the home page where you can find more information.

Table B.3 Linux implementations on non-PC architectures.

Project	Home Page
Alpha	*http://www.azstarnet.com/~axplinux/*
Acorn	*http://www.ph.kcl.ac.uk/~amb/linux.html*
ARM Linux	*http://whirligig.ecs.soton.ac.uk/~rmk92/armlinux.html*
Fujitsu AP1000+	*http://cap.anu.edu.au/cap/projects/linux/*
Linux/68k	*http://www-users.informatik.rwth-aachen.de/~hn/linux68k.html*
Linux/8086	*http://www.linux.org.uk/Linux8086.html*
Linux/PowerPC	*http://www.linuxppc.org/*
MkLinux	*http://nucleus.ibg.uu.se/macunix/*
MIPS	*http://lena.fnet.fr/*
SPARC Linux	*http://www.geog.ubc.ca/sparclinux.html*

Books

This book focused on the Slackware distribution of Linux on the accompanying CD-ROM. Should you wander away from this distribution, you may want to check out alternative sources of Linux information. Also, because this book doesn't cover the UNIX operating system or the X Window System in any depth (it takes entire forests to cover these topics in any depth), you may want to look for another UNIX/X book or two. The following lists should fill most of your needs.

Other Linux Books

Running Linux, Matt Welsh and Lar Kaufman, O'Reilly & Assoc., 1995. This nonspecific Linux primer covers both Linux and some general UNIX commands. It's not tied to any specific distribution of Linux, so some of the information won't apply to the accompanying CD-ROM. Welsh deals with some advanced topics not covered in this book.

Linux Network Administrator's Guide, Olaf Kirch, SSC, 1994. This technical overview of Linux networking should cover whatever you need to know about Linux on the network. Although this book is written from the viewpoint of a technically sophisticated user, it's still useful for anyone who needs to deal with Linux on the network.

UNIX Books

Teach Yourself ... UNIX, third edition, Kevin Reichard and Eric F. Johnson, MIS:Press, 1995. OK, so we're biased. This book provides an overview of the UNIX operating system with topics ranging from system configurations and shell scripts to the Internet. Some computer experience is assumed.

UNIX in Plain English, Kevin Reichard and Eric F. Johnson, MIS:Press, 1994. This book covers the major commands in the UNIX command set and most of the information should be directly applicable to Linux.

UNIX Fundamentals: The Basics, Kevin Reichard, MIS:Press, 1994. This book is for the true UNIX neophyte who knows little or nothing about UNIX—or computing, for that matter. It's part of a four-book series covering UNIX fundamentals (the other titles are *UNIX Fundamentals:*

UNIX for DOS and Windows Users, UNIX Fundamentals: Communications and Networking, and *UNIX Fundamentals: Shareware and Freeware).*

Programming Books

Teach yourself ... C, Al Stevens, MIS:Press, 1992. This book provides a beginner's introduction to C programming and goes far beyond the brief introduction found in Chapter 2.

Graphical Applications with Tcl and Tk, Eric F. Johnson, M&T Books, 1996. This book covers Tcl scripting on UNIX, Linux, and Windows. You can create a lot of neat applications with very little effort using Tcl.

Cross-Platform Perl, Eric F. Johnson, M&T Books, 1996. While the syntax may appear to have come from someone who's possessed, Perl provides many useful capabilities for system administrators and Web page developers.

X Window Books

The UNIX System Administrator's Guide to X, Eric F. Johnson and Kevin Reichard, M&T Books, 1994. This books focuses on topics related to UNIX and X, including configuration and usage. There's also some information about XFree86. An accompanying CD-ROM contains all the UNIX/X freeware detailed in the book.

Using X, Eric F. Johnson and Kevin Reichard, MIS:Press, 1992. This book covers X from the user's point of view, covering both usage and configuration issues.

Motif Books

Power Programming Motif, Eric F. Johnson and Kevin Reichard, M&T Books, 1994. This second edition covers OSF/Motif programming through version 1.2 most of which matches LessTif as described in Chapter 3.

Java Books

Java Programming Basics, Edith Au, Dave Makower, and the Pencom Web Works, MIS:Press, 1996. This is one of a vast number of Java books on the market.

Magazines

If you're serious about your Linux usage, you'll want to check out *Linux Journal* (SSC, 8618 Roosevelt Way NE., Seattle, WA 98115-3097; 206/782-7733; $19 per year; *http://www.ssc.com*; subs@*ssc.com*). This monthly magazine covers the Linux scene, offering practical tips and profiles of the many interesting people in the Linux community.

The number of UNIX-specific magazines has fallen to the wayside in recent years (a trend, admittedly, that baffles us). *UNIX Review* is our favorite, if only because two-thirds of the writing team contribute a monthly X Window column.

OSF/Motif and Linux

OSF/Motif, as licensed from the Open Software Foundation, is commercial software. OSF/Motif is actually many things, including a style guide, a window manager, and a set of programming libraries. (You learned about Motif in Chapter 3.)

Because OSF/Motif is licensed commercial software, it's not included on the accompanying CD-ROM. (Instead because OSF/Motif is beginning to be a prerequisite for any serious commercial UNIX development, you may at some time need to find OSF/Motif for your Linux system if you're looking at any professional installations.

MetroLink (4711 N. Powerline Rd., Fort Lauderdale, FL 33309; 305/938-0283; *http:www.metrolink.com*; *sales@metrolink.com*) offers OSF/Motif for Linux.

Linux How-Tos

The collective wisdom of the Linux community has been distilled into a series of text documents, called *How-tos*, that describe various portions of the Linux operating system. We've included the latest version of these documents on the accompanying CD-ROM (in the **/docs** directory), but if they don't answer your questions, you may want to see if a more recent version is available via the Internet. You can find them in many sites, but the official repository of these documents is at *sunsite.unc.edu* in the **/pub/Linux/docs/HOWTO** directory.

Linux Text Editors

In Linux, the chore of text editing falls on a few different editors, which vary greatly in terms of capabilities. Basically, however, you have two choices for your main editor in the main Slackware Linux distribution: **emacs** or **elvis** (a **vi** clone). We're not going to get into a religious war about **vi** or **emacs**; we'll present explanations of both.

Using the Elvis Text Editor

The full-screen **elvis** text editor is a clone of the **vi** text editor, which appears on most (but not all) UNIX systems. (Because you're not technically using the same **vi** found on other UNIX systems, we'll use the proper terminology here and refer to **elvis**. However, whenever you see **elvis** as part of a command, you can substitute **vi** if that's what you're used to.)

Elvis is used for editing text (ASCII) files, which have a wide application in the Linux operating system; text files are used for shell scripts, input to text processors, input for electronic mail, and programming source-code files. **elvis** works from the command line, and you can invoke it without a file loaded:

```
gilbert:/$ elvis
```

or with a file loaded:

```
gilbert:/$ elvis textfile
```

You can also invoke **elvis** using the following command lines:

```
gilbert:/$ vi
gilbert:/$ ex
gilbert:/$ view
gilbert:/$ input
```

These command-line variations can be a tad confusing, because they all call up the **elvis** editor. Basically, you can think of **vi** and **elvis** as doing the same thing. If you run **view** with a file specified, you're starting **elvis** in read-only mode. (This is the equivalent of **elvis -R** run from the command line.) And if you run **input** with a file specified, you're starting **elvis** in input mode.

Input mode? Yes. **Elvis** works with two modes (as does **vi**): command and input (input mode is the same as insert mode, for you **vi** users out there). The two modes are pretty straightforward: *command mode* is used to send a command to **elvis**, while *input mode* creates the text making up the file. You'll notice the difference immediately if you load **elvis** from the command line and then assume you can begin typing immediately into the file; chances are good that you'll end up generating a series of annoying beeps, because **elvis** begins in command mode and won't accept most keyboard input. The exception is if you accidentally type **i**, which puts **elvis** in input mode.

When in input mode, you can go ahead and type away. When you do, you'll notice that **elvis** doesn't insert line breaks at the end of the line; the line shifts to the right, with previously input text scrolling off the page. Line breaks (in the form of an **Enter** keystroke) must be entered at the end of the line by you.

When you're ready to save the file, you must switch to command mode and enter the proper command. Pressing the **Esc** key will switch you to command mode; by default **elvis** won't tell you if it's in input or command mode. (If you're not sure you switched to command mode, go ahead and hit the **Esc** key again. If you are in command mode, the only damage you can do is generate an annoying beep.) To enter a command in **elvis**, you must preface it with a semicolon (**:**). For example, the following would save a file in **elvis**:

```
:w file
```

where *file* is the name of the file to be saved. To save a file and quit **elvis**, use the following command:

```
:wq file
```

where *file* is the name of the file to be saved. (The command **ZZ**—sans leading colon—does the same thing.) To quit **elvis** without saving a file, use the following command:

```
:q!
```

Elvis and Memory

There's one important thing to remember when dealing with **elvis**: As you edit a file, you're editing a file that's been loaded into your system's RAM (or, in **elvis** parlance, a *bufffer*). You're not making a single change to the copy of the file on your hard drive. You can delete all the contents of the file loaded into RAM or you can make a set of drastic changes, but the changes will be meaningless until you explicitly save the file to disk in the manner described in the previous section. If you're not happy with the changes, you can quit **elvis** without saving the file with the following command:

```
:q!
```

If you are happy with the changes, save the file to disk, and the previous version of the file is gone. Poof.

Creating a Text File

Elvis can be as simple or as complex as you want to make it. On the one hand, it's really easy to create or edit a text file; all you need to know are the following steps:

- Launch **elvis** from the command line.
- Switch to insert mode by typing **I**.
- Type away.
- When you want to save the file and exit **elvis**, press the **Esc** key (which moves you to command mode), type **:wq** *filename* (use your own filename here), followed by **Enter**. The file is saved, and your command prompt reappears.

Moving Through Your Document

If you're running **elvis** from the command line (as opposed to running it under the X Window System), you'll find that your mouse won't help you much. If your documents get too long, you'll need to learn about some of the shortcuts used to move through a document.

The easiest way to move through a document in **elvis** is to use the cursor and page-movement keys on your keyboard (**PageUp**, **PageDown**). The **PageUp** and **PageDown** keys will move you up and down a single page; if there's less than a page of text to scroll to, you'll be placed at the beginning or end of the file. Similarly, the up and down cursor keys (↑ and ↓) can be used to move the cursor through the document; if you press the up cursor key (↑) at the top of the screen, the previous line will scroll to the top.

However, there's one quirk with **elvis** (which maintains compatibility with **vi**, by the way): the left and right cursor keys (← and →) can be used only to maneuver through the current line of text. If you're at the end of the line and expect to use the right cursor key (→) to move to the following line, you'll be greeted by a beep and a cursor stuck on that last character, because only the up and down cursor keys (↑ and ↓) can be used to move between lines.

For the most part, the cursor and page-movement keys should serve your scrolling needs in **elvis**. However, should you require some additional capabilities, Table C.1 list some useful additional cursor and scrolling commands.

Table C.1 Elvis cursor and scrolling commands.

Command	Result
0 (zero)	Moves the cursor to the beginning of the current line
b	Moves the cursor to the beginning of the current word
)	Moves the cursor to the end of the document
$	Moves the cursor to the end of the current line
e	Moves the cursor to the end of the current word

continued…

Command	Result
w	Moves the cursor to the beginning of the next word
*n*G	Moves the cursor to the beginning of line *n*
H	Moves the cursor to the beginning of the file
G	Moves the cursor to the beginning of the last line in the file

Undoing the Last Command

Elvis can undo the last command (unless you've saved the file to disk, in which case all changes are set in stone); to do so, go to command mode with **Esc** and type **u** (for *undo*).

elvis Information

This is about all you'll need to know about **elvis**. To be honest, it's not a very complex application, and given your probable text-processing needs, there's little need to spend much time mastering its every nuance. There are a lot of other options to **elvis**, but most of them are of interest only to the hard-core user. To see what additional actions you can take with **elvis**, use the following command line:

```
gilbert:~$ man elvis
```

Using Emacs

Elvis is a pure text editor; all it does is open or create a text file and edit it in a full-screen layout. (It also performs this basic capability in a very confusing manner, forcing you to distinguish between command and input modes.)

The **emacs** text editor goes a little further in its capabilities and is easier to use. Created by Richard Stallman and controlled by the Free

Software Foundation, **emacs** has evolved into an essential piece of software for most UNIX users, even though **emacs** ships with relatively few commercial implementations of UNIX; its appeal is such that system administrators are willing to go the extra mile and obtain it for use on their systems.

Although we're not going to get into the religious war that separates **vi** and **emacs** editors, we do think that **emacs** is worth checking out, especially if you've not used either text editor extensively. **Emacs** offers many things not found in **vi**:

- **Emacs** allows you to edit more than one file at a time with the added ability to cut and paste between files.
- **Emacs** features online help, a rarity in the Linux/UNIX world.
- A spelling checker, based on the UNIX **spell** command, can be accessed from a pull-down menu.
- With pull-down menus and a graphical interface (though, sadly, without what-you-see-is-what-you-get capabilities), **emacs** comes closest to a true word processor in the Linux world.

Programmers will probably get a little more out of **emacs** than other Linux text-editing tools, if only because **emacs** works in modes specifically designed for creating and editing source-code files (C, Lisp, and even Java), and the basic commands are always available in pull-down menus. In addition, **emacs** can be used for many other functions, including the reading of electronic mail and Usenet news.

This discussion will center around the X Window version that ships with the Slackware distribution of Linux (version 19.31). If you've decided to forego the joys of X, you should have installed the non-X version of **emacs** that was available during the Linux installation process. You can go back and install that version if you're not using X; however, if you installed the X Window version of **emacs**, you should remove that version from your system before installing the non-X version.

If you do use the non-X version of **emacs**, you'll still be able to follow along in this section of the appendix, for the most part. We'll provide keyboard equivalents to the commands listed here.

To launch **emacs** without a file loaded, type the following command line in an **xterm** window:

```
gilbert:/# emacs
```

You can also load **emacs** with a file loaded, specifying the file on the command line:

```
gilbert:/# emacs filename
```

where *filename* is the name of the file. (Remember that if *filename* isn't found on your *PATH* or in the current directory, you'll need to list an absolute filename.)

If you've used any other computing system or another X Window application, you'll feel fairly comfortable in **emacs**. There are some changes in terminology that might throw you off; for example, you don't edit separate files (you edit buffers), and the mechanism for showing your position in a document is not called the *cursor*, but the *point*. (In this chapter, we'll use the term *cursor*.)

Emacs and Commands

With **emacs**, there is usually more than one way to perform a command, especially with the X Window version of **emacs**.

One method is through keyboard shortcuts. Every **emacs** function can be performed via the keyboard, usually in conjunction with the **Ctrl** and **Alt** keys. (In some **emacs** documentation, there will be references to the **Meta** key rather than the **Alt** key; this reference is more for the users of other UNIX systems that lack an **Alt** key on their keyboard. This is, of course, not the case with Linux.) Most of the time the **Ctrl** and **Alt** keys are shortcuts for full commands, which you could enter if you were truly inclined.

There's one thing to note when working with keyboard sequences: When you see notation like **Ctrl-x Ctrl-f**, this means you hold down the **Ctrl** key and then press the **x** and **f** keys in sequence. (No, you don't need to release the **Ctrl** key between the **x** and **f** keys.)

The other method is through a pull-down menu. **Emacs** provides some pull-down menus (Buffers, File, Edit, and Help). Be warned that these menus don't work the same way as pull-down menus in the Microsoft Windows, Macintosh, or OS/2 environments. In these situations, a menu choice acts as a gateway to another action, either a dialog box or another menu.

Essentially, pull-down menus in the **emacs** environment act as gateways for the **emacs** command line, which can be found on the bottom of the screen. For example, choose **Open File** from the File pull-down menu (or the keyboard equivalent of **Ctrl-x Ctrl-f**) You won't see a fancy dialog box that allows you to choose from a list of existing files. Instead, you'll see a line at the bottom of the **emacs** window that lists the current directory, as shown in Figure C.1.

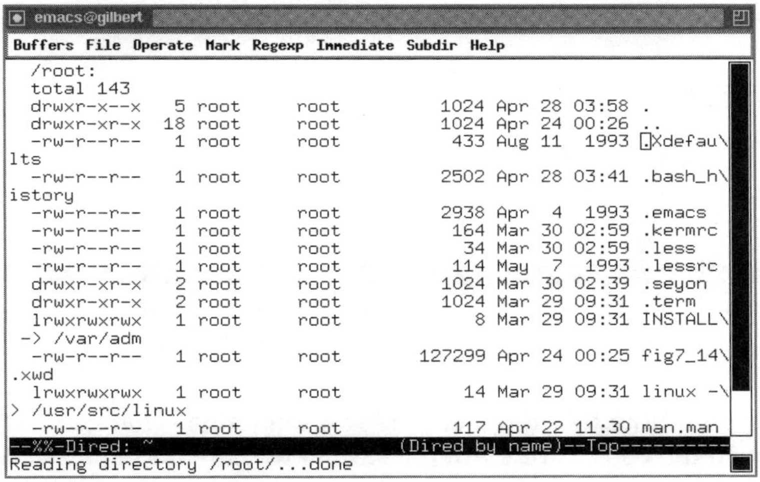

Figure C.1 Emacs with the listings of a directory.

If you look at Figure C.1 closely, you'll see that the pull-down-menu choices have dramatically increased. Depending on the context, **emacs** will display varying sets of pull-down menus.

The listings from Figure C.1 are meant as a way to show you options; the contents are read-only, and you can't scroll between them to select a file or directory. Instead, you continue to choose **Open File** from the File menu (**Ctrl-x Ctrl-f**) and manually insert the file or directory name. In short, the **Open File** menu choice is a shortcut to both the **emacs** command line and the **ls -l** command line.

After you choose a file, you'll see something like Figure C.2, assuming, of course, that your file contains more than the gibberish shown in the figure.

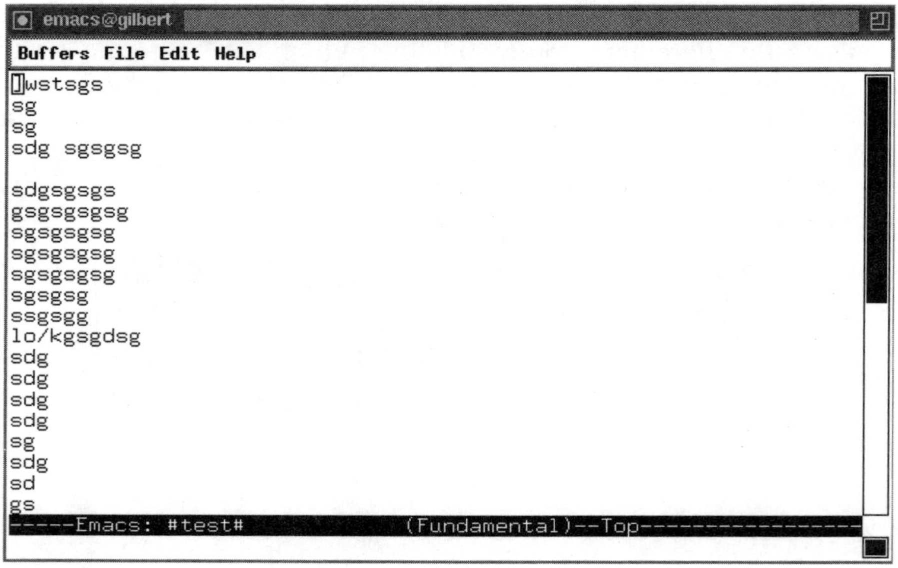

Figure C.2 Emacs with a file loaded.

Again, you'll note that the menu bar for **emacs** has changed slightly, in reaction to the context of editing a simple text file. In Figure C.2, **emacs** gives us the name of the file (*test*), the mode (*Fundamental*), and the amount of the file that is displayed on the screen (in this case, *22 percent*).

The Many Modes of Emacs

You've already seen **emacs** change behavior when presented with a different context—the example being different pull-down menus for different chores. Another sign of **emacs**' flexibility is in its support of modes, which essentially changes **emacs** depending on the usage.

For example, Figures C.1 and C.2 showed **emacs** in Lisp Interaction mode. If you were a LISP programmer, this mode might be important to you. However, most of you will be interested in other **emacs** modes—particularly the mode found in Figure C.2, Fundamental mode. This is the mode used to edit ASCII files. There are other modes for **emacs** that you may end up using, however, such as the modes for editing C and **TeX** source-code files.

Creating and Editing Files

Most of what **emacs** does is pretty straightforward; as you've already learned, most actions can be done from the pull-down menu or from keyboard equivalents.

After you launch **emacs** from a command line, you're presented with a blank screen. If you're creating a new file, you can go ahead and type. **Emacs** will wrap words at the end of a column, but in an unusual manner, displaying a slash (/) to indicate that a word is continued on the following line.

With the version of **emacs** found on the accompanying CD-ROM, **emacs** performs just like any other text editor when it comes to cursor commands and such; there are a few quirks to watch for, however:

- The cursor keys (↑, ↓, ←, and →) are used slightly differently than you'd think. The up arrow (↑) moves the cursor to the beginning line of the current paragraph; pressing it twice moves the cursor to the beginning of the file. The down arrow (↓) moves the cursor to the end of the current paragraph; pressing it twice moves the cursor into the following paragraph. However, the left and right arrow keys (← and →) work as you would expect them to.

- The **PageUp** and **PageDn** commands apply to the position of the document in the **emacs** buffer. If the entire document is displayed in a window, these commands won't do anything.

- The **Home** and **End** keys are used to mark text, in addition to positioning the cursor at the beginning or end of a document.

- The **Backspace** and **Delete** keys should work as you'd expect. (This is one of the advantages of Linux on the PC architecture; Linux assumes there's standard PC equipment present, and by and large that assumption is valid. There are mechanisms for remapping keys should Linux not work as you'd expect, but these sorts of problems are minimized under Linux and XFree86.)

In addition, there are a host of keyboard commands for maneuvering through a document, as listed in Table C.2.

Table C.2 Emacs cursor commands.

Command	Moves...
Ctrl-a	the cursor to the beginning of the current line
Ctrl-b	the cursor backward one character
Ctrl-e	the cursor to the end of the current line
Ctrl-f	the cursor forward one character
Ctrl-n	the cursor to the next line
Ctrl-p	the cursor to the previous line
Ctrl-v	the document ahead one page
Alt-v	the document back one page
Alt-<	the cursor to the beginning of the document
Alt->	the cursor to the end of the document

Buffers

In UNIX parlance, a *buffer* is a portion of memory set aside for a specific task. In **emacs**, a buffer can contain an existing file or a new file in progress. When a file is in a buffer, it exists separately from something stored on the hard disk; you can make changes to the buffer, but they won't be reflected in the version stored on disk. Only when you explicitly save the file to disk will the changes be made permanent. This sometimes trips up new computer users, who assume that whatever appears on the screen is exactly mirrored at all times on the disk.

Emacs allows you to view multiple buffers and to cut and paste between the buffers. To see which buffers are currently open, select **Buffers** from the menu bar (or type **Ctrl-x Ctrl-b**).

Emacs and Help

There's one additional area where **emacs** is better than most other Linux text-editing tools: the presence of true online help. To access the online help, you can choose **Help** from the pull-down menu, which gives you a list of selections. Some of the help is context-sensitive, responding to what you're doing at the moment (such as the help for modes), while there are also general help topics and a tutorial.

A good place to start with the online help is with the Info menu choice (**Ctrl-h Ctrl-I**), which provides a general overview of **emacs** online help. And **Ctrl-h Ctrl-t** provides a decent tutorial.

A Basic Emacs Tutorial

Many Linux users won't care about **emacs'** bell and whistles; they only care about creating and editing a document. In that spirit, we present this minitutorial that covers the creation and editing of text files under **emacs**.

You already know how to load **emacs**. If you want to create a new file, you can go ahead and type away. If you want to load an existing file and didn't specify the file on the command line, you can open it by selecting **Open File** (**Ctrl-x Ctrl-f**) from the File menu.

To edit the file, you can use the basic movement and editing keys on the keyboard. When it's time to save your file, you can select **Save Buffer** (**Ctrl-x Ctrl-s**) from the File menu; if you're working with an existing file, you should select **Save Buffer As** (**Ctrl-x Ctrl-w**) from the File menu, but use the existing filename.

To quit **emacs**, select **Exit Emacs** from the File menu or type **Ctrl-x Ctrl-c**. If you haven't saved any changes to the file, **emacs** will make sure you want to quit and give you the option of saving the file at that time.

The Undo Command

Emacs also allows you to undo your most recent action; naturally enough, the **Undo** menu selection from the Edit menu does this. (The keyboard equivalent is **Ctrl-_**.)

Editing Text

When you edit existing text, you can go one of two ways. Old-time UNIX and **emacs** users make a big deal about the scads of commands used to delete and edit text. Because we're modernists (relatively speaking), we're into the more recent (and handier) methods to do things.

For example, to cut and copy text, there's a host of commands for cutting existing text, saving it to a buffer, and then reinserting the buffer in either the existing file or a new file. We find it's easier to use the mouse to mark a section of text and then use the menu choices in the Edit menu to make the changes (**Cut, Copy,** and **Paste**). If you're used to this trinity of choices from the Windows, Macintosh, or OS/2 worlds, you'll feel comfortable with them under Linux:

- The **Cut (Ctrl-w)** menu choice cuts the marked text and saves it to another buffer.
- The **Copy (Alt-w)** menu choice copies the marked text to a buffer, leaving the marked text intact.
- The **Paste (Ctrl-y)** menu choice pastes the text in the buffer where the cursor is positioned on the page.

There are two things to note here: The keyboard equivalents for these mechanisms aren't the same as the keyboard equivalents under Windows, Macintosh, or OS/2, and marked text is grayed when you select it with the mouse, but not when you release the mouse. The text is still marked; you just have no way to tell.

Deleting text involves the same sort of mechanisms: Marking text with the mouse and then using the **Clear** menu choice (no keyboard equivalent, interestingly enough) from the Edit menu to delete the text. (You can't use the **Backspace** or **Delete** key to delete marked text.) There are also a host of keyboard commands for deleting text (if you're a devoted touch-typist and can't bear the thought of using a mouse), as listed in Table C.3.

Table C.3 Delete commands in emacs.

Command	Deletes...
Delete	the character to the left of the cursor
Backspace	the character to the left of the cursor
Ctrl-d	the character beneath the cursor
Ctrl-k	all characters to the end of the line
Alt-d	to the beginning of the next word
Alt-Delete	all characters to the beginning of the previous word

Finally, **emacs** features a slew of keyboard commands for changing existing text. Most of these selections aren't found in a menu, so you'll need to perform them from the keyboard. We list them in Table C.4.

Table C.4 Additional emacs editing commands.

Command	Result
Ctrl-t	Transposes the character under the cursor with the character before the cursor
Alt-t	Transposes the word under the cursor with the word before the cursor
Ctrl-x Ctrl-t	Transposes the current line with the next line in the document; remember that under **emacs** a line can be a paragraph if there's no carriage return at the end of a line
Alt-l (*ell*)	Changes the case of a word to lowercase; if your cursor is positioned in the middle of the word, **emacs** only changes the case of the letters in the remainder of the word
Alt-u	Changes the case of a word to uppercase; if your cursor is positioned in the middle of the word, **emacs** only changes the case of the letters in the remainder of the word
Alt-c	Capitalizes the word, provided the cursor is at the beginning of the word

Searching and Replacing

When it comes to searching and replacing text, **emacs** is not a very sophisticated player, but you'll probably have little need for the more extensive search-and-replace facilities found in a commercial word processor.

To search for a specific string, select **Search** from the Edit menu. The bottom of the window will feature the following input mechanism:

```
Search:
```

At that point you can enter the string of text to look for, moving forward through the document from the current cursor position, not from the beginning of the file.

If you choose **Ctrl-s** from the keyboard, you'll get a slightly different search mechanism, as you'll see by the bottom of the window:

```
I-search:
```

The search is *incremental*, which means that **emacs** is moving through the document based on your first keystroke (if you type **t**, it will move to the first *t* it finds).

To perform a search-and-replace operation, select **Query-Replace** from the Edit menu. **Emacs** will prompt you for the text to search and then the text to replace. Armed with this, **emacs** will move to the first occurrence of the search text in the buffer, asking if you want to replace the text (type **y** or **n** to choose).

Spell-Checking

Emacs features a spelling checker that's really an extension of the UNIX **spell** command, **ispell**. If you select **Spell** from the Edit menu, you'll see a host of choices that allows you to check the spelling in the buffer, of a particular word, or using a different or foreign-language dictionary. This menu also allows you to make changes to a dictionary (a good thing, especially if you're writing a book and use a lot of words not in the standard dictionary).

Linux also supports the **spell** command if you wish to run it from the command line.

Printing in Emacs

To print a file in **emacs**, select **Print Buffer** from the File menu (there's no keyboard equivalent). This has the same effect as running **lpr** from the command line.

Quitting Emacs

The sequence **Ctrl-x Ctrl-c** will save the current buffer and quit **emacs**. You can also use the **Exit Emacs** choice on the File menu.

There's a lot more to **emacs** than what we list here; realistically, all we can do is offer an overview of **emacs** and let you poke around the rest, figuring out which of **emacs** many capabilities best fits your situation.

Xedit

A considerably less sophisticated editing tool is **xedit**, but it's one you might find useful nevertheless. **Xedit** is a simple text editor, where the screen is split into different areas for editing text and creating drafts of text.

You can launch **xedit** from the **fvwm** menu or from an **xterm** window. If you specify a file on the command line, that file will be loaded into **xedit**. For an X Window application, there's not much to do with the mouse; you basically can load and save a file via buttons, as well as select text, but the rest of the action is accomplished via a set of **Ctrl-** and **Alt**-key combinations. These combinations are listed in Table C.5.

Table C.5 Important editing actions with xedit.

Key Combination	Action
Alt-Del	Deletes the previous word
Alt-Backspace	Deletes the next word
Alt-<	Moves the displayed text to the beginning of the file
Alt->	Moves the displayed text to the end of the file
Alt-]	Moves the displayed text ahead one paragraph
Alt-[	Moves the displayed text backward one paragraph
Alt-b	Moves the cursor to the beginning of the previous word
Alt-d	Deletes the word after the current cursor position
Alt-f	Moves the cursor to the beginning of the next word
Alt-h	Deletes the word prior to the current cursor position
Alt-i	Inserts a file
Alt-k	Deletes the text to the end of the current paragraph
Alt-q	Makes the current text into a paragraph, with indent and newline
Alt-v	Moves the cursor to the beginning of the previous page
Alt-y	Inserts the selection to the current cursor position
Alt-z	Scrolls the displayed text one line down
Ctrl-a	Moves the cursor to the beginning of the line
Ctrl-b	Moves the cursor backward one character
Ctrl-d	Deletes the character after the cursor
Ctrl-e	Moves the cursor to the end of the line
Ctrl-f	Moves the cursor forward one character
Ctrl-h	Deletes the character before the cursor
Ctrl-j	Inserts a newline character and indents the following line
Ctrl-k	Deletes to the end of the line
Ctrl-l	Redraws the display
Ctrl-m	Inserts a newline character
Ctrl-n	Moves the cursor to the next line
Ctrl-o	Inserts a newline and moves the cursor to the previous line

continued...

Key Combination	Action
Ctrl-p	Moves the cursor to the previous line
Ctrl-r	Performs a search-and-replace before the current cursor position
Ctrl-s	Performs a search-and-replace after the current cursor position
Ctrl-t	Transposes the characters on either side of the cursor
Ctrl-v	Repositions the page to the following page
Ctrl-w	Deletes the selected text
Ctrl-y	Undeletes the last text deleted with **Ctrl-w**

For more on **xedit**, check out its online **man** page, best viewed with **xman**.

Textedit

If you're coming from a Sun Microsystems environment, you may be more comfortable with the **textedit** text editor:

```
gilbert:$ textedit
```

This text editor features the familiar Open Look buttons for opening and managing files. It's a basic text editor, complete with search-and-replace capabilities and the ability to copy selections to a Clipboard.

To get more information about **textedit**, check out its online **man** page:

```
gilbert:$ xman
```

Other Text-Editing Tools

If these text editors don't fit your needs, you're welcome to try some of the other text editors:

- **Vim** is a **vi**-compatible text editor (only the **q** command is missing). It adds to the basic **vi** command set with several shell-like features, including command-line history, filename completion, and more.

- **Jove** is Jonathan's Own Version of Emacs; it works pretty much like **emacs** in the major ways, using buffers and such. If you yearn for **emacs** in text mode and installed **emacs** to run under the X Window System, you can use **jove** and pretty much feel right at home (although there are some areas where **jove** differs significantly from **emacs**; you can read all about it in the online **man** pages).

- **Joe** is Joe's Own Editor (notice how these software creators name things after themselves?). It's basically a text editor that supports some old WordStar conventions. (History lesson: WordStar is a text editor that used to be very big in the MS-DOS world; Windows pretty much wiped it out.) When you think of WordStar, you should think of **Ctrl**-key combinations used to perform basic tasks, and that's exactly what you'll find in **joe**.

- If you're a UNIX old-timer, you might feel comfortable with the **ed** text editor (which can also be summoned under the **red** command). The Slackware Linux version is very limited; you can only edit files in the current directory and you cannot execute shell commands.

- Finally, you'll want to poke around the CD-ROM for other editors. We've included **nedit**, a Motif-based editor, and other programming tools.

Index

A

ansi2knr command, 132
ash shell, 36
ar command, 126
Athena widgets, 165-168

B

bash shell, 36
BASIC, 228-229
binutils, 36
bison parser, 132
bitmaps, creating, 312-313

C

C programming language, xvii, xix, xx, 36, 115, 116, 117, 118, 119, 120, 121, 122, 123, 124, 125, 126, 127, 133, 182, 213, 218, 250, 254, 313
C++ programming language, xvii, xix, xx, 116, 117, 126, 133, 176, 182, 218, 250, 254, 288, 313
cc command *see GNU C compiler*
cjpeg command, 312
cmp command, 278
comm command, 278-279
cpp command, 122

D

diff command, 132, 276-278
diff3 command, 279-280
djpeg, 312

E

Eiffel, 238-242
   Small Eiffel, 239-242
ELF format, 124
elvis text editor, 36, 117, 352-370
emacs text editor, 36, 117, 266-267, 308, 352-370

F

find command, 283-287
flex parser, 132
Free Software Foundation, xviii, xix, xx, 116
Frequently Asked Questions (FAQs), 246
Fortran, 116, 133, 231-232
   g77, 133, 231-232
Fresco, 176-178
ftp command, 316-317

G

gdb debugger, 117, 131, 254-265, 266, 267
GNU C compiler (**gcc**), 117, 118, 119-120, 122, 123, 125, 131

GNU libraries, 126
GNU Public Licenses, xx
grep command, 282-283
grof command, 132
guavac, 225

H

hexdump command, 132, 290-291
How-Tos, 246-247

I

IBM, 22
imake utility, 117, 131, 139-142
info command, 247-250

J

Java, xvii, xx, 217-226, 268
jdb debugger, 268-273
joe text editor, 36, 370
jove text editor, 36, 370

K

Kaffe, 224

L

ldd command, 290
LessTif, xvii, xx, 144-163
libc, 36
Linux, xvii, xviii-xix, 1, 2, 3, 4, 5, 6, 8, 9, 10, 11, 12, 13, 14, 15, 16, 19, 20, 21, 22, 23, 24, 25, 26, 27, 28, 29, 30, 31, 32, 33, 34, 35, 37, 38, 39, 40, 41, 42, 43, 44, 45, 46, 47, 48, 49, 50, 51, 52, 53, 54, 55, 57, 58, 59, 60, 61, 62, 63, 66, 67, 69, 72, 79, 97, 103-104, 116, 117, 118, 119, 120, 121, 123, 124, 125, 126, 130,
131, 132, 133, 182, 204, 209, 210, 211, 229, 233, 238, 239, 244, 245, 246, 247, 254, 266, 268, 276, 282, 283, 288, 290, 294, 308, 309, 311, 314, 319-336
boot floppies, creating, 3
booting, 21, 54
disk sets, 33-34
documentation, 244-245
and **FDISK.EXE**, 16
FIPS, using, 13
and **FORMAT.COM**, 16
gpm, 35
hard-disk names, 23
hardware compatibility, 319-336
and help, 59
installing, 2, 30
installing from floppies, 41-42
installing from hard drive, 41
installing from tape, 42-43
and JPEG, 311-312
kernel, installing, 37-38
kernel, recompiling, 50
kernel modules, 58
LILO, configuring, 39
and **LOADLIN**, 46-49
modem, configuring, 38
mouse, configuring, 39
partitions, 12
and PCMCIA devices, 62
and **pkgtool**, 51
printer, setting up, 61
rootdisk image, choosing, 8
run levels, 103-104
shutting down, 60

and swap disk, 25-26, 31

UMSDOS, 9-10, 53

upgrading, 51-52

and UPS, 63

users, adding, 55-56

and Windows 95, 48

linuxinc, 36

LISP, 236-238

M

make utility, 117, 127-131

manual pages, 244

Midnight Commander, 36

Modula, 235

Modula-2, 235

Modula-3, 235

Motif, xvii, xx, 64, 65, 66, 144-163, 290

    mwm, 65-66, 113

MS-DOS, 9-24, 25, 26, 29, 31, 32, 39, 40, 41, 42, 46-47

N

NCSA Mosaic for X Window, 20

O

Oberon, 236

objdump command, 132, 287-290

Objective-C, 116, 117, 133, 232-233

OS/2, 14, 16, 21, 25, 26, 29, 31, 32, 39, 40, 41, 42

    and **FDISK**, 21

P

Pascal, 233-234

Perl, xvii, xix, xx, 203-215, 250

    associative arrays, 208-209

    subroutines, 214

    variables, 206

PPP, 38

R

ranlib command, 132

rcp command, 315

Revision Control System (RCS), 117, 132, 292-308

rlogin command, 314-315

S

screen shots, making, 309-311

sdiff command, 280-281

Slackware96 *see Linux*

Slackware Linux *see Linux*

SLIP, 38

SmallTalk, 239

strace command, 132

T

Tcl, xvii, xix, xx, 182-201, 250

    and Motif, 184

    procedures, 192-193

    scripting, 185, 194

    variables, 189-191

    widgets, 184

TCP-IP, 38

tcsh shell, 36

textedit, 369

Torvalds, Linus, xviii

U

UNIX, xviii, xix, 2, 37, 43, 64, 65, 82, 97, 98, 103, 116, 123, 126, 128, 129, 133

    run levels, 103

V

vi text editor, 36, 117, 370

vim text editor, 36, 370

X

X Window System, xvii, xviii, 35, 36, 63, 64, 65, 66, 67, 68, 69, 73, 74, 78, 79, 80, 83, 85, 86, 88, 90, 92, 95, 96, 97, 98, 99, 100, 102, 103, 105, 106, 107, 108, 109, 110, 112, 114, 116, 117, 126, 135-179, 312 *see also XFree86*

    resource files, 99-100

    window manager, 65, 110, 137

    xterm, 96-97, 99, 100, 101, 102

xedit, 367-369

XForms, xvii, xix, 168-173

XFree86, 26, 36, 66, 67, 68, 69, 70, 71, 72, 73, 74, 75, 76, 77, 90, 94, 95, 110 *see also X Window System*

    font server, 77, 108-109

    fvwm window manager, 110-114

    installing, 68

    and laptops, 73

    servers, 70-71

    starting, 92

    stopping, 94

    xdm, 102-103

    XF86Config file, 72, 75, 76, 84, 85, 86, 87, 88, 89, 90, 91

    xf86config program, 89, 90

    xinit, 67, 68

xpaint program, 313-314

xv graphics editor, 37, 308-311

XView, 174-176

xxgdb debugger, 117, 131, 142, 266

Z

zsh shell, 36

About the CD-ROM

The accompanying CD-ROM is formatted under ISO-9660 standards, with Rock Ridge extensions. You can read the contents from both PCs and UNIX workstations. However, long UNIX filenames can't be read by MS-DOS.

Most of the tools listed in this book are installed during the course of a normal Slackware Linux installation, so there's no need to separately install C and C++ compilers, Perl, Tcl, and X Window System programming libraries. When additional programming tools are highlighted in the text, their file locations on the CD-ROM are listed.

This CD-ROM also contains the Java Development Kit (JDK), as ported to Slackware Linux.